My Los Angeles in Black & (almost) White

Andrew Furman

Syracuse University Press

First Edition 2010
10 11 12 13 14 15   6 5 4 3 2 1

Author's Note: Some (though not many) of the names that appear in this book have been changed.

∞ The paper used in this publication meets the minimum requirements of the American National Standard for Information Sciences—Permanence of Paper for Printed Library Materials, ANSI Z39.48-1992.

For a listing of books published and distributed by Syracuse University Press, visit our Web site at SyracuseUniversityPress.syr.edu.

ISBN: 978-0-8156-0959-9

Library of Congress Cataloging-in-Publication Data
Furman, Andrew, 1968–
    My Los Angeles in black and (almost) white / Andrew Furman. — 1st ed.
        p. cm. — (Sports and entertainment)
    Includes bibliographical references.
    ISBN 978-0-8156-0959-9 (cloth : alk. paper)
    1. Basketball—Social aspects—California—San Fernando Valley. 2. Granada Hills High School (Los Angeles, Calif.)—Basketball. 3. Furman, Andrew, 1968– —Anecdotes. 4. School integration—California—San Fernando Valley. 5. Segregation in education—California—San Fernando Valley. 6. San Fernando Valley (Calif.)—Race relations. 7. San Fernando Valley (Calif.)—Social Conditions. 8. Los Angeles (Calif.)—Race relations. 9. Los Angeles (Calif.)—Social conditions. I. Title.
    GV885.73.L67F87 2010
    796.32309794'94—dc22   2010033492

For Sophia

Andrew Furman teaches in the MFA program in creative writing at Florida Atlantic University. He is the author, most recently, of the novel *Alligators May Be Present* (2005). In addition, he has published numerous essays on a variety of topics in *Poets & Writers, Ecotone, Oxford American, Agni Online, Image, ISLE, The Chronicle of Higher Education, The Forward,* and elsewhere, and he is a frequent book reviewer for the *Miami Herald.* He is currently working on a novel and a collection of essays that examine Florida's ecology.

Contents

Illustrations

Acknowledgments

I OWE A SPECIAL DEBT to the following people, without whom this book would not have been possible: my teachers within and without the Los Angeles Unified School District during the 1970s and 1980s, who extended their best efforts toward a dreamy and distracted student; coaches Bob Johnson and Lou Cicciari, and all of my teammates on the 1986 Varsity Basketball squad at Granada Hills High School, for an experience that extended well beyond the realm of sport; Mark Slothower, John Walsh, and all of their colleagues at the offices of the LAUSD, who patiently and professionally responded to my interminable queries and data requests; Paul Ardoin, our graduate research assistant, for his expert sleuthing; the talented editors and readers at Syracuse University Press; my colleagues in the Department of English at Florida Atlantic University, who have always supported my work; my colleagues in the Peace Studies Program at FAU, who provided travel funding for this project; the left-coast Furmans—Richard, Leila, Daniel and Ruth; Buddy and Joanne Bloomfield, for taking me in way back when, and for welcoming me back; Anthony Lockhart, for opening up the basketball gym to all comers Saturday mornings at Boca Raton High School (age, race, gender, and skill level aside); and, finally, my parents, Nancy and Stephen Furman, who never quite knew what I was up to with all of my pestering questions about those hazy Valley days.

My Los Angeles
in Black & *(almost)* White

Photograph

THIS STORY BEGINS with a photograph. Or, rather, a curious circumstance surrounding the composition of a photograph. I'm looking down now at the black-and-white image in my 1986 high school yearbook, having retrieved the album, encased in its protective plastic jacket, from the uppermost shelf of my most remote back hallway closet in Boca Raton, Florida. It seems strange that the yearbook has managed to stick doggedly with me over the past twenty years, given my cross-continent peregrinations since graduating from Granada Hills High School in the San Fernando Valley of Los Angeles. It's open at my side, the pages unyellowed, scarcely worse for the wear. Yet here it is!

This must mean something. That having achieved a near seamless and deliberate escape from the smog-choked Valley of my childhood, I have clung to this remnant of those faraway days, as I suppose many of us do for all the obvious nostalgic reasons, and for other less explicable reasons—the reasons, perhaps, most worthy of contemplation.

"Undefeated in league: leads to city playoffs" the caption reads just below the small photograph, the varsity basketball team photograph at the upper-left corner of the page. There I am. Fourth from the left. An unsmiling, altogether too serious expression on my face. All twelve of us teammates wear the same sober expression, as if we had discussed it beforehand. *Okay, nobody smile. This is serious. We're ballers.* But I can't remember any such orchestration. What I do remember is the photographer instructing us to stand in a curve around the midcourt circle, the school's seal and motto, "Home of the Highlanders," emblazoned in white, green, and black on the glossy hardwood before us. The coach and

1

assistant coach pose paternally at either end. I remember the photographer looking down into the viewfinder of his fancy camera, then looking up at us again, gazing toward us for a moment without saying anything, as if he has noticed something troubling through the lens but isn't quite sure how to address the problem. Recognizing the photographer's discomfiture, our graying coach, Bob Johnson, a man as mild as his name, breaks his pose and peers over toward his players, taking us in.

"Okay, I think we better mix it up a little over here. This doesn't look so good," I can remember him saying, giving audible expression to what was certainly on the poor photographer's mind. A quick look about and his meaning is clear. The five black players on our squad all stand at one side (I can't quite remember which side), while the rest of us had congregated together on the other side of our semicircle. Coach is right. It doesn't look so good.

I don't remember this as a particularly tense or dramatic moment. We all pretty much laughed it off as we mixed up our ranks. It took a mere moment to arrange a satisfactorily integrated tableau. There was some horsing around, some tugging at one another's arms and jerseys to redistribute the real estate. We looked once again toward the camera, affecting our too serious, earnestly intimidating expressions. The photographer, appeased, snapped the photo and we were done. We headed toward the mildewed locker room to change out of our home game jerseys and green rip-away sweat pants—which seemed fancy and even venerable to me at the time—and into our more comfortable tanks and shorts, threadbare cotton. Time for practice.

What a funny coincidence, I remember thinking. That all of us white players and Sam, our tall and talented Thai-American player, gathered together to one side of the frame, while our black teammates gathered together at the other side. There was little, if any, racial strife on our team. Certainly nothing overt. So what a funny coincidence.

Still, if it were merely a coincidence, if the occasion were so arbitrary and insignificant, then why do I remember the scene so vividly after all of these years? It must have meant more to me at the time than I remember it having meant, if this makes any sense. Yes, we often know (don't we?) more than we know that we know. A part of me, that is, must have recognized something emblematic in this fleeting scene. For though we enjoyed an easygoing esprit de corps on the basketball court, there was no disputing that the black players and the white players on our squad lived in strikingly contrastive worlds. Our traffic with one another pretty much dissipated once we stepped off the glossy hardwood.

Simple geography accounted for much of this curious situation. While my nonblack teammates and I lived near campus in the middle-class northwest Valley neighborhoods of Porter Ranch, Granada Hills, and Northridge (epicenter of the devastating 1994 earthquake, just over the horizon)—neighborhoods increasingly Jewish and Asian American—our black teammates lived roughly an hour south over the hill in more hardscrabble inner-city L.A. neighborhoods. They participated in the Los Angeles Unified School District's voluntary busing program, Permits With Transportation (PWT), created in 1977 along with the city's magnet program for the express purpose of desegregating the public schools in L.A. These two programs represented a kinder, gentler integration of L.A.'s public schools than the more contentious and short-lived forced busing program of the late 1970s. My teammates' route both ways would travel opposite rush hour traffic along some combination of the Golden State, San Diego, Santa Monica, and/or Ventura Freeways (who knew, precisely, where in the faraway city my teammates lived?), but these main arteries were frequently clogged, regardless. I didn't know the whereabouts or names of these neighborhoods, only that my teammates, as they revealed, arose in the predawn darkness to meet the yellow buses that transported them to our school, and that it was often dark by the time they arrived home on the last bus after practice in the evening.

And so, naturally, when the photographer asked our varsity basketball team to pose for our photograph, we stepped-to and arranged ourselves according to the prevailing pattern that defined our lives, and that would probably continue to define our professional and social networks in the years after graduation, whether we decided to remain Angelenos or to venture elsewhere about the country. Somehow, I think I glimpsed all of this as an awkward seventeen-year-old Jewish Valley boy. Eager as I was to escape once and for all what I considered my largely ignoble adolescent career on the left coast—half an eye was already trained on the East

Coast, where I would attend a small liberal-arts college—I think I knew that there was something strange and of value in my senior season with the varsity, that the experience was, and would remain, significant to me in ways I wasn't yet prepared to understand. And so just as I had for some inexplicable reason toted around my 1986 high school yearbook from apartment to apartment in various Pennsylvania towns before settling in south Florida, I had toted around my memory of the circumstances surrounding that small black-and-white photograph nestled inside on page 92, knowing that it might be of use some day, in some way. More, that it presented a challenge, of sorts, a challenge that I would eventually be compelled to meet.

Precipitating this challenge was a business envelope I received in the mail early in 2006. The envelope was rather nondescript and fairly approximated junk mail, except for that curious black-and-white graphic branded across the adhesive flap. It was a graphic I recognized with a start as the Granada Hills High School seal, an impish Scotsman dancing a jig, feet aflutter beneath his kilt, the elbow of one arm cocked above the waist, the hand of the other arm stretched theatrically toward the sky. I knew before breaking open the envelope that inside lay an invitation to my twentieth high school reunion. I had been found.

As sad as it sounds (as sad as it *is*, perhaps), I haven't kept in touch with any of my high school classmates, or any of my childhood friends for that matter. Despite my comfort on the basketball court, I was something of a loner amid Granada's gargantuan student populace—nearly twenty-five hundred strong during my senior year—skirting the periphery of several cliques (the brains, the jocks, the partyers) yet never fully absorbed into any of these social networks. I remember the high school experience, generally, as a rather brutal period of my life for which I was woefully unprepared, on levels mostly emotional, an experience defined by an overarching sense of alienation, accented by daily humiliations and embarrassments. All of which is to say that the experience for me approximated that of scores of high school students nationwide. And so, like these many others, I made a clean break of things. Only that was far easier for me than for most as my parents pulled up the stakes from L.A.'s San Fernando Valley as well, my father having accepted a new job in Philadelphia.

My official high school reunion held little interest to me. Primarily attending, I suspected, tossing the invitation into my kitchen trash-bin, would be a rag-tag assortment of old Valley friends and the more exalted members of those Valley cliques that held sway twenty years ago. Either these former classmates would once again flaunt their restored hegemony over the rest of us or, more likely—and somehow worse—they would be impossibly welcoming and kind. This wasn't the reunion that somehow seemed required of me. Rather, the invitation compelled me to trek toward the uppermost shelf of my most remote back hallway closet, where that small black-and-white photograph on page 92 of my high school yearbook awaited.

The accounting I feel compelled to pursue, this self-styled reunion of sorts, isn't so much about me, but how someone like me came to live in the San Fernando Valley while half of my teammates lived over the hill. How did this highly segregated diversity, defining the greater Los Angeles area in those days, impact the childhoods afforded to us? What forces—socio-economic, legal, and political—combined to thrust my teammates and me on the same San Fernando Valley junior varsity and varsity squads, and what does the team at our old high school look like now? How did our experiences in the LAUSD in the 1970s and 1980s compare? What was it like, in short, to be a black child from the inner city, or a white Jewish child from the Valley, during the most turbulent period of school desegregation, when students throughout the greater Los Angeles area were bused—often against their will—to schools in faraway neighborhoods? Playing on the varsity meant one thing to me. But what did it mean to my teammates, black, white, and Asian American? Does it mean anything at all to them now? It's only been twenty years, not fifty, but will they even remember who I am?

I look down at those young faces in my team photograph, the faces of my PWT teammates particularly. Jeff Inzar, one of my better friends on the team, stands to the right of me. Sean Brown stands to my left. He was a superlative three-sport athlete, Sean, a sophomore during my senior year, who would go on to play tight end on the University of Colorado's national championship football team. Dennis Bishop, those super-long arms of his hidden behind his back, stands beside Sean. Finally, Thomas McBride

1. Granada Hills High School 1985–86 varsity basketball team. Photograph courtesy of Granada Hills Charter High School/Chris Davis.

(TMac, we called him, never Thomas or Tom) stands a few players down. I'll find these old teammates. My coaches too, if they're still alive.

"They say people in your life are seasons," the lyrics of a Kanye West song go, and our varsity season together is long past. Increasingly, it occupies a mere blip across the screen of our collective experiences. But something in me won't accept this erasure. Curiously, these high school basketball days—these Valley days, generally—seem to exert their power over me with increasing heft as my specific memories of this season, of these teammates and coaches, fade. Is this essential dynamic, the disproportionate power of distant days, what Faulkner glimpsed when he observed that "The past is never dead. It's not even past"?[1] Inscribed just below the team photograph in my yearbook is a note by Gary Gray, our team's star player. "We will have to get the old team together for a 5-5 full court at Castle Bay," he closes. He included a P.S., too, at the bottom, evocative in its understatement: "Alumni Game." Just beside his signature, to the right, Gary scrawled his phone number, most likely defunct by now. But there are ways of reaching people.

First, though, a word about the structure of this book. My overarching goal from the beginning, as I hope I've made clear, was to explore the meaning of school desegregation for myself and for my basketball team-mates. I soon discovered that it was impossible to pursue this goal in ear-nest merely by reconnecting with former teammates, coaches, childhood friends, and neighbors. I would have to examine, as well, the socioeco-nomic, political, and judicial realities and events that impacted the child-hoods (and, by extension, adulthoods) afforded to us. Consequently, while I draw heavily upon elements of the conventional memoir, I also incorpo-rate episodes of scholarly inquiry (e.g., my extended analysis of crucial federal, state, and local judicial decisions regarding school desegregation in chapters 3 and 11). As such, the book will strike most readers, I imagine, as something of a hybrid: part memoir, part scholarly text.

Fair enough. But just to be clear: my research and writing of the book's most "academic" moments felt, and still feels, highly personal to me. Given my stake in the issues at hand, it seemed as if I had unearthed old family letters as I pored over those dusty judicial decisions from the 1970s. If I realized this reunion at all, I realized it through enacting and documenting both my physical journey to my old stomping ground and, just as crucially, through enacting and documenting my intellectual jour-ney through the written record of our collective history. I stand by these aesthetic terms. Whether or not I meet them successfully in the pages that follow, I leave for readers to decide.

Valley Boy

I WAS ONLY FIVE YEARS OLD in December 1973 when our blue Oldsmobile Vista Cruiser station wagon pulled up to our new home in the San Fernando Valley. My siblings and I had flown with our mother from the Newark Airport (close to our South Orange, New Jersey, neighborhood) the day before to join our father, who had flown into L.A. earlier to settle things in preparation for our arrival. Although I was young, I remember this first full day in Northridge. Rather, I remember a particular scene, looking out the window of our station wagon as we approached our white, ranch-style house on the corner. The car slowed. I'm sure that my father pointed out the house to us for our inspection, but my attention was elsewhere, as I had already spotted the two children on the sidewalk beside the macadam street. They were playing an odd-looking game, which involved a hard plastic ball and a set of hand grips. The grips seemed equipped with some sort of suction device through which my new neighbors had been attempting, none too successfully, to catch and throw the ball. I remember them stopping abruptly to peer inside my window, taking in this strange boy who was sizing them up just as deliberately. Before the moving van even arrived, my mother tells me, my siblings and I were playing with our new neighbors out on the street. My parents knew that they had chosen a good neighborhood for us.

Had my across-the-street neighbors not been playing this odd game, I doubt I would remember my first day on Wystone Avenue. I don't remember my first impressions of our new house, per se. But I must have taken note of the odd-looking glossy leaves of the rubber tree beside the front door, which I would soon discover oozed a white, gluey substance when shorn in half. The expansive sunken living room to the right of the foyer must have looked immediately formal and forbidding dressed in its stiff white carpet. Reaching the sliding door in the family room leading to the backyard, I must have been impressed upon glimpsing the expansive covered patio (my father would soon set up a Ping-Pong table), the large swimming pool down the few cement steps, and the veritable mini-orchard of orange trees just beyond, holdovers from our subdivision's citrus grove days. From the patio, I'm sure I gazed awestruck toward the Santa Monica Mountains off into the southern distance at the other end of the Valley. The closer Santa Susana Mountains loomed over us like a schoolyard bully to the north, just blocks away.

A child doesn't think of his experiences in terms of demographic trends or other apposite statistical realities. My parents didn't think in these terms, either. Yet, in hindsight, their westward move to the San Fernando Valley might be seen as part of the mass postwar migration of Jewish Americans, principally from the Northeast, to the Sunbelt cities of Miami and Los Angeles. "After World War II," a *Los Angeles Times* journalist reported in 1978, "the trickle from the East became a torrent, with hundreds of thousands of Jews stuffing their belongings into '47 Nash sedans for the drive west."[1] Nearly a half million Jews lived in Los Angeles by the 1950s, which made L.A. the second largest Jewish community in the United States after New York City. The Jewish population in California, generally, grew 730 percent between 1930 and 1994, as the political scientist Raphael J. Sonenshein notes, while it illustratively dipped by 16 percent in New York State.[2]

Had my parents been a generation or two older, they most likely would have settled in Boyle Heights, the most ethnically integrated enclave in urban L.A., which attracted an especially high concentration of Jews, and sizeable Mexican and Japanese American populations as well. In my teens, I would have attended Fairfax High School, known as "a Jewish High School" in the 1950s, as the historian Deborah Dash Moore remarks in her book *To the Golden Cities*.[3] The heavily Jewish Fairfax High, interestingly, would become one of the few public schools in L.A. to desegregate without a court order, once its district boundaries were redrawn in 1968. Its Jewish basketball coach, Marty Biegel, especially welcomed the influx of talented African American players, many of whom continue to stay in touch with their aging former coach and mentor.[4] By the time I was in high school, however, Boyle Heights, and Fairfax High, were populated almost exclusively by African and Mexican Americans. (The area is largely populated by Latin Americans today.) The old-timers had mostly passed away, and the younger Jews had moved on, contributing their share to the broader white flight phenomenon plaguing urban areas across the country in the postwar years. As early as the 1950s, that is, Jews were increasingly settling in more affluent—and less integrated—areas beyond Boyle Heights. The truly wealthy sought properties in Brentwood, Beverly Hills, and Westwood, where coastal breezes cooled the summer temperatures, while "the agricultural San Fernando Valley," as Moore observes, "north of the Hollywood hills and separated by mountains from the rest of Los Angeles, particularly attracted Jews."[5]

The San Fernando Valley emerged as an affordable and attractive option to scores of economically middle-class Jewish arrivals like my parents. It was decidedly hotter, the Santa Monica Mountains effectively, and unfortunately, obstructing the salty sea breezes. The smog, which on some days settled visibly like a sulphurous blanket across the Valley floor, was also particularly oppressive across our expansive basin, twenty miles long and twelve miles wide. But oh the property values! "Five bedrooms, a three-car garage, *and a pool*," my father, sixty-five years old now, brays excitedly over breakfast about his long-ago real estate find. "For only $81,000!" Small wonder that by 1978, just five years after our arrival, Valley Jews were 150,000 strong.[6]

It wouldn't have occurred to me as a five-year-old to consider the pros and cons of my parents' relocation three thousand miles across the country. My immediate family was the only true constant in my life. One day, we had all lived in a small Tudor home in a leafy New Jersey suburb; the next day, we were living in a much larger house, where the weather was oddly warm for December. I doubt it much fazed me. But it must have taken a great degree of courage for my parents to relocate with three small children to a place where they had no family and no social network whatsoever to offer them ballast. My mother, in fact, tells me that she didn't want to go. They had already been the first in their immediate families to leave Scranton, a wintery Pennsylvania backwater of Italian, Polish, Irish, and Jewish immigrants where life was provincial, yes, but safe and comfortable, too. Moving to New York City, then to South Orange, New Jersey, was as far away from her parents, her siblings, and her extended family as my mother intended to roam.

My father's Big Eight accounting firm, however, had promised to make him a partner soon if he agreed to accept the westward relocation. Moreover, upon further inspection, L.A. seemed chock full of advantages. "Lots of sun, not much rain, no snow or icy streets to deal with, ba-da, ba-da, ba-da," my father sings in rhythmic, yiddishe fashion, recalling this important family decision long ago. "Plus," he says, pausing here contemplatively, sifting through his home fries for his thoughts, "everything we knew about L.A. told us that it was a more"—he pauses here to locate just the right word—"*open* community, open to new ideas businesswise, and socially too more open and accepting. I suppose there was something of the pioneer spirit involved." Here, my father might as well have been one of Moore's primary sources. As one of her L.A. Jewish subjects observes, "'On the West Coast . . . particularly in L.A., the people are very wild, very open minded. . . . People are not fixed in their ways, they are searching.'"[7] The longer I speak with my parents about their westward migration, the clearer it becomes that L.A. to them represented social mobility in the material sense, but also a shift in ethos transcendent of mere economics. L.A. offered the promise of realizing a new Jewish American life for themselves and for their children, one less hemmed in by the rigorously fortified boundaries of the older Jewish (and non-Jewish) communities in the East, a life defined primarily by promise and possibility rather than by duty and expectation.

Why had my parents settled in Northridge, specifically? When I ask my mother, she recalls that with the assistance of my father's firm they had hired a relocation consultant, who had steered them toward the area. Topeka Drive Elementary was a good school, the consultant assured them, and there already existed a burgeoning Jewish community in the area with a Conservative synagogue, Temple Ramat Zion, complete with a Hebrew School. I doubt that matters of race came up explicitly in any of the conversations between my parents and their relocation consultant.

When I pose the question to my parents, as neutrally as possible, they affirm my expectations. But it would have been understood, I'm certain, that phrases like "good schools" and "growing Jewish community" signaled implicitly to my parents that Northridge was primarily a white enclave, one hospitable to Jews, which would allow them to pursue their continued incursions into mainstream (read: white) America.

That Northridge existed as a viable residential option for my parents illustrates, in one sense, how Jewish Americans during the last century navigated their transition, for all intents and purposes, from a disenfranchised "racial" minority to "whiteness." This transition was by no means simple or complete. From the moment Jews arrived in the United States, they struggled to locate themselves somewhere amid America's implacable black-white dichotomy, a problematic paradigm Jews still find themselves grappling with today. In *The Price of Whiteness*, Eric L. Goldstein examines with great probity these complex, dynamic, and, above all, ambivalent negotiations from within. But such internal negotiations, as Goldstein makes clear, have always been informed by the pressures from without (i.e., white Protestant America). As Karen Brodkin notes in *How Jews Became White Folks and What That Says about Race in America*, "It is certainly true that the United States has a history of anti-Semitism and of beliefs that Jews are members of an inferior race. . . . American anti-Semitism was part of a broader pattern of late-nineteenth-century racism against all southern and eastern European immigrants, as well as against Asian immigrants, not to mention African Americans, Native Americans, and Mexicans."[8]

It was certainly good for the Jews, to coin a phrase, that the United States opened its doors to them in the late nineteenth century, allowing my great-grandparents to count themselves among the 1.7 million Jews to emigrate to the United States between 1880 and 1914. But this massive ingathering of Jews, and other immigrants from southern and eastern Europe, also provoked a Nativist furor that effectively fixed Jews into a category of racial inferiority. As nonwhites, Jews (like the Italians and Irish, to a certain extent) were subject to official and unofficial exclusion from any number of bastions of "white" privilege, including neighborhoods, universities, and professional organizations such as a state bar associations and laborer guilds. Small wonder that Jews in America—while drawn powerfully to racial language as a positive means for self-description—largely acceded to mainstream America's eventual willingness in the twentieth century to absorb them as deracinated "white" Americans.[9]

The San Fernando Valley was precisely the type of place from which my family would have been barred earlier in the twentieth century. As Kevin Roderick documents in his excellent study of the Valley, *The San Fernando Valley: America's Suburb,* racial exclusion was a salient feature of the postwar development boom that carved the agricultural Valley into residential subdivisions. While Mexican, Japanese, and African Americans were among the Valley's relatively few inhabitants prior to the war, builders after the war envisioned the broad swath of yet undeveloped Valley land as an exclusively white domain. The 1950 census revealed precipitous growth of the African American population in Los Angeles County, yet of the 402,538 Valley residents, only 2,654 were African-Americans (with other nonwhites contributing only 2,189 to the overall population). A Davenport Institute report notes that, "As recently as the 1960s, about nine out of ten Valley residents were Caucasian."[10] As Roderick pithily puts it, "Racism has been a Valley tradition. As early as the original subdivision of Tract 1000 lands, deeds on town lots specified that the property could never 'at any time be sold, conveyed, leased or rented to any persons of African, Chinese, or Japanese decent.'"[11] Mexicans were excluded from this particular clause only to ensure the accessibility of this vital laboring class, who were channeled into segregated communities. Other typical San Fernando Valley real estate covenants read, "No part of the property could ever be leased, sold, used or occupied by an persons other than those whose blood is entirely that of the Caucasian race."[12]

The Supreme Court declared such deed restrictions unconstitutional as early as 1948, but unofficial redlining by real estate brokers and developers continued for years to restrict minorities—Latinos and African Americans, primarily—to San Fernando and Pacoima at the eastern edge of the Valley and, later, into newer minority neighborhoods in Canoga Park, Reseda, Panorama City, and Van Nuys. Northridge, historically, was dis-integrated to the extreme. It wasn't that my hometown was ever particularly affluent. Tarzana and Encino, at the southern rim of the Valley, were tonier areas. And I should probably note here that even before Frank and Moon Zappa's wildly popular song "Valley Girls" ruthlessly satirized Valley mores in 1982, the entire area had ever been viewed as declasse, if not a joke altogether, by the truly affluent Angelenos living in various exclusive communities over the hill, and even by less affluent, but more hip, L.A. residents. All the same, had the parents of my black basketball teammates relocated to L.A. in 1973, it's doubtful that a relocation consultant or real estate agent would have shown them properties in my town. It wasn't until 1961, in fact, that the first black family, the Rices, moved into a Northridge home, and their arrival hardly precipitated a mass migration of African Americans to the area. One Pacoima activist, Bill Burwell, noted of the late 1960s that "It was unheard of to find a black person in Northridge."[13]

The dearth of African American students at the local college, San Fernando Valley State, which would later become California State University, Northridge, was emblematic of the broader exclusion of African Americans from Northridge neighborhoods. As Roderick notes, "In the Fall of 1968, only about 200 of the 18,000 students were African Americans."[14] My future high school, Granada Hills High, was just as starkly Caucasian—so much so that athletic contests against the mostly black and Latino San Fernando High just a few miles to the east took on the character of race battles. A fight in the stands, in fact, brought the city championship football game between the two schools to an abrupt end in 1970. As late as 1975, according to the LAUSD's Racial and Ethnic Survey, Granada Hills High boasted a gargantuan populace of 3,579 students, 94 percent of whom were white.

Things were beginning gradually to change by that time, owing to deliberate desegregation efforts at the federal and local levels. Many of these efforts were met with fierce resistance. A series of sit-ins and demonstrations for black rights at Valley State in 1968 and 1969, for example, were effectively quashed by local police. The most notable incident involved twenty-seven black students, who took over the administration building in 1968 to protest the antiblack racism alleged against the school's football coach. Although no one was injured, then governor Ronald Reagan saw to it that the local district attorney vigorously pursued charges against the students, many of whom served prison sentences. Still, the Valley State protests of the late 1960s heralded the beginning of the Valley's transition—which continues apace today—from a Caucasian redoubt to an ever more minority and immigrant enclave.

The minority population in the Valley would increase markedly over the years that I lived there. Moreover, the PWT desegregation program encouraged the more vigorous integration of my high school from a 94 percent white student populace in 1975 to the 56 percent white, 13 percent black, 12 percent Asian American, and 18 percent Hispanic student populace of my senior year, 1986. By the mid 1990s, no single ethnic group formed a majority at California State University, Northridge and Granada Hills High had "become a symbol of the Valley's diversity," according to Roderick, its students speaking twenty-eight native languages other than English.[15] Census data reveal that between 1990 and 2000, Northridge saw a modest overall population increase of 5 percent, but its African American population increased by almost 80 percent, its Latino population increased by almost 50 percent, and its Asian American/Pacific Islander population increased by almost 45 percent. Hopeful statistics, one would think, for proponents of integration. Yet, on the whole, the migration pattern reflects, more than it belies, the ongoing "segregated diversity" (to borrow the title phrase of one recent demographic study) that largely defines the relationship between whites and minorities in the greater Los Angeles area,[16] for the white population in Northridge between 1990 and 2000 declined by almost 15 percent. In 2005, white students accounted for only 39 percent of the student population at Granada Hills High (and an arrestingly low 9 percent of the students enrolled district-wide). A relocation consultant today might very well steer an African American family toward a Northridge property, but only as its white residents grow increasingly scarce. White flight began as a phenomenon plaguing our urban centers. My hometown would appear to serve as a prime example of white flight in its second, suburban phase.

As a youngster I was blissfully unaware of the problematic racial history of the Valley. In the mid-1970s, my Little League and Pop Warner football practices were held on the expansive grass fields at the northern edge of the CSUN campus. I took note of the odd-looking high-rise dormitory across the street, but it wouldn't have occurred to me to wonder about the demographics of its student residents. Nor would it have occurred to me as a child to contemplate the significance of my subdivision's name, "Scottish Terrace," built by the same Scottish-American developer, Mac-Adams, who developed several other subdivisions in the Valley. Many Valley subdivisions boasted equally pastoral names, such as Sherwood Forest, Pepper Tree, and Devonshire Country Estates, courting a distinct demographic to which even my Jewish family didn't quite adhere.

Nor, finally, would have it occurred to me to wonder why there was only one African American child in my class at Topeka Drive Elementary. A girl. Her name was Angela. She tamed her thick shock of hair high up on her head in a tightly braided ponytail, and she carried a mysterious array of gleaming keys on a chain around her neck. Angela was a true latchkey child, though I wouldn't have known to apply this term to her. A silver whistle also dangled from the chain. This intrigued me, and it would provoke the only conversation I can remember having with my classmate. "What's the whistle for?" I asked. We were playing on the single elevated zinc bar on the black, rubber-matted playground. Sitting atop the bar with one leg over, Angela could drop forward and flip herself all the way around, making as many furious revolutions as she wanted, her disciplined ponytail thwacking against the rubber ground on each down-swing. Impressive. The whistle was for protection, she told me, in case someone "messed" with her. She wasn't particularly friendly toward me, Angela; I probably wasn't too friendly toward her, either. I remember, frankly, being somewhat frightened of her. Black girls could fight even more fiercely than black boys. You didn't "mess" with them. (Angela had nothing to worry about from me.) This bit of essential knowledge was about as much as we knew about our few black schoolmates. Funny that I remember Angela, her actual first name, while I can barely remember anyone else from Topeka. It suggests, perhaps, the strangeness of her presence in my public school district at the time. After all, 94 percent of my peers at Topeka were white as late as the fall of 1975 (my second-grade year), according to the LAUSD's Racial and Ethnic Survey.

Northridge. When people ask me where I'm from, I'm always careful to specify that I grew up in Northridge, in the San Fernando Valley of Los Angeles. During my first years as a young adult in Pennsylvania, I had responded to such queries with the more recognizable answer, L.A., which every once-in-an-annoying-while would provoke a response something like the following: "Oh, really? I'm from Pasadena." At which point I'd stare dazedly back at my acquaintance, not quite knowing what to say next. Substitute Pasadena with any number of other L.A. enclaves—Hollywood, Santa Monica, Glendale, Palos Verdes—and my nonplused reaction would be the same. These somewhat awkward interactions drove home for me, in the years just after I left the Valley, the exceedingly circumscribed nature of my childhood experience.

Isolated would be one word to describe the dailiness of my life as a youngster growing up in Northridge. Yet "isolated" smacks of unsavory connotations. Self-contained more accurately captures the essence of my early childhood years. Rarely was there a reason for my family to leave the Valley, or even Northridge. We had parks, grocery stores, the largest mall in the Valley, two movie theaters—a small one called the Pepper Tree and a larger one on Parthenia Street—a fair variety of Italian, Mexican, and Chinese restaurants, and a Jewish delicatessen, Brent's, to boot. On the expansive grounds at Devonshire Downs, within a couple of miles of my house, we enjoyed the annual San Fernando Valley Fair, a circus from time to time, and I hazily recall concerts, as well.

My father's life was necessarily more complicated. He would awake in the predawn hours to make his long commute to downtown Los Angeles, a place that seemed (and still seems) distant, strange, and foreign to me. We weren't shackled to our Valley home. I don't want to misrepresent things. We semi-regularly ventured over the hill as a family during the summer, when we'd travel the distance to Zuma or Santa Monica Beach. On occasion, we'd traverse Topanga Canyon to reach the coast, a rustic wooded pass with steep precipices and dilapidated wooden storefronts here and there; it seemed like another country to me. My parents also belonged to Brentwood Country Club, the Jewish club over the hill, but it was pretty far away. Other than my bar mitzvah reception and the Fourth of July celebrations, I remember only intermittent visits. Unlike my brother, I never developed a passion for golf. There was the odd trip to a Dodger game or to Disneyland, too, and an occasional meal in Chinatown. Yet I think it's fair to say that I lived my childhood mostly in Northridge at a safe remove from 99 percent of the sprawling, expansive region that we regard loosely as L.A., a sheltered existence that was precisely what my parents had in mind for their children.

All the same, I wasn't sheltered in the sense that we shelter our children today. Scrupulously arranged "play-dates" were unheard of. This wasn't the era of the overscheduled child. My time, outside of school, was pretty much my own. I led a rather rugged, almost Thoreauvian, childhood that I only wish I could provide to my own youngsters, but can't (mostly on account of south Florida crime, traffic, and rampant overdevelopment). Given what Northridge and the surrounding areas look like today, it's hard to imagine how rustic the environs truly were, how near at hand and available the unconstructed realm lay for my friends and for me to explore. Our subdivision itself was a fairly typical suburban neighborhood, if not quite as ruthlessly stuccoed or homogenous as more recent developments plaguing the country's landscape. But it wasn't so thoroughly zone-restricted that I couldn't convince my parents to allow me to build an enormous coop, where I raised a teeming flock of homing pigeons. This was an unusual hobby for a young boy in the neighborhood, to be sure, but not so unusual that there wasn't a feed store nearby in Canoga Park, where I bought my enormous bags of seed and smaller bags of red grit. "Squab?" the man at the counter asked before ringing me up. I knew enough to nod, for if you ate your pigeons you didn't have to pay taxes on their food.

A couple of lots on our block had yet to be leveled. The dusty swatches of tumbleweed and thistle-rich earth were excellent sites to hunt for blue-bellied lizards or to shoot through a whole red roll of caps during epic cowboy-and-Indian battles, or test the ruggedness of our knobby-tired bicycles on trails we cleared of weeds and rocks. A decent BMX bicycle meant freedom in those days, freedom to explore beyond the few blocks of our subdivision to less residential areas just beyond. If we rode our bikes just outside the subdivision to Vanalden and crossed the street, we could feed and pet through the fence the horses that lolled about lazily on a sprawling ranch. Pedaling only a short distance north on Vanalden, then west on Devonshire, led to Tampa Avenue, the gateway to the rugged, undeveloped Santa Susana foothills adjacent to the neighboring town of Porter Ranch. We'd ride on the sidewalk just a few blocks up the winding slope of Tampa Avenue, then veer off into the undeveloped, scrubby hills to the left. The broad boulevard continuing clear up the hill past Rinaldi Street heralded the randy rate of residential development that would eventually catch up to us. But in those days, the developers had yet to pave over the hilly chaparral and cactus landscape or plant their ochre streetlights like so many matchsticks. There were few signs of human encroachment across these acres, which seemed infinitely vast to me at the time. Traversing the unmarked rocky trails (one stretch, in fact, was called "Rocky Road") was tough going, which was the point. We'd work our quadriceps to exhaustion, competitively testing our physical prowess and the toughness of our bikes, as we made our slow way up toward the mountain proper. On occasion, I'd bring a few of my pigeons along in a brown Ralph's grocery bag, then release them to see if they would beat us home. (They always did.) Red-tailed hawks, cooper's hawks, kestrels, and rabbits were plentiful. Spotting coyotes lurking warily about and rattlesnakes curled in corkscrews was common, too, yet thrilling all the same. For a time, I fancied myself a budding wildlife biologist, so I toted along my off-brand portable tape player, into which I breathlessly recorded my wildlife observations. "Two *accipiter cooperiis* are soaring roughly seventy-five feet high a mile away! We're in pursuit!"

A landmark called Three Trees could be glimpsed at the peak of the mountain. My friends and I vowed to reach this quasi-mythical destination one day. From our homes in the Valley, we could see these three oaks at the summit, which seemed to sprout from the otherwise barren mountain like broccoli florets, motionless and toylike off into the distance. Three Trees seemed an apt name for the locale, but there were actually four trees, insisted the older boys who claimed to have reached the summit. The fourth tree, purportedly, stood behind one of the others, which was why you couldn't see it from the Valley. My friends and I never quite made it all the way up to Three Trees. The trails pretty much stopped halfway up the mountain. There were fences and no trespassing signs, too. Getty Oil owned the land up on the hill. Usually, we didn't even make it to that point, the rugged trails, the heat, the dust and smog taking their toll. Rather than make our way back the arduous way we came, we'd turn east to Tampa Avenue. Once safely on cement, we'd pick the thorny burrs from our tube socks ("land mines," my son calls such burrs today), then coast at breakneck speed down the winding, broad—but at that time still largely unmotored—avenue back down toward our Valley homes. After hours of laborious pedaling in the hills, it always surprised me how little time it took to descend once again to Devonshire Street and civilization.

Early childhood in the Valley seemed an endless succession of blithe carefree days. I weathered my share of domestic trauma, but nothing particularly remarkable. In retrospect, the Valley offered me a childhood chock full of strange wonderments: earthquakes rumbling or rolling wavelike (the seismic effects varied), sending us diving under table-tops; the occasional nighttime glow of brush fires in the chaparral hills just to the north or at the far south beyond Ventura Boulevard; the light dusting of snow that every once in a magical while powdered Three Trees and the surrounding mountainside; curious pea-soup drifts of fog that would greet us some mornings. Forces from without would alter the landscape, diminishing (I'm afraid) the childhoods of subsequent generations growing up in my Northridge neighborhood. New Porter Ranch subdivisions would soon obliterate the last wild remnants of the northern Valley; every acre of the horse ranch, closer to my home, was bought up and transformed by residential real estate developers even earlier, as were the few undeveloped tracts in my neighborhood. But even before all that, a separate phenomenon threatened to interrupt my halcyon Valley days, a judicial phenomenon that had been simmering even before my parents moved to the Valley: the effort to desegregate the schools in the LAUSD.

Integration Efforts and Agonies

GROWING OLDER, despite its numerous drawbacks, carries with it certain advantages. One's life, I've only recently discovered, gains a sort of historical resonance, and even richness, as the years march by. My birth year, 1968, looms over my shoulder as perhaps the most tumultuous year in modern American history. The social upheaval that defined the 1960s reached its bloody crescendo in 1968 with the Vietnam Tet offensive, the assassinations of Martin Luther King, Jr., and Robert Kennedy, the student and worker uprisings in Paris, and the police riot at the Democratic National Convention in Chicago. The assassinations of King and Kennedy represented a crushing blow to the Civil Rights movement, but the tragedies also galvanized the resolve of many Americans to fulfill the promise of the landmark Civil Rights Act of 1964. Of particular concern here, the era of my childhood would represent the zenith of our country's efforts—at the federal and local levels—to desegregate our public schools. The thorny racial quandaries surrounding public education; the embattled school assignment policies within school districts; the legal wrangling at every judicial level— these realities defined my experiences, and the experiences of my teammates, in the LAUSD of the 1970s and 1980s. Moreover, these controversies remain a current event in L.A., south Florida, and throughout our nation.

Litigation in the Los Angeles Superior Court and the U.S. Supreme Court, in addition to various ballot initiatives and state executive orders in other states, threaten today to accelerate the rapid resegregation of our public schools, a resegregation that began in earnest just after my graduation from high school in 1986. I will return to these recent developments

21

later. But given the currency of the issues at hand, given all that's at stake, it seems crucial to examine the terms of those early judicial efforts to desegregate the schools in L.A., which provided a particular integrated educational experience for my teammates and me. I will locate these teammates, as many of them as I can find, shortly. A trip to L.A., I know, looms on the horizon. But before there was a Jeff Inzar, a TMac, a Sean Brown, a Dennis Bishop, before there was a me, there was a Jay R. Jackson, Jr. First things first.

Jay R. Jackson and his wife, Lucia, I imagine, had only noticed in 1961 what most families with children in the Washington Junior High School zone of the Pasadena City School District probably noticed. A separate, predominantly white, junior high school in the area (attended primarily by students graduated from the predominantly white Linda Vista Elementary) had recently withdrawn from the district, leaving it to the school board to rezone these students to a new junior high school. From a geographical standpoint, Washington was the obvious choice to absorb the Linda Vista graduates. Washington was closer to Linda Vista than any other junior high school in the district. However, a voluble constituency of Linda Vista parents, alarmed by this imminent prospect, exerted pressure upon the board to assign their children to McKinley Junior High School, instead, populated by a considerably smaller percentage of minority students. The board acquiesced to these demands, essentially gerrymandering the McKinley zone to accommodate the white students.

Why does it surprise me to learn about this episode? I suppose it has something to do with the prominence and sheer power of the landmark 1954 *Brown v. Board of Education* decision in our popular imagination. This was the decision, of course, in which the U.S. Supreme Court—overturning their *Plessy v. Ferguson* (1896) "separate but equal" doctrine—held that separate schools were inherently unequal and therefore violated the constitutional rights of minority children. Like most educated Americans, I suppose, I knew about those isolated pockets of resistance in Birmingham and in other deep south locales in the immediate aftermath of *Brown*. But, as naïve as it sounds, I had always assumed that willful segregation in the rest of the country pretty much ended the day after the *Brown* decision. So it surprises me to discover that efforts to maintain segregated schools—effectively, if not ostensibly—were fairly typical and transparent (to anyone paying attention) throughout the country after *Brown*.[1] The Jacksons had only noticed what most people living in the Washington Junior High School zone of the Pasadena City School District had probably noticed. The Jacksons, however, possessed the wherewithal and will to pursue a legal remedy.

From the current vantage, the circumstances precipitating the Jackson's lawsuit seem obviously, even shamefully, actionable. As Mr. Jackson, a bank executive and Morehouse College alumnus, tersely put it to a *Los Angeles Times* reporter in 1967, "If Washington wasn't good enough for their children [the white children of Linda Vista] I didn't believe it was good enough for mine."[2] Yet the Jacksons and their lawyer, the Pasadena NAACP president, Samuel Sheats, were up against a longstanding cultural legacy of legally segregated schools in the nation, and in California specifically—a legacy of apartheid that wouldn't be so easily jettisoned after the *Brown* decision. A California statute from 1870 stipulated that public schools be "open for admission of all white children," and that "the education of children of African descent, and Indian children, shall be provided for in separate schools."[3] The statute was challenged periodically in the state courts over the next century (perhaps most significantly in the 1924 *Piper v. Big Pine School District*), but segregated schools were the order of the day in California, and on the whole accepted as such, until the *Jackson* case.

The Jacksons only won their case upon their appeal to the Supreme Court of California in 1963. Two years earlier, the Pasadena Superior Court had granted the defendant's demurrer, dismissing the complaint. My wife, fortunately for me, is an attorney, and helps me through the legalese. What this means, she patiently explains to me over dinner at our kitchen bar, scanning the decision I've printed and foisted upon her, is that the court upheld the defense argument that even if the plaintiff's allegations were substantiated, the complainant nonetheless held no legal recourse, or "standing." As far as the court was concerned, the Pasadena City School District's right to establish school attendance zones within the district, to determine the area that a particular school shall serve, and to require the students in that area to attend that school, trumped the allegations of racial discrimination that may or may not have influenced these decisions.

The California Supreme Court's reversal of the lower court's decision makes for compelling reading—even for a lay reader like myself—both for the sheer power of its language (refreshingly uncluttered by jargon) and for the broad sweep of its claims vis à vis the school district's responsibility to desegregate its schools proactively. While the court acknowledged early in its opinion that local boards of education retained the power, "in the exercise of reasonable discretion," to establish school attendance zones, the court also tilted its hand as to its ultimate ruling by clarifying that such decisions might always be checked by the higher authority of constitutional law.[4] "It is obvious, however," the court argued, "that the general powers of the board with respect to attendance zones are subject to the constitutional guaranties of equal protection and due process."[5] One of the defendant's key arguments in the case was that its actions did not change the physical boundaries of the Washington district or its racial composition. The court was unmoved by this argument and invoked compelling phrases from recent legal precedent to apply to the Pasadena School District's actions, phrases such as "evasive schemes for segregation" and "zoning is merely a subterfuge for producing or perpetuating racial segregation in a school."[6] The court affirmed the plaintiff's allegation that "the existing imbalance has been intensified by purposeful and unreasonable action," elucidating that "a racial imbalance may be created or intensified in a particular school not only by requiring Negroes to attend it but also by providing different schools for white students who, because of proximity or convenience, would be required to attend it if boundaries were fixed on a nonracial basis."[7] Despite the defendant's claims to the contrary, then, the court held that their actions constituted an intentional discriminatory action.

The California Supreme Court might have stopped there and ruled accordingly for Jackson. Had they done so, the ruling would have been fairly typical of its day, as state courts across the nation, post-*Brown*, were busily striking down intentional acts of school segregation wherever they came across such violations of the Fourteenth Amendment. With regard to unscrupulous zoning practices specifically, the California Supreme Court would cite ample recent precedent from a diverse panoply of state courts: *Cooper v. Aaron* (Arkansas), *Taylor v. Board of Education of City School District of New Rochelle* (New York), *Clemons v. Board of Education of Hillsboro* (Ohio), *Buchanan v. Evans* (Delaware), and *Gomillion v. Lightfoot* (Alabama). It's amazing, truly, the spate of local desegregation judicial decisions in the wake of *Brown*. While most of us only think of *Brown* when we think of school desegregation, and only think of the eventual Supreme Court justice Thurgood Marshall, a host of lower court cases, lawyers, and judges would, just as crucially, bolster the essential precepts of *Brown* through their arguments and decisions in the late 1950s, 1960s, and 1970s. We were a nation on fire, suddenly—state by state, county by county—to integrate our public schools. But the California Supreme Court went one significant step further than most of these district and state courts, holding that school boards must not only refrain from intentional acts of segregation (e.g., gerrymandering school zones) but must seek actively to integrate schools where a substantial racial imbalance exists.

The court surely knew that its ruling would do little, otherwise, to change the facts on the ground in school districts throughout California, but particularly in the L.A. area. In reality, most local schools would retain their segregated character as long as geography, primarily, dictated school boundary zones. The separatist impulses of the school board members plotting these precise boundaries with their pens—both white members and some minority members, as well—would only exacerbate matters. Indeed, it had long been accepted as a given in L.A. that some schools would serve a disproportionately high percentage of minority students, and vice versa, given preexisting residential segregation. The court reserved its strongest language to assail this apparently inexorable reality of the status quo. "Residential segregation is in itself an evil," the court argued,

> which tends to frustrate the youth in the area and to cause antisocial attitudes and behavior. Where such segregation exists it is not enough for a school board to refrain from affirmative discriminatory conduct. The harmful influence on the children will be reflected and intensified in the classroom if school attendance is determined on a geographic basis without corrective measures. The right to an equal opportunity

for education and the harmful consequences of segregation require that
school boards take steps, insofar as reasonably feasible, to alleviate racial
imbalance in schools *regardless of its cause.* (emphasis mine)[8]

Only after issuing such strong directives did the court reverse the lower
court's judgment, noting that the demurrer should have been overruled.
The ruling was a shot across the bow of school boards throughout the
state and the nation.

Given its clear, uncompromising principles, one would think that
school boards throughout the LAUSD (and in California, generally) would
have set to the task of addressing diversity in their schools in a substantive
way. And, to their credit, the Pasadena City School District implemented
the Geographic and Controlled Open Districting program the year after
the *Jackson* decision to increase diversity in its public schools. The plan,
essentially, designated a formerly minority zone as an "open" zone. The
parents of the primarily black students in this neighborhood were encouraged to volunteer to have their children bused crosstown to a predominantly white school. As only a few families volunteered, however, this
initial plan did little to integrate the Pasadena schools. Consequently, the
board—in a further attempt to adhere to the spirit of the Jackson ruling—
initiated a more rigorous rezoning effort in 1967, called Plan A. This plan,
however, was met with fierce resistance in the community and was soon
repealed by incoming board members. "The State Supreme Court ruling
was just an opinion," argued one white board member, Steve Salisian.
"We don't have to do anything."[9]

This imperious stance seems to flout rather brazenly the court's order
in the *Jackson* case. Yet, upon inspection, the court's decision contained
enough qualifying language to offer such views just enough traction.
School boards, after all, were only instructed to take "reasonably feasible" steps to alleviate racial imbalances in particular schools.[10] Further,
toward the end of its opinion, the court specified that school authorities
were "not required to attain an exact apportionment of Negroes among
the schools, and consideration must be give to the various factors in each
case, including the practical necessities of governmental operation."[11]
School authorities, finally, were instructed to balance the extent to which

a racial imbalance in a particular school affects the opportunity for education with the "difficulty and effectiveness of revising school boundaries
so as to eliminate segregation" or make available "other facilities to which
students can be transferred."[12]

What constitutes a "reasonably feasible" step to alleviate a racial imbalance? At what point does the "difficulty" of revising a school boundary to
achieve integration outweigh the effected benefits? When ought "practical necessities" preclude the pursuit of lofty, egalitarian goals? These are
arguable questions, of course, and local citizens and school board members throughout the greater L.A. area wrangled, and continue to wrangle,
over precisely these issues.

It would be easy, from the current vantage, and given my progressive
predilections, to vilify those like Salisian who vigorously opposed those
first, more toothy plans to integrate the Los Angeles schools in the 1960s.
I take in his grainy, black-and-white photo printed in an old *Los Angeles
Times* article and, reflexively, see that broad smile of his as a self-satisfied
smirk (whereas the more sober expression worn by the Pasadena NAACP
president, Sheats, printed just above, seems to me the model of steadfast
integrity). But, in fairness, it should be noted that these plans were not,
in any sense, uncomplicated or uncontroversial. The intense residential
segregation of the sprawling area would challenge even the best intentions to desegregate individual neighborhood schools. The elephant in
the room, which few citizens were willing to face in these early years,
was that to effect substantive integration in the most racially imbalanced
schools, children of all races (if the plan were to be fair) would have to
travel, sometimes over significant distances, to attend schools in unfamiliar neighborhoods.

The neighborhood school was, and remains, a powerful institution in
our collective ethos. Even many, if not most, black families resisted the prospect of busing their children miles away from home. Again, only a fraction
of minority families in the "open" district of the Geographic and Controlled
Open Districting program in Pasadena volunteered to have their children
bused to the more distant, predominantly white schools. Certainly, a considerable number of families with the available means would simply withdraw their children from the public school system rather than accede to

having them bused some thirty miles or more. And what would happen to the quality of the public schools if the most affluent (read: white) families abandoned the system to enroll their children in private schools? While racial integration seemed an admirable goal, perhaps allocating a greater share of resources to predominantly minority schools would ameliorate, to a more significant degree, the racial inequities plaguing the public schools. At the end of the day, perhaps it simply *wasn't* feasible or practicable to alleviate racial imbalances in schools, regardless of its cause.

In any case, the challenge to integrate the schools proved insuperable for the Pasadena community, so insuperable that in 1970, the Pasadena City School District would become the first district outside the southern states, post-*Brown*, to be ordered by a federal judge (U.S. district judge Manuel Real) to desegregate. By this time, of course, it was far too late for Jay R. Jackson, Jr. By the time the California Supreme Court overruled the lower court's decision, he was no longer a junior high school student, and the case was not continued. The protracted case had taken a clear, emotional toll on the family, and upon Jay R. Jackson, Jr., specifically. While the boy and his family might have been hailed as heroes of the Civil Rights movement, the more salient reaction at the time, even (and perhaps especially) within the African American community, was one of resentment and distrust. Five years after the trial, Mr. Jackson recalled that his son's peers had harassed him for requesting the transfer out of the Washington district with taunts such as "'What's the matter, are you too good for this school?'"[13] Such hostility from within the African American community exemplifies the crabs-in-the-barrel syndrome that has concerned civil rights leaders as far back as W. E. B. Du Bois. All the same, it should be noted that the crabs didn't put themselves in the barrel. "It seemed that neither acquaintances nor teachers, Negro nor white, could understand we were just trying to achieve better schools," Mr. Jackson continued.[14] His son would quit high school after two years, join the marines, and serve in Vietnam as a combat soldier.

It would take another court case in L. A. to force local boards to take meaningful and substantive action to integrate its schools—a case that would make its way back and forth from the United States Supreme Court during a dizzying array of decisions and appeals over a nearly twenty-year period. It was a case that would ultimately affect my own experience in the LAUSD as an elementary school student and would later play a major role in determining the roster of my JV and varsity basketball teams at Granada Hills High School. There is no book-length study devoted to the case, but I readily access the court opinions at the local, state, and federal levels and also manage, mostly online, to unearth the energetic and often bitter wrangling over the case in the local and national press. I track down and speak with a couple of the major players on both sides. Given my personal stake in the case, all these old documents, all these old people, don't seem old at all. The case may be history, but it's living history. The case—yet another of those local, post-*Brown* desegregation cases that we ought not forget—was *Crawford v. Board of Education of the City of Los Angeles.*

The wheels of justice spin slowly, the old saying goes, but the manifold twists and turns of the *Crawford* case brings to mind Charles Dickens's Jarndyce and Jarndyce case in *Bleak House,* the story line through which Dickens excoriates England's byzantine legal system. The class action was originally filed on August 1, 1963, just a few months after the California Supreme Court issued its decision in the *Jackson* case. Emboldened by that decision, a group of minority students enrolled in the LAUSD filed the suit to compel the district to desegregate two of its high schools. The two schools were located less than two miles from each other, yet one school served an almost entirely white student population while the other school served an almost entirely African American student population. The American Civil Liberties Union represented the plaintiff's case, which would eventually be expanded to include the entire school district. Interestingly, the case would not go to trial in the Los Angeles Superior Court until 1968. During the intervening years, the plaintiffs sought in vain to persuade the LAUSD to initiate voluntarily a meaningful plan to desegregate its schools.

The judge assigned to the case was Alfred Gitelson, who had been appointed to the superior court in 1957 by Governor Goodwin Knight. This first phase of the trial would occupy the court for over two months. Recognizing the significance of the outcome, the plaintiffs marshaled ample evidence to support their contention that (1) the LAUSD was not only segregated but becoming *increasingly* segregated; (2) the school board had failed to take meaningful steps to alleviate this worsening unconstitutional condition; and had even (3) taken affirmative steps to contribute to and perpetuate the racial and ethnic segregation of the district. As the California Supreme Court would later note, "a tremendous quantity of evidentiary material was introduced in the course of a lengthy trial; the reporter's transcript on appeal runs to 62 volumes."[15]

The evidence supporting the segregated character of the LAUSD was particularly compelling. While the student population in the district as a whole was roughly half minority and half white in 1968, the plaintiffs were able to highlight a substantial proportion of individual schools in the district wherein either minority or white students represented 90 percent of that school's total student population. By the time the case would reach the California Supreme Court, the court would cite a 1971 enrollment survey conducted by the federal Department of Health, Education, and Welfare, which determined that the LAUSD was among the most segregated in the entire country, with 86.6 percent of black pupils (including my future PWT basketball teammates) attending schools that were more than 80 percent black.[16] Indeed, even at the trial court stage, the statistical evidence was compelling enough that the defendants did not challenge the plaintiff's claim that substantial segregation existed.

Judge Gitelson was particularly moved by the evidence presented by the plaintiffs elucidating the serious harm that minority children suffer when their education takes place in segregated public schools, especially as these minority segregated schools in the Los Angeles district were, as the court affirmed, "of poorer quality than the plant, teachers, physical facilities and curriculum at its predominantly white schools."[17] To illustrate the deleterious effects of segregated schools upon minority children, the plaintiffs referenced both measurable indicators, such as academic performance, and the less measurable psychological harm imposed upon minority children, averred in the *Brown* decision. The rhetoric surrounding the issue of lagging minority student performance in the school district, and the school board's associated responsibilities to address the problem, occasionally grew heated. Perhaps the most racially charged episode during the initial trial occurred when the school board claimed that it was "agnostic" about whether or not African American mental abilities were inferior to the mental abilities of white students, but that a school board could not be expected to attain equality in achievement if, in fact, the races were different in their capacities.[18]

In its circuitous way, I suppose that the school board meant to dissociate the segregated condition of its schools from the poorer academic performance of its minority students, while also suggesting the likely futility of any efforts to enhance minority academic performance through integrating its schools. Such measures, the logic goes, wouldn't necessarily raise the graduation rates or SAT scores of minority children, who may, after all, simply possess inferior mental capacities. The school board may have been moved to pursue such inflammatory arguments because it couldn't claim that it had taken any steps to desegregate its schools. The defendants claimed, instead, that they were not convinced that the educational value of a desegregation program would outweigh the financial detriment that such a program would entail. Here, the school board clearly sought relief in the qualifying language of the *Jackson* decision, which only mandated "reasonably feasible" steps to alleviate racial imbalances in schools and noted that school boards must balance the extent to which a racial imbalance in a particular school affects the opportunity for education with the "difficulty and effectiveness of revising school boundaries so as to eliminate segregation" or make available "other facilities to which students can be transferred."[19] As far as the school board was concerned, the difficulties inherent to any substantive integration plan outweighed any of its prospective—and perhaps even unlikely—benefits.

Judge Gitelson disagreed, finding it unacceptable that the school board had refused to devise or implement a desegregation program. Moreover, evidence presented by the plaintiffs convinced the court that the school board had actually taken steps to exacerbate the segregated condition of its schools, that it had, in the words of the court, "knowingly, affirmatively and in bad faith . . . by and through its affirmative policies . . . and practices, . . . segregated, *de jure*, its students."[20] The *de jure–de facto* distinction would be a crucial one in this case, and in subsequent desegregation court cases, which continue today. *De jure*, for the uninitiated, and as my attorney-wife affirms, translates roughly as "of law." Schools authorities found to have segregated its students, *de jure*, have directly intended or mandated such segregation. *De facto* translates roughly as "flowing from the fact of," meaning that instances of *de facto* segregation occur inadvertently or without the assistance or collusion of authority, but by social, economic, and/or other factors. Judge Gitelson highlighted several *de jure* discriminatory policies and practices in his 103-page ruling, including the construction of new schools in geographic sites that, based upon the "neighborhood school" assignment policy, would inevitably be segregated; the gerrymandering of boundaries defining neighborhood zones to exacerbate the segregated condition of specific schools; and the implementation of open transfer policies, ostensibly to allow minority students access to predominantly white schools, but which in practice (and as the school board surely recognized) more readily permitted white students to transfer out of minority segregated schools, given the burden upon the transferring students to provide their own transportation.[21] Thus, Judge Gitelson entered a judgment ordering the defendant school board to prepare and implement a reasonably feasible plan for the desegregation of its schools, and, most controversially, designated specific racial and ethnic percentages to which schools must adhere. No school, the judgment specified, may deviate by more than 15 percent above or below the overall minority population of the school district after desegregation is completed. The district's racial breakdown at the time—in the parlance of the day—was 58 percent Anglo, 20 percent Negro, 18 percent Spanish surname, and 4 percent Oriental and American Indian.

However one might feel about the moral propriety of Judge Gitelson's order, there could be little dispute regarding the amplitude of the corrective actions he ordered. He had issued his *Crawford* decision in February 1970 and ordered the school board to develop by September a desegregation plan that would be fully implemented by the following fall. Any such plan or network of plans would represent an enormous undertaking. The LAUSD covered a sprawling 714 square mile area to serve its 730,000 students in its 579 schools!

From our current vantage—or is this just *my* current vantage and that of others sharing my sensibilities?—the Gitelson ruling, at least its broad stroke to compel the school board to implement a desegregation plan, seems abundantly just. Yet it's fair to say that the ruling was poorly received by a broad swath of citizens within and without Los Angeles. In fact, the decision proved disastrous for Judge Gitelson's career. Although the phrase "activist judge" had yet to enter into our collective vernacular, the most voluble critics of the Gitelson decision excoriated him in that spirit. President Richard Nixon opined that the ruling was "probably the most extreme judicial decree so far."[22] The governor of California at the time, Ronald Reagan, called the ruling "utterly ridiculous," while the mayor of Los Angeles, Sam Yorty, worried that the ruling could "polarize public opinion to the point of setting the nation against itself."[23]

While Gitelson never proposed forced busing, specifically, in his ruling, his political opponents tarred him as the "busing judge," a label that stuck. The vitriol leveled against Gitelson in letters to editors and op-eds was particularly severe. In April 1970, the police even uncovered an assassination plot against the judge by members of a right-wing extremist group.[24] The undercover policemen were contracted by the group to shoot the judge and drive a nail into his head with a note reading, "This is for the niggers."[25] Later that year, Gitelson would lose his seat on the court in an election that couldn't have been timed worse for the judge. He would respond bitterly to the defeat, attributing his loss to "enough people who are truly racists."[26] Reflecting more coolly and eloquently upon the *Crawford* case two years later, Gitelson remarked, "We were about to lose the equal protection of the laws."[27] His decision, he asserted self-deprecatingly to a *Los Angeles Times* reporter, did not represent a great act of courage but was "mechanical."[28] In his view, the appropriate judgment in the case was rather obvious, and he appears to have been nonplussed by the resulting acrimony inveighed against him. "I took the law and the facts and applied them," he noted. "The evidence was overwhelming."[29]

To add insult to injury, the school board proved intransigent to Gitelson's decision. Attorneys for the board appealed the trial court order, and the court of appeal stayed its enforcement for several years. The court of appeal's decision would hinge upon the distinction between *de facto* and *de jure* segregation. We must remember the *Jackson* decision had rendered such distinctions irrelevant. "Where such segregation exists," the court declared, "it is not enough for a school board to refrain from affirmative discriminatory conduct. . . . The right to an equal opportunity for education and the harmful consequences of segregation require that school boards take steps, insofar as reasonably feasible, to alleviate racial imbalance in schools *regardless of its cause* [emphasis mine]."[30] The *Jackson* ruling, that is, required school boards to fix the problem of segregation even if a school board could demonstrate that it hadn't caused the problem. In the several intervening years between the Gitelson ruling and the appeal court ruling, however, several courts across the land would issue more defendant-friendly verdicts that, in essence, declared that school boards must only take active steps to desegregate schools to remedy *de jure* segregation. The U.S. Supreme Court, for example, held in *Swann v. Charlotte-Mecklenburg Board of Education* (1971) that courts ought only to address "state-imposed segregation."[31] Two years later, in *Keyes v. School District No. 1, Denver, Colorado,* the U.S. Supreme Court stated that plaintiffs in segregation cases must prove a defendant school board's "purpose or intent to segregate."[32]

Judge Gitelson's ruling, of course, did not rely upon the court's declaration in *Jackson* that school boards were responsible to repair *de jure* or *de facto* segregation. Schools in the LAUSD, he noted, were not merely segregated *de facto*. Rather, the school board had taken several affirmative steps to maintain and intensify the segregated condition of its schools. Nonetheless, the court of appeal was not persuaded by the ample evidence of intentional *de jure* discrimination presented by the plaintiffs and highlighted by Judge Gitelson in his lengthy decision. At most, the three-judge panel declared, the school board failed to give significant consideration to the matter of the effect of its acts or omissions upon the prevailing condition of racial and ethnic imbalance. Such possible negligence, according to the appeal court, did not amount to an intentional act of segregation. As *de facto* segregation was no longer actionable, according to more recent federal precedent than *Jackson,* the court of appeal reversed the trial court's decision. It was 1975, nearly five years after Gitelson had issued his ruling. Within a year after this reversal, former superior court judge Gitelson, at age sixty-nine, would die of a heart attack on a cruise ship off Panama.

There are no books about Judge Gitelson. The *Crawford* case, the various old newspaper articles covering it, and the judge's untimely death, provide only scant information about this man, who captivates me—not least of all because he was a Jew. The newspaper article photos reveal a face that looks not unlike my great-grandfather Harry. For those unacquainted with my great-grandfather, Gitelson, with his protuberant ears (old-world ears, they seem to me), hawkish nose, and white, slicked-backed hair, could pass for the better-looking brother of the actor Fievel Fivush. He, purportedly, was rotund. Here's what else I know about Gitelson: He was born in New York City in 1906. He was the son of a builder and land developer. The family moved to southern California when Alfred was still a baby. After breezing through college and law school at UCLA and USC, respectively, he worked in private practice for thirty years, specializing in corporations, partnerships, and trusts, before accepting his less lucrative appointment to the L.A. Superior Court bench in 1957. He was married to Gail Olsher, of Chicago. The couple raised a son and two daughters, who produced seven grandchildren for their parents.

There is little mention of Gitelson's Jewishness in the articles devoted to him, though his olive complexion is noted at least once. Gitelson himself, never alludes to his Jewish identity in the quotations attributed to him, the ones I can find, at any rate. This seems unremarkable to me. One's minority identity wasn't exactly something that public figures, or those aspiring toward public office, bandied about forty years ago. A judge, in particular, grounds his or her decisions upon the law, which, ideally, transcends the politics of personal identity. Gitelson, in fact, had sought to armor his decision in *Crawford* against any suggestion that it arose from personal passion. It was an obvious decision, he had remarked—one that he had issued mechanically, as he put it. Despite his protestations (and, in part, because of them), it's difficult for me to believe that Gitelson's Jewishness didn't in some way influence his 103-page ruling. What did Gitelson know of cultural marginality? Had such knowledge rendered him more sensitive to the plight of those darker-than-olive minorities in his midst?

Although Gitelson wouldn't live long enough to see it, the California Supreme Court would affirm his original ruling within a year after its reversal by the court of appeal. What makes the court's decision particularly interesting is its frontal challenge to the recent federal court decisions, which held that school boards need only take steps to remedy *de jure* segregation. The state court, importantly, needn't have reentered this morass to overturn the court of appeal's decision, as ample evidence had been presented at both previous stages of the case to support the plaintiff's contention of *de jure* segregation. And, in fact, the supreme court notes in its decision that "The findings in this case adequately support the trial court's conclusion that the segregation in the defendant school district is de jure in nature."[33] Still, the court explicitly refused to rest its decision on these grounds, taking pains instead to address and affirm its earlier, more plaintiff-friendly precedent, articulated in *Jackson*.

The opinion begins, in fact, with an allusion to the language of the *Jackson* decision thirteen years earlier, specifically to its declaration that "'[the] segregation of school children into separate schools because of their race, even though the physical facilities and the methods and quality of instruction in the several schools may be equal, deprives the children of the minority group of equal opportunities for education and denies them equal protection and due process of the law.'" "We held," the *Crawford* opinion continues, "that as a consequence school boards in this state bear a constitutional obligation to undertake reasonably feasible steps to alleviate such racial segregation in the public schools, *regardless of the cause of such segregation*."[34] The court highlighted this last phrase, as it cut to the heart of its judgment that the *de facto–de jure* distinction was a meaningless one, at least in terms of a school board's responsibility to desegregate its schools.

The court, however, might also have italicized the phrase, "school boards in this state," to emphasize the spirit of its current, *Crawford* decision. For what the court argued, in essence, was that its own precedent, vis à vis particular instances of segregation in California, trumped the precedent of the federal court. Indeed, the state supreme court fairly admonished the court of appeal for privileging the precedent of the federal court over its own state court precedent: "In focusing on these federal decisions, however, defendant ignores a significant line of California decisions, decisions which authoritatively establish that *in this state* school boards do bear a constitutional obligation to take reasonable steps to alleviate segregation in the public schools, whether the segregation be de facto or de jure in origin" [emphasis mine].[35]

It would be easy to chalk up the California Supreme Court *Crawford* decision cynically as a mere turf battle between the federal and state branches of the judiciary. But, upon close inspection, the decision does not so much contradict the spirit of recent federal precedent as establish, instead, the latitude such precedent allowed for individual state courts to mandate active remedies to segregated schools, even in the absence of demonstrable *de jure* discrimination. Racial and ethnic segregation in the LAUSD was *unusually* extreme and entrenched; the facilities in the minority schools were *particularly* substandard. These disconcerting facts on the ground warranted more vigorous judicial intervention in California, the court suggested, than the more restrained, federal standard imposed. To administer justice based upon arguable *de facto–de jure* distinctions in the case of the schools in the LAUSD was to descend into absurdities:

> Finally, and most fundamentally, even if courts could satisfactorily distinguish de facto from de jure segregation and even if the effect of such judicial effort would not provide a haven for intractable school boards, the judiciary must still face the ultimate reality that in California in the 1970s the de facto–de jure distinction retains little, if any, significance for the children whose constitutional rights are at issue here. Although the educational experts may disagree on many aspects of the desegregation controversy, there is virtually no dispute that the practical effect of segregated schooling on minority children does not depend upon whether a court finds the segregation de jure or de facto in nature; the isolating and debilitating effects do not vary with the source of segregation.[36]

The court would allude to the more restrained federal *Keyes* decision to add the final flourish to its argument. "Thus," the decision reads, "the final blow against an adoption of the de facto–de jure distinction is that, as Justice Powell has pointed out, the distinction is simply 'a legalism rooted in history rather than present reality.'"[37] Consequently, the state supreme court found the trial court's order compelling the school board to prepare and implement a reasonably feasible desegregation plan "completely justified," except for its definition of a 'desegregated' school in terms of specific percentages.[38] With this one caveat, the court affirmed Gitelson's ruling and remanded the case for proceedings consistent with its opinion. It was June 28, 1976.

It would take six months for the parties and a supervising judge to name a replacement for the deceased Judge Gitelson. The replacement would be Paul Egly, who had been appointed to the superior court by Governor Reagan in 1968. Egly was perhaps the obvious choice, as he had recently served on the bench for a school segregation case in neighboring San Bernardino, issuing a judgment consistent with Gitelson's. The *Crawford* case couldn't have been considered a plum appointment, given the political repercussions Gitelson suffered. Yet Judge Egly, unlike Gitelson, still had five years left in his term. As he reflected in a recent interview, "I figured I was safe. . . . I thought I'd have a couple years to recover."[39]

The state supreme court had made its position clear in *Crawford:* it considered it a last resort for a court to intervene in designing and implementing any school desegregation plan. That was a job best left to the experts. Ideally, the school board itself would design and implement its own viable plan for ameliorating the segregated condition of its schools. "Experience has taught that the task of integration is an extremely complex one," the court declared,

> which entails much more than the assignment of specified percentages of pupils of different races or ethnic groups to the same school. . . . In light of the realities of the remedial problem, we believe that once a court finds that a school board has implemented a program which promises to achieve meaningful progress toward eliminating the segregation in the district, the court should defer to the school board's program and should decline to intervene in the school desegregation process so long as such meaningful progress does in fact follow.[40]

Consistent with the supreme court's directive, Egly instructed the school board to submit to the court its "reasonably feasible" plan for integrating the schools.

Perhaps predictably, the LAUSD initially submitted in the spring of 1977 a fairly toothless, mostly voluntary, plan. The language of the supreme court's decision in *Crawford*, consistent with its earlier *Jackson* decision, contained just enough qualifying language to encourage such a conservative plan. The court took pains, after all, to emphasize that the judicial branch should "stay its hand," rather than impose a specific integration plan, even if it felt that its own plan would more effectually integrate the schools than a given plan developed by the district.[41] The school board, thus, might reasonably have expected Judge Egly to demonstrate judicial restraint by accepting its plan. Egly, however, could not be convinced that the board's plan represented a viable strategy toward which to achieve "meaningful progress." He rejected the plan, describing it as "wholly ineffective," and demanded that the board submit to him an alternative plan within ninety days. As Egly recently reflected, he "didn't want to cause a revolution in the city," but he "couldn't accept that plan."[42]

He's still alive, Judge Egly, and teaches at the La Verne School of Law just east of L.A., which he founded before taking his seat on the bench. I'll contact him and speak with him about these bygone days, and about the current state of diversity in our public schools. But later.

It would be Egly, in fact—and not Gitelson—who would compel the board to institute a desegregation plan that included forced busing. The board acceded, finally, submitting its plan, which Judge Egly ordered to be implemented by fall of 1978, the beginning of the next academic year. The voluntary and mandatory portions of the plan involved roughly 260 of the district's 558 schools and over 85,000 students—roughly 15 percent of the district's projected enrollment in 1978–79.[43] Although these numbers may seem modest on the surface, the plan at the time represented one of our nation's most substantial and comprehensive desegregation efforts ever to be initiated. According to the plan, 54,300 students in grades 4–8 would be desegregated through a variety of integrated school pairings, clusters, and midsites (i.e., forced busing); 11,000 students had signed up for 45 magnet programs designed to attract an interracial cohort; 1,300 students were expected to attend four integrated "alternative" schools; and about 20,000 students were expected to ride in the district's voluntary Permits With Transportation (PWT) program, which would bus mostly minority students to predominantly white schools elsewhere in the district.[44]

The plan predictably unleashed a furor across the district. There would be an onslaught of desperate legal activity initiated by groups of mostly white Angelenos opposed to the forced busing component of the plan. The leading organization, in fact, adopted the name Bustop. A significant—if smaller—cohort of minority residents in L.A., it should be noted, also opposed the forced busing component of the plan. The proposal to transfer what amounted only to a small percentage of their children to historically white schools in the Valley and elsewhere seemed to them little more than a smoke-and-mirrors ploy to facilitate the continued diversion of much needed resources from inner-city schools. "Our demand," one minority parent argued, "is to improve our present programs and not to take money from our neighborhood schools and place it where only a few of our children will benefit from it."[45] The legal activity would once again involve the court of appeal, the state supreme court, and even the U.S. Supreme Court this time.

A definite pattern had developed since *Jackson*, in which the court of appeal routinely overturned the superior court's more plaintiff-friendly rulings, after which the state supreme court upheld the trial court's decision. In any event, the U.S. Supreme Court would ultimately deny Bustop's request for a stay, upholding the California Supreme Court's rationale that it possessed the authority to impose more rigorous desegregation standards than strictly mandated by federal law. "While I have the gravest doubts that the Supreme Court of California was *required* by the United States Constitution to take the action it has taken in this case," Supreme Court Justice William Rehnquist held, "I have very little doubt that it was *permitted* by that Constitution to take such action."[46] Just days later, on September 12, 1978—as the *Los Angeles Times* ran an editorial titled "A Time for Calm"—1,200 school buses rolled out of parking lots and garages throughout the greater Los Angeles area.[47] The drivers, several of them only certified last minute by Taylor Bus Lines, would crisscross the sprawling district in a tangled yellow web with their precious cargo, playing their small role in integrating the nation's most highly diverse, yet heretofore highly segregated, student populace.

The Blacks and the Jews

I WAS TEN YEARS OLD in the summer of 1978, having just completed
fourth grade at Topeka Drive Elementary. I had no idea that my sheltered
suburban school zone had emerged as the epicenter of one of our country's most significant and divisive school desegregation efforts. Topeka
was my neighborhood public school in Northridge, which I had attended
since kindergarten. Like many of the public schools in the Valley, particularly in the most distant northern and western parts of the Valley, Topeka
was a predominantly white school, still 84 percent white, to be precise,
in the fall of 1977. For this reason, Topeka, like a number of other Valley schools, was earmarked to participate, starting in the fall of 1978, in
the forced busing program to desegregate grades 4–8. Topeka was paired
with Griffin Avenue Elementary, a mostly Mexican-American school over
the hill in Lincoln Heights. The distance between many of the paired
schools in the desegregation plan was great, particularly when schools
in the faraway reaches of the Valley were involved. The Topeka-Griffin
commute of over thirty miles was no exception. The onerous logistics of
desegregating Valley schools accounted in large part for the fierce resistance against forced busing among Valley residents. A *Los Angeles Times*
survey of eighty-five schools affected by the mandatory desegregation
plan found that "only 35 percent of the youngsters scheduled to ride the
bus from the predominantly white western and northern San Fernando
Valley to minority schools had turned up" by the end of the first week of
school.[1] At my public school, Topeka, only 21 of 130 students showed up
to ride the buses to Griffin Avenue.[2]

Despite the significant white attrition from the district, there could be little doubt that the integration plan "worked," insofar as it dramatically integrated the remaining student populace at both Topeka and Griffin. Topeka went from an 84 percent white school in 1977 to a 54 percent white school in 1978; the Hispanic student populace rose from 5 percent (28 students) to 25 percent (85 students), while the black student populace rose more modestly from 8.5 percent to 13 percent. The demographic change was more gradual at Griffin Avenue, owing in part to the attrition of white students from the district in 1978. The school was 91 percent Hispanic in 1977, and only slightly less so in 1978. By 1979, however, Griffin Avenue suddenly boasted an irrefutably more integrated student body, including 204 white students (from a mere 21 white students the year before). White children suddenly represented 38 percent of the student body at Griffin Avenue.

I would like to claim that I was one of the 21 students who rode the bus to Griffin Avenue. But I wasn't. Rather, I was among the majority of Topeka children for whom alternative arrangements were made. In short, my parents withdrew me from the public school system that year and enrolled me in one of the several private schools that had been sprouting up throughout the region at a randy rate. I feel a certain embarrassment upon the disclosure. Wasn't my family on the wrong side of this story, the side that resisted the morally upright efforts of the courts and, ultimately, the school board to deliver a program of education that hewed to the egalitarian spirit of the Constitution? The side that could afford to coddle their youngsters rather than send them to more hardscrabble inner-city schools? My parents, true, were not among those most vociferous opponents of forced busing. They didn't attend the contentious PTA and local school board meetings during this period. "We weren't really very politically active or even aware in those days," my father remembers. Still, they voted with their feet, or, rather, with my feet.

I might have ridden the bus, like some of my peers, to faraway Griffin Avenue. Who knows how this immersion amid Latino/a students, teachers, and administrators would have altered the texture of those days? Might this more integrated learning environment have contributed to the creation of a different—perhaps better—me? Minority students, after all, were envisioned as the primary, but not the sole, beneficiaries of integration. As the California Supreme Court affirmed in *Crawford*, "The elimination of racial isolation in the schools promotes the attainment of equal educational opportunity and is beneficial to all students, both black and white."[3] My parents had, in effect, decided to preserve the "racial isolation" of my elementary school experience. Why?

"It wasn't all about busing," my mother tells me now, from a chaise lounge at her community pool. "We were thinking of sending you to private school anyway. You were doing horribly at Topeka. They were experimenting with a more open curriculum when you were in fourth grade. Something Montessori-like. There were all these learning centers throughout the class, and you kids were pretty much on your own. There were no set expectations. Not even any grades. There was no structure," my mother—someone always fond of structure, of set expectations, of grades—fairly shouts. "All you did was sit in the corner and read." In retrospect, this doesn't seem to have been such a terrible waste of my time. But I suppose I can understand my mother's concerns. I was never a particularly strong student in the conventional sense, which is to say by any measurable standard. I was, on the whole, dreamy and distracted. Overly sensitive to boot. To exacerbate matters, my older brother *was* a strong and disciplined student. He possessed a competitive, fiery spirit that eluded me at the time. SAT glory, the Ivy League, and law school awaited him, even without the intervention of private primary or secondary schooling. I must have seemed, well, dim compared to my diligent and perspicacious brother. My parents, in fact, felt certain that I was afflicted with some nondescript neurological disorder. When I was about five years old they worriedly took me to a psychologist, who studied me in private for an hour, then called my parents back into his office. "Well, your son is fine," he told them. "Now what's wrong with the two of you?!"

My mother, curiously, grows defensive when I pursue the role that race, specifically, played in their decision to remove me from the system. "It wasn't that we had anything against integrated schools," she recollects. "Nobel was already integrated." (Nobel was my brother's public junior high school, just blocks from our house.) "We didn't have anything against blacks coming to *your* school," she insists. She would repeat this particular argument during several of our conversations on the matter, as if fearing that it had failed to register with me. "But you would have had to travel over an hour on the bus at God knows what time in the morning, to a school and neighborhood we didn't know anything about. We didn't think you were ready for that." Who knows? Maybe my parents were right. I can't say with any certainty, despite my progressive predilections, that I would have sent my child off on a bus to a faraway, inner-city school had I the means to pursue alternatives. I think now of my own eight-year-old son: dreamy, distracted and, yes, as overly sensitive as his father once was. Each morning I walk him and our younger daughter (made of sterner stuff) to their public school in our little burg, heralded recently as the fiftieth safest city in the nation by the Morgan Quitno publishing company.[4] I stop at the gate as they continue on to their classrooms, watching after them with just a tinge of anxiety as they slip past my field of view. This is hard enough. I can't imagine walking either of them to a bus that would take them some thirty miles north or south to an inner-city school in West Palm Beach (the seventh most dangerous city, according to the Morgan Quitno study) or Fort Lauderdale (the forty-sixth most dangerous).

While some of my anxiety might be attributed to the post-Columbine world we now occupy, the 1970s and 1980s in L.A. weren't exactly violence-free days, either. I remember, quite vividly, my basketball team's contest against Los Angeles High School, located over the hill on West Olympic Boulevard. Or, rather, I remember the general blight of the grounds, the curious bars on all the windows. I remember being escorted to a bleak locker room by a walkie-talkie-wielding administrator. "Open up those doors," the fellow warned, pointing toward a set of heavy doors that presumably opened to the street, "and every gang in Los Angeles will be up in your face." I remember my teammate, TMac, who wore a lacquered 'fro and couldn't have lived far from that campus, strutting toward those doors in mock bravado just after the administrator left us to change into our uniforms. I remember the rest of us laughing, yet leaping to our feet to restrain him just in case. School violence, indeed, on a modest and even a grand scale, predates Columbine. No, despite my best efforts, I can't honestly muster up any significant distance from my parents' long-ago decision to counter, in effect, these particular desegregation efforts of my hometown.

The rival perspectives of Jewish families toward *Crawford* is particularly interesting. Sharp divisions split L.A. Jews, a rift that stands today as a textbook example of the rightward political shift of several Jewish Americans nationwide during this period. While Jewish Americans would continue to register and vote overwhelmingly Democratic during the 1970s (as they do today at nearly 80 percent), they would increasingly find their own interests at odds with progressive initiatives aimed at benefitting other minorities, initiatives that they could formerly be counted upon to champion. Simultaneously, a more radical strain of political expression, increasingly distrustful of Jewish motives, emerged on the African American side.

Scholars have usefully interrogated the notion that there was ever an uncomplicated, golden age of Black-Jewish relations in America.[5] But it is just as true that Jewish Americans had, collectively, represented one of the more voluble and engaged groups to support early, modern civil rights initiatives. Jews had helped to found the NAACP in 1909. Jewish brothers, Joel and Arthur Spingarn, would serve successively as presidents of the organization, and another Jew, Herbert Seligman, served as its publicist. Stanley Levison, a radical Jewish businessman and lawyer, was a key advisor and close confidant of Martin Luther King, Jr. Jewish lawyers, indeed, would occupy central positions of advocacy on behalf of civil rights cases, including the famous *Scottsboro* case, in which nine black youths were falsely accused of raping two white women in Alabama, and the later *Brown* case. Jack Greenberg, a lawyer on the *Brown* team, would succeed Thurgood Marshall as head of the NAACP's Legal Defense Fund. Before his appointment to the U.S. Supreme Court, Felix Frankfurter actively recruited talented lawyers for the NAACP. While lawyers were, perhaps, the most visible and influential Jewish cohort to champion civil rights initiatives, they only reflected the collective Jewish support for the cause. A disproportionately high number of Jews, for example, would count themselves among the young white volunteers who participated in the "freedom rides" during the summers of 1961 and 1964. These volunteers, mostly from the North, traveled to the most racist outposts of the South to work on behalf of black voting rights. Two Jewish volunteers, Andrew Goodman and Michael Henry Schwerner, would be murdered along with their black coworker, James Earl Chaney, by the KKK in June of 1964.

The bridge, however, between African and Jewish Americans began to buckle during the late 1960s. The very titles of recent book-length studies on the relationship between these two minority groups betrays the rupture of this once strong coalition: *What Went Wrong? The Creation and Collapse of the Black-Jewish Alliance* (1995), *Struggles in the Promised Land: Toward a History of Black-Jewish Relations in the United States* (1997), *Broken Alliance: The Turbulent Times Between Blacks and Jews in America* (1988), *Blacks and Jews: Alliances and Arguments* (1994). During the 1960s and 1970s, African and Jewish Americans increasingly found themselves in conflict over pressing issues of the day, including Zionism, Black Nationalism, and various Affirmative Action initiatives. The school campus would represent a pronounced site of contention. Black-Jewish tensions came to a head, for example, in the Ocean Hill–Brownsville teacher's strike of 1968, which pitted several Jewish teachers in the Ocean Hill–Brownsville school district in New York against the predominantly African American population of the area. In their effort to claim greater control over decisions affecting the education of their children, black parents threatened to decentralize and disempower the predominantly Jewish United Federation of Teachers.

On the left coast, it would be the specter of forced busing that illustrated for an increasing number of Jews that their interests no longer meshed seamlessly with the interests of other American minorities, particularly African Americans. The official leadership of the L.A. Jewish community, in keeping with the Jewish American tradition of advocacy toward progressive causes, filed a "friend of the court" brief during the appellate phase of *Crawford,* supporting court-ordered integration even if it meant busing. That was only a few years after the Ocean Hill–Brownsville turmoil. But a large cohort of L.A. Jews rose up to oppose the specter of forced busing. According to a 1970 survey, conducted by a UCLA professor, 61 percent of Los Angeles Jews disagreed that "Busing Jewish children to racially mixed schools is a good idea."[6] The Jews who most stridently opposed forced busing tended to live in the Valley. A *Los Angeles*

Times article on the Jews of L.A., published in January of 1978—as buses were being prepared to roll in the fall—made it clear how powerfully the imminent threat of forced integration bore down upon Jewish families in the Valley. "Sometimes in the Valley at late night kaffeeklatsches," Robert Scheer reported, "that's all one hears—buses are coming—a crackling message from home to home, the end of the Valley, the end of a dream."[7]

The rift between the official position of the Jewish Federation Council and those Jewish families who opposed forced busing boiled down in part to an economic rift within L.A.'s Jewish community. Influence in the Jewish Federation Council was dominated by the more affluent Jews, who tended to live in Beverly Hills, Bel-Air, and Brentwood. (Judge Gitelson, incidentally, lived in Beverly Hills.) The strongest opponents of forced busing lived in the decidedly middle-class Valley where I was raised. It was easy for Beverly Hills Jews to champion integration, no matter the cost, many Valley Jews insisted. They wouldn't have to live with the consequences of their idealism. Should the buses roll, Jews in Beverly Hills could afford to pay for private schools for their children, if their children weren't already enrolled in private schools. Many Valley Jews couldn't afford this luxury. It seemed bitterly ironic for many of them. That they lived in the Valley in the first place was a testament to their hard-fought success in the American meritocracy. They had scrimped and saved for years to afford homes in suburbia, beyond Boyle Heights and other hardscrabble urban centers throughout the country, where they were most likely raised. Many of them had attended dilapidated urban public schools. Their children, they had hoped, would attend safe high-quality neighborhood schools in suburbia. That's why they had moved to the Valley in the first place. *Now* they were being told that their children would be forced to ride buses back to those faraway schools over the hill? No thank you!

It would be a Jewish parent from the Valley, Bobbi Fiedler, who would lead Bustop, the organization of mostly white citizens in Los Angeles that issued a series of desperate legal challenges against the mandatory busing plan. Interestingly, she would deploy provocative and inflammatory language from the Holocaust to assail the forced busing plan. In January of 1978, the busing threat imminent, Fiedler sat with a *Los Angeles Times* reporter to reflect upon what inspired her to form Bustop:

> I was sitting in my living room. My walls are paneled and the light was
> dim and there were shadows from the fluttering of the leaves outside
> and it just seemed to begin to move, almost, in my mind. And I began to
> see what I viewed as the cattle cars that hauled off so many Jews during
> the course of the Holocaust. And I could never understand as a child
> how they could go down without a fight. And I made a commitment at
> that time that I would not go down without a fight.[8]

Recent scholars of the Holocaust might seize upon Fiedler's reductive take
on the European Jewish response to the atrocity. (Without a fight?) Even
so, her very allusion to the cattle cars is arresting and illuminating on
any number of levels. Most obviously, it suggests simply the grand scale
of the busing threat, as it was perceived by some Jewish Valley residents.
It also betrays the centrality of the Holocaust upon the collective Jewish
ethos during these post-Holocaust years. The European catastrophe, quite
simply, was the prism through which many Jews—even those who didn't
experience the Holocaust directly—were likely to view any threatening
political event affecting the Jewish community.

Perhaps most intriguingly, Fiedler's allusion to the European atrocity crystallizes one principle source of the growing rift between African
and Jewish Americans during this period. Given the progressive leg-
islation of the 1950s and 1960s, histories of persecution and victimization finally seemed to translate into political clout. Amid this zeitgeist,
African and Jewish Americans would increasingly challenge the nature
and intensity of their respective persecution in what one writer has aptly
described the "foolishness of comparative victimizations."[9] In essence,
African and Jewish Americans—once mutually recognized minorities
bound together in a shared struggle—began to challenge one another's
bona fides as authentic American minorities. James Baldwin perhaps
most famously challenged the minority (i.e., persecuted) status of Jewish
Americans in his 1967 essay, "Negroes Are Anti-Semitic Because They're
Anti-White." Baldwin clearly believed that Jews in America had milked
their status as victims for too long given their upward mobility during
the postwar years. "One does not wish, in short," Baldwin writes, "to be
told by an American Jew that his suffering is as great as the American

Negro's suffering. It isn't, and one knows that it isn't from the very tone in which he assures you that it is."[10]

Fiedler's allusion to the Holocaust exemplifies the kind of talk from the Jewish side that so rankled Baldwin and other African Americans. For what was Fiedler up to here but claiming and deploying this most catastrophic episode of human suffering in the twentieth century to trump any African American claims of victimization, which had supported the school desegregation efforts? Jews had suffered enough in recent years, hadn't they? They were the true victims of history, truer victims than African Americans, Fiedler implicitly (and perhaps unconsciously) argued. Which begs the question: where, exactly, were the minorities of the inner city positioned in Fiedler's provocative analogy, anyway? If Jewish school children from the Valley, like me, faced the threat of becoming modern-day Jewish victims, forced onto the cattle cars, who were the minority children already residing at the figurative concentration camps? Were they the Nazis or were they fellow victims?

That Fiedler's analogy cannot accommodate—or refuses to accommodate—these mostly non-Jewish, minority students at the ramshackle public schools over the hill poignantly illustrates the growing chasm between the felt lives of Jewish and African Americans by the 1970s. By this time, Jews had mostly moved out of the embattled urban enclaves where other minorities still lived and struggled. The most egregious bulwarks of institutional racial and ethnic discrimination having been dismantled, Jews had managed to participate fully in the heady promises of the American meritocracy. Many (though not necessarily Fiedler) couldn't understand why African Americans simply couldn't do the same. Simultaneously, it appeared to an increasing number of African Americans that Jews had rather callously lifted up the ladder after they had scaled it. Where there was once accord and good will, there was now increasing distrust and antipathy. But at root, and as the elision of Fiedler's analogy suggests, African and Jewish Americans simply couldn't, and didn't, see one another anymore.

Fiedler's prominent role during the forced busing controversy emboldened her to run for a seat in the U.S. House of Representatives, and she was elected as a Republican to the ninety-seventh and two succeeding

Congresses, serving from 1981 to 1987. Given all the time that has passed, I wonder what Fiedler thinks now (and *if* she thinks now) about these tumultuous days. My amateurish Internet search, to my surprise, turns up her address and telephone number within minutes. Apparently, Fiedler still lives in the Valley, in Northridge, as a matter of fact, just blocks from my former home. Rather than call her cold, I send a letter asking if I might speak with her. Within days, I'm greeted by her message on my office voicemail. She'd be happy to talk with me. She leaves a phone number. She doesn't "do e-mail," her disembodied voice confesses, which immediately warms me to her.

"Oh yes, of course I think about those days," Fiedler tells me over the phone once I muster the courage to return her call. It takes little prompting to elicit her memories and her current views on these issues, which seem not to have changed over the years. "You could just see what was going to happen. Los Angeles never violated the laws in the way they were violated in the South. There was no deliberate segregation. It took place as a result of people moving into certain areas, so there shouldn't have been any legal basis for forced busing. But it was a very liberal school board in those days. You could just see what was going to happen," she repeats, adding "I was always very good at that." Somehow, this doesn't sound boastful, but matter-of-fact. I had expected a certain lingering stridency on these matters, even abrasiveness perhaps, but there is little heat in Fiedler's remarks. She speaks with the calm clarity of someone who knows that she has already won the argument. "Parents," she declares, "black and white, should be able to send their children to public schools in their own neighborhood if they choose"; "racial assignment," as she puts it, is wrong. "It really comes down to equal protection of the law."

Deliberate segregation. People moving into certain areas. Equal protection of the law. I might pursue these loaded issues with Fiedler, given the nuanced arguments and counterarguments in the court transcripts. But I don't care to press her, knowing, pretty much, the side on which she remains. What more truly interests me is that quotation from nearly thirty years ago, as the buses prepared to roll. How does she feel now about her provocative Holocaust rhetoric? I'm just about to ask, when Fiedler surprises me with a question of her own, out of the blue.

"Are you Jewish, Andrew?"

"Only on my mother's and father's side," I offer my stock response. She chuckles.

"Now don't put this in your book," she warns me, "but I was seven years old when we all learned about what happened in Europe. And I could never understand how the Jews went down without a fight. Now I know that they did resist in Poland, and elsewhere, but that was my perception, anyway, as a seven-year-old. And I always told myself that if something like that happened to me, I wouldn't go down without a fight." As I listen, transfixed, Fiedler proceeds to repeat, nearly verbatim—right down to the cattle cars and the shadows of fluttering leaves in her paneled living room—the provocative quotation attributed to her in 1978. I tell Fiedler this, with some trepidation, after she's through speaking, at which point she concedes, "Well, I suppose you can go ahead and use it, then."

Try as I might, I can't quite greet the moment with the cynicism it might appear to merit. Fiedler's regurgitated remarks, some thirty years later, seem less a carefully scripted talking point than a genuine formative experience, etched into her memory, and naturally tapped upon my prompting. What had I noted about countless American Jews of Fiedler's generation? The Holocaust was the prism through which they viewed the world. I don't think I understood what this meant, precisely, until my telephone conversation with Fiedler. The unignorable presence of the atrocity in one's consciousness; the Jewish anxiety over modes of mass transport (whether a fleet of cattle cars or school buses); the impossibility of seeing the world through an alternative frame of reference; the recognition, all the while, that non-Jews simply cannot understand, and will likely disparage, such ways of seeing. (*Now don't put this in your book . . .*) Which isn't to say that *I* see the world, and the issues at hand, in a manner wholly, or even mostly, consistent with Fiedler.

"Should an integrated learning environment be a goal, at any rate, of education?" I press, some moments later.

"I think education should be the principal goal of education," Fiedler declares.

I suppose that my parents, who plucked me from public school upon the threat of forced busing, agreed with Fiedler. The private school I attended during this episode was somewhat selective. Prospective students were required to pass an entrance exam. I, perhaps predictably, failed the exam on the first try, and so my parents hired a tutor to help me study. I managed to pass just in time to matriculate in the fall of 1978. To inform me of the good news, my mother scrawled a congratulatory note in red lipstick on the mirrored, sliding panels of my bedroom closet. I don't remember the exact words, but it was an unusually dramatic gesture from my mother, which may reflect how important it seemed to her that I had successfully eluded Griffin Avenue. My new private school was named appropriately enough after a pastoral town in England—Egremont. The elementary school campus, where I finished out fifth and sixth grade, was located just down the street on Devonshire. I remember very little, only that my crush on a fetching Catholic classmate named Ann-Marie posed the only significant inter-ethnic threat.

The junior high Egremont campus was located at the more affluent southern rim of the Valley in Encino, nearly a half hour away depending upon traffic. My parents, by this time, were somewhat worried that in protecting me from forced busing they might have been coddling me, to my later detriment. It seemed that some toughening up was required, my mother tells me now. Toward this end, she insisted that I take public transportation each morning to school, the RTD bus, rather than ride on the small yellow school bus from Egremont's nearby northern campus. The irony of the situation wholly eluded me at the time, but it doesn't now. My parents had protected me from forced busing, yet—to offer their sheltered son a more measured exposure to the rough-and-tumble world—implemented their own regimen of forced busing. I'm not sure exactly what my parents hoped I would see, but the rear seating section of the RTD offered ample exposure to an array of pot-smoking adolescents and one serial public masturbator, who managed the strange, spastic exercise with enough discretion, turned sideward against the wall of the bus, that I would only figure out what it was exactly that he was doing some time later, after shedding the outmost layer of my sexual ignorance.

By the time I was in eighth grade, the forced busing episode in L.A. had run its course. Fiedler and her cohorts who opposed mandatory busing had successfully passed Proposition 1, an amendment to the

California state constitution that—after another protracted bout of wrangling at every court level—precluded the state from exercising more rigorous standards for desegregation than federal law required. Predictably, school demographics throughout the LAUSD returned instantaneously to their former, segregated character. In 1980, for example, the student bodies at Topeka and Griffin Avenue were again over 80 percent white and Hispanic, respectively. I might have attended our neighborhood junior high, Nobel, at this point, which was apparently good enough for both my older brother and younger sister. Yet my parents felt it would be in the best interest of their most unmotivated, if not quite slow, child to finish out junior high at Egremont.

There is little of note to retrieve from these junior high school days, only that it was clear to me from the fancy Encino and Tarzana hillside homes of my new, mostly Jewish, classmates that my family was suddenly less wealthy than the families of my new peers. My comparatively humble origins in the déclassé northern reaches of the Valley must have embarrassed me to an appreciable extent, for I remember two emblematic moments rather clearly. The first was a weekend afternoon I spent playing paddle-tennis at the opulent Encino estate of a pretty Jewish classmate named Jacqueline. She sported a perpetual tan and wore her hair feathered, the style of the day. The plan—or at least *my* plan—was for me to take the RTD bus line back home toward the end of the day. (My mother by this time was a busy real estate agent and didn't cater to my social agenda.) The weekend route schedule was different, so I had jotted down the few times when the bus would pass the nearby Louise Avenue stop. I still remember the name of the street! When it came time for me to leave, however, Jackie's mother insisted upon driving me the half hour clear across the Valley in their behemoth black Mercedes. It occurred to me, only upon hearing my vigorous, and ultimately futile, protests that I didn't want Jackie or her mother to see our more modest environs to the north. The second occasion I recall with greater embarrassment. It was the morning of the day of one of our school dances. My parents, in an unusual turn, would be picking me up at school that evening after the event. Before leaving the house for the RTD, I turned toward my mother and issued my request: "Bring the nice car."

How thoroughly, and shamefully, I had internalized the shallow, materialistic values of the Valley. It all seems so comically pathetic now. Me, this Jewish child of relative affluence hoping desperately to fit in with those Jewish children of somewhat greater affluence. It does make one wonder, though. If this RTD ride across the Valley—from one Caucasian Jewish redoubt to another—meant so very much to me at the time, what did those more dramatic student migrations back and forth over the hill mean to those involved—my varsity basketball teammates, in particular? I've dawdled in safe, scholarly mode for long enough. It's time to pursue this reunion in earnest.

Contact

THE TORN SHEET of scrap paper with assistant coach Lou Cicciari's current telephone number scrawled across it in my nearly illegible hand sits for nearly a week at the far corner of my office desk. Between my completion of various mundane administrative tasks—returning e-mail queries and complaints from students and prospective students, drafting recommendation letters for colleagues up for university research awards, tinkering one last time with the upcoming spring 2007 course schedule— the torn leaf captures my eye, vies for my attention. I should pick up the phone already and call my old coach. I *need* to call him if I'm at all serious about this undertaking. Yet something keeps me from doing so. One good thing about my job is that I can always rely upon an ever-replenishing list of mindless, ten-minute tasks to distract me from the harder, and more essential, work at hand. *Tomorrow,* I tell myself, on any number of tomorrows. *Tomorrow will be a better day to call.*

I can't quite chalk up my procrastination (though I try) to the onerous workplace demands upon my time, or to the three-hour time delay, which only slightly complicates matters. I think it only seems to me somehow not quite right that it can be so easy to make contact, that between workaday administrative duties I can simply pick up the phone, stab the keys, and in mere moments be speaking with the assistant coach I haven't spoken with in twenty years. A more gradual, more rigorous, effort seems required. I had, in fact, begun this effort to reconnect in deliberate, distanced fashion, having written a query letter "to whom it may concern" and sending it off to Granada Hills High School, a charter school now, I discovered online. Would they, by any chance, have any records from the 1986 varsity basketball season? Any contact information for players and coaches that might be of use? Coach Johnson had been somewhat long in the tooth back then. Did they know, even, whether he was still alive? Within days, I received a telephone call at my office from the athletic director at Granada Hills. An academic administrator myself, I can just imagine how this job was delegated to the poor shlub from the main office. *Here,* you *deal with this? Tell this guy what he wants to know and get him off our backs.* The young athletic director didn't know about Coach Johnson (hadn't heard of him, in fact) but Lou Cicciari was still coaching at Granada Hills! The girls basketball team. "Lou?" I asked him, incredulously. "*The* Lou? The guy who uses a wheelchair?" One and the same, apparently. The athletic director would mention my name to Lou, see if he remembered me (he did), and see if it was okay with Lou to give me his telephone number (it was).

And so here it is, Coach Lou's telephone number, resting like a challenge at the far corner of my desk. *For God's sake, Andy,* I finally admonish myself in third-person, *just pick up the goddamn phone and call already!*

"Andy Furman. It's been a loooong time," Lou exclaims at the other end of the line, his voice throaty, high-pitched, and instantly familiar. Yes, it certainly *has* been a long time, I agree. I hadn't exactly practiced what I would say. There was just so much *to* say, given all the time that has passed. Lou goes first. He was married now, and had a daughter. He had coached the boys varsity at Granada Hills for a few years after Coach Johnson retired in 1993. Bob Johnson was still alive (!) and enjoying an active retirement, globetrotting with his wife to any number of exotic destinations for several weeks of the year. Lou had only coached the boys for a few years, then moved over to coach the girls, instead, as their schedule didn't interfere with his own daughter's basketball schedule. I congratulate my old coach. He was single when I knew him, and finishing up his education degree at CSUN. It occurs to me only now that Lou—who twenty years ago as "coach" seemed to occupy an entirely separate stratosphere—is actually only a few years older than I am.

Lou remembered, somehow, that I had gone to college somewhere in Pennsylvania, which compels me to fill in the blanks, breathlessly, and with abandon. I had gone on to graduate school in Pennsylvania too, I tell him. Penn State. I was a professor now. The chair of an English Department in Boca Raton, Florida. And a writer. And I had gotten married. I had two kids, eight and six. I had played basketball for a year and change at Franklin & Marshall. I had continued playing full-court hoops long after, competitively, in several community leagues. I had actually grown into a much better player than I was in high school, I assure my old coach. *Much* better. It turned out I was a late bloomer, wouldn't you know. . . .

It occurs to me—and probably to Lou—that I'm hoping quite ludicrously to impress him with my athletic prowess. What is it about the relationship between coaches and their players? Twenty years have passed. I've done pretty well in the years since I left the Valley. Yet none of this seems to matter, at least not to me. I am once again that awkward seventeen-year-old boy, bounding up and down the hardwood floor. Only a few minutes into the conversation with my old assistant coach and here I am, clamoring for his approval.

Here Coach. Look at me!

I didn't actually "make" the varsity in the fall of 1985. Not exactly. There should be no great shame in the admission, especially not at this late date. Granada Hills High School, only a tenth grade through twelfth grade institution in those days, nonetheless boasted an enormous student body populace of nearly twenty-five hundred students, replete with sterling athletes, many from downtown L.A. We were especially proud to count John Elway as our most distinguished alumnus. Four separate boys' basketball leagues accommodated our robust populace. The Cee and Bee teams at Granada were reserved for the less athletically gifted players. One could play in either of these leagues up through senior year. The boys endowed with greater athletic prowess tried out for junior varsity and varsity. John Elway, a three-sport phenom at Granada Hills—but more prodigiously talented at football and baseball—played on the Bee basketball team. So, again, it should provoke no great shame in me to admit that I had originally been cut from the varsity in the fall of my senior year. Yet how to explain the flush I feel in my face as I recall the vital circumstances? How promptly the heat rises in me upon a moment's reflection on these bygone days! My visceral reaction must betray the great magnitude of those circumstances to me at the time, its emotive heft that refuses dilution after all these years. There's something in these early athletic contests in our lives, something that marks us profoundly and indelibly, something that makes many of the subsequent challenges we face as adults seem small by comparison.

Making the JV as a junior was something of a coup for me. I didn't play on one of the organized basketball teams as a sophomore. I was too small for JV or varsity and was too proud, if memory serves, to play on the Cees or Bees. I remember my general state of bedazzlement upon attending a few of the varsity games as a sophomore: the anticipatory buzz in the packed stands, the rap music pounding from the speakers when our team finally took to the court, our players' fancy rip-away green and white game sweats, the effortless manner in which most of the players leapt toward the glass backboard, slapping it with both hands during one choreographed warm-up exercise, the multiple slam-dunks during the subsequent lay-up drill. All this, before the game even started. I'm sure it was all pretty standard high school athletic fare—that high school teams today amply trump these theatrics—but at the time these older athletes seemed flashy and brilliant and totally beyond my reach. Thankfully, I enjoyed a sudden growth spurt between my sophomore and junior year, gaining several inches in height and roughly forty pounds in weight, realizing the essential proportions I've maintained throughout my adulthood. These new proportions made JV and varsity basketball viable possibilities.

It qualified as a pretty big deal to make either squad, so plenty of my classmates crowded the wooden bleachers in the cavernous gym for JV try-outs junior year. Efficiency was the key to the process, given the volume of eager student-athletes. Each of us was paired arbitrarily with another hopeful player, and the pairs were set off against each other for brief two-on-two, half-court contests, or public displays of mortification, depending upon one's skill level. Coach Johnson and Coach Lou sat together conspiratorially at a remove from the rest of us, with wooden clipboards. They scribbled copious notes while the four players squared off, and while the rest of our group waited anxiously, higher up on the bleachers, for our names to be called.

I remember the classmate with whom I was paired. His name was Fidel and, oddly enough, we had played basketball together on the same team three or four years back in the Northridge Park youth league. A few of the would-be players at try-outs were former star players in the recreational league. Although I had made the All-Star team, I wasn't one of its better players, and I remember these few formerly stronger teammates in the bleachers looking at me askance before I took my turn on the court, even mumbling into each other's ears what I imagined were uncharitable thoughts regarding my presence. I wasn't wrong. One of those players who would make the team, Kevin (he would become one of my better friends) would admit to me later that he, Fidel, and a couple others were fairly shocked by my nerve.

Fidel was one of the best players in our park league back in those days. He had matured early and was bigger than most of us. But the intervening years weren't favorable ones for his development. He was no longer as tall for his age as he was then, and his movements on the court, once he and I were summoned, seemed awkward now, uncoordinated, as if his hands and feet had grown estranged. Moreover, from the start he labored for breath on the court as if he smoked cigarettes. By contrast, I was all hustle and managed to outperform any expectations I might have harbored for myself. Many of my outside shots fell through the hoop, and I snatched a few rebounds, taking special pains to demonstrate my fundamentally sound "box-out" technique.

For the life of me, I can't remember exactly how I was notified that I had made the JV team—whether I was notified immediately, or whether there was some list that the coaches posted somewhere a day or two later—which seems odd given its import to me at the time, and given other things I so vividly recall. All I know is that I was notified somehow that I had made the squad. Fidel had not been so fortunate. And while I'm sure that this was fair enough, and while it certainly shouldn't bother me now, I wonder somewhat guiltily whether my own single-minded purpose during the try-out, my fierce determination to score and rebound, cost Fidel his spot when I probably could have taken greater pains to make him look better. There's something brutal about athletic competition, a zero-sum quality that goes a long way toward making participation (as an observer or athlete) so thrilling. As competitive as I remain about a good many things, part of me as an adult finds this fierce, implacable quality of sport difficult to abide, too. Perhaps I'm mellowing as I enter middle-age.

I remember little of note of my junior year on the JV team. Just that I played in the 1-guard and 2-guard positions capably but with little true prowess, certainly with none of the outsized skill that Coach Johnson hoped I possessed after my JV try-out. Immediately after my performance, he tested me for a few practices with the varsity, but it became clear pretty quickly that I wasn't near ready for the challenge. During that JV season junior year, I was positioned in the rotation such that I knew that making the varsity squad next year would be a struggle. Not every junior from the JV squad would make the varsity squad as a senior. It was a simple case of mathematics. There were only a certain number of spots, and talented incoming juniors (and, on rare occasion, sophomores) would always be given priority over less, or even equally, talented seniors. These were the terms we all knew and accepted. A junior, after all, could contribute two full years to the squad; a prodigiously talented sophomore, three. And so I knew going into senior year that earning a spot on the squad would be difficult and would depend largely upon a wild-card factor—those new incoming sophomores, juniors, and seniors.

A racial dimension loomed large here. There was a summer league at Grant High School in the Valley in which our provisional incoming varsity team participated before fall. The Watts Games in L.A. was another, shorter summer league, of sorts. I played on our summer varsity team in both of these programs during the summer of 1985. But it was rarer for the black kids bused in from L.A., over the hill, to participate in either of these summer leagues, even the Watts Games, closer to their neighborhoods. I suppose that the logistics were too complicated, that the LAUSD didn't provide the requisite transportation to and from these unofficial summer leagues. The upshot was that most of the new and returning students from over the hill wouldn't arrive until the first day of school; a certain number would certainly try out for the JV and varsity. It was a factor of which I was fully aware and even fearful.

I don't remember any outright feelings of racial resentment I might have harbored going into the fall season. These black kids, that is, living in some other faraway attendance zone, descending upon *my* school, threatening *my* spot on the varsity. As clueless as I was regarding the politics and policies that ultimately designated Granada as their high school, too, it didn't occur to me to question the validity of their presence in these terms. It only occurs to me now that I might have. At the time, I accepted that a certain number of black players would be arriving and that if they outperformed me on the court they would make the team and I would be cut. Again, these were the terms, fair terms, and I accepted them. Yet before congratulating myself for my equanimity, I should also note that it had never occurred to me until now to ponder the real advantages I enjoyed over my peers from L.A. After all, while I enjoyed several summer weeks of additional coaching and organized play, they . . . Well, I don't know exactly what they were up to over the hill, just that they weren't privy to the same access to the team afforded to me during the off-season, and that I took this advantage of mine wholly for granted.

My fears going into fall would be realized. There were so many talented new players from over the hill that our single full court in the gym was too small to accommodate our numbers. For the first few weeks of the term, our too-large prospective varsity team scrimmaged on the two smaller full courts in the dimly lit practice gym, adjacent to the main court. I wasn't the worst player out there, and Coach Johnson would cut several players from both sides of the hill before my spot would be in jeopardy. Yet I knew, doing the math, that my spot was, indeed, in jeopardy. There was one new bused-in player who seemed a particular threat to my place in the rank and file. His name was Jeff Mays and, like me, he could play the point-guard or shooting-guard position. He was lanky, sported a wispy black mustache, and carried himself on the court with a sort of cocksure confidence that eluded me.

"Give me the rock!" I can remember him pleading falsetto to one of our peers in mock agony. At this point in the sociocultural history of the sport—at least in L.A.—"rock" still qualified as a strange and new slang term for the basketball. I can remember Coach Lou and several teammates laughing on the sidelines upon Jeff's comic outburst. In many regards, Jeff was everything I was not. While I was workmanlike, tight, and humorless on the court, his style was loose and carefree. He took clear pleasure in the game, was flippant and funny, and I remember not particularly liking him for it. It seemed to me, as impossibly earnest as I was, that things came too easily to him, that he somehow didn't respect the sport, that he was a punk. All of which is to say that Jeff was the better player, and I must have known this. Moreover, I'm sure that the self-righteous indignation he inspired in me—though I can never remember him uttering a harsh word to me or to anyone else—offered me curious comfort from this truth.

Coach Lou knew how much it meant to me to make the varsity. That may have been why he approached me one day—I can't recall the precise context—and posed the question: "What would happen, really, if you *didn't* make the team?" I don't remember exactly what I said in response, but I wasn't prepared to be philosophical. I'm fairly certain that I expressed, one way or another, how devastating it would be for me not to play with the varsity. For as long as I could remember, with the exception of my sophomore year, basketball had simply been there, part of my routine, a constant ingredient offering texture to my days, weeks, and years. Coach Lou might have known at that point that I would be cut. Yes, he had probably approached me out of kindness to prepare me for the blow in Coach Johnson's office. The two of them had probably already discussed the positions, their depth at the 1- and 2-guard positions. It was a pity, I can imagine them thinking. I was a hard worker. A good kid. But there just wasn't room for me on the team. Jeff was the better player.

I would be summoned to Coach Johnson's office some time after my encounter with Coach Lou. It was in the middle of a trigonometry class. I knew at the moment I opened the note some unknown student handed me announcing Coach Johnson's summons that I was cut. The specifics diverge little, I'm sure, from the circumstances common to any of us who have been cut from a competitive athletic team. I walked lugubriously to his small office next to the gym, my face cold with sweat. It was the one and only time I would be in his office, and I remember thinking that it was small, and dark, and cluttered. Coach Johnson was kind enough about the whole thing. He told me to take a seat, gesturing to a dilapidated plastic chair beside his desk. "I'm sorry that I have to say this, Andy," I remember his lead-in. Why is it that we remember only these brutal episodes word for word? "You work as hard as anyone out there. Harder. But you've been introduced to a wonderful sport that I'm sure will be important to you for a long time." Here, he seemed to be rationalizing his harsh decision on the spot, offering himself, as much as me, some measure of solace. It would turn out that he was right about this, more right than he could possibly know. Basketball *was* a wonderful sport, and it *would* be important to me for a long time after high school. Yet at the time I was in no state to receive these words. I don't remember challenging the decision. I believe that I accepted its justness. Again, Jeff was the better player. Our conference couldn't have lasted more than a few minutes. Coach Johnson offered me a dry hand. We shook, and I departed.

It was some days after this conference with Coach Johnson that Coach Lou approached me during phys ed on the battle-scarred blacktop outside the gym, the desultory session of physical exercise that now replaced formal basketball practice. "Jeff Mays is gone," he revealed tersely, and somewhat cryptically.

"Gone?" I inquired. I had no idea, as cut off as I suddenly was from the realm of athletics at Granada. *Cut.* It's a particularly illustrative word as far as words go. The advanced placement courses I endured (performing yeomanlike, I suppose, but without distinguishing myself in the least) were populated mostly by Asian American and Jewish American peers, only few African Americans, and only few athletes, period. I, truly, had been cut from the team's social fabric.

"He's not at Granada anymore," Lou clarified. I slowly absorbed the significance of this news. Several of the bused-in boys from try-outs had chosen, before cuts were even made, to return to their neighborhood schools. The long commute on the bus in the darkness of morning took its toll, I'm sure, among other variables. But most of these decisions were made by the end of the first week or so of classes. It was unusual for Jeff to have waited so long before deciding to return to his neighborhood school, as I assumed he had decided.

"So does this mean there's a spot for me now?" I tried to keep my excitement at bay.

"You could ask Coach?" he suggested, then wheeled off.

I took a moment to glean the context as best as I could. It seemed unlikely that Coach Johnson had asked his assistant coach to contact me. It probably hadn't crossed Bob Johnson's mind when Jeff quit that he might now offer me the unused uniform. Without me they would still have eleven better players, which was plenty. Only the top seven or eight would see significant game time. Had the team truly needed my services, Coach Johnson surely would have contacted me himself. Still, it didn't occur to me to contemplate Lou's kindness at the time. I was too singly focused upon the task at hand. In short, I marched to Coach Johnson's office, I asked him for my spot back, and he acquiesced, without (it must be said) any particular enthusiasm. I'm sure that I hardly registered the lackluster tenor of his welcome back. I was on the team. This was all that mattered to me at the time.

In retrospect, my meeting with Coach Johnson, which clearly took him by surprise, betrays the extent of Coach Lou's kindness in approaching me with the news of Jeff's departure. It may have only been an afterthought to him, something he figured—while he had a moment before practice—that he might as well mention to me, and something that he might not have done had he been more pressed for time or less charitably disposed. This brief gesture probably ranked rather low on Lou's mental list of priorities, given his abundant duties and obligations. I doubt he remembers this moment at all. As an educator myself, I am ever reminded of this powerful, and downright frightening, dynamic between my students and me, the potentially large impact of even my smallest act of kindness, or cruelty. A teacher's most casual gestures of encouragement or discouragement might make or break a student's entire semester and might even set the trajectory for a student's future after school. It's something I try to keep in mind.

Over the telephone, twenty years later, Coach Lou and I continue to share what we remember about that bygone season, those bygone players, piecing together the puzzle that lies before us as best we can. Gary Gray was awarded a full basketball scholarship at UC Santa Barbara. (Yes, I remember stumbling across one of his games by chance on ESPN in my college apartment in Lancaster, Pennsylvania.) Gary, Lou tells me, went on to enjoy a long and fruitful professional career in Europe. He lived in Las

Vegas now. Lou would find me his telephone number. Todd Lytle had entered the Air Force, Lou thought but wasn't sure. Sam Puathasnanon had gone to college out east. Columbia. The news cheers me. Sam, a year younger than I, had talked incessantly about Columbia. He had returned to L.A., Lou said. How did he know this? Sam's younger brother, Donald (who I only vaguely recall) was now the volleyball coach at Granada Hills. Go figure.

Curious that neither of us knows much of anything about my PWT teammates, who seem to have disappeared (like me) the moment after graduation. Lou does have some memories to share about Sean Brown, however, my teammate who had earned a full ride as a football player at the University of Colorado and played tight end on their National Champion-ship team in 1990. Sean, a soft-spoken guy, strong as an ox, had been touted as the best three-sport athlete at Granada Hills since John Elway. (John Elway was, and probably remains, the touchstone against which any athlete of promise tended to be compared.) Lou remembers a miraculous baseball throw that Sean had executed from deep in left field, throwing out on the fly the runner who had tagged up from third base. "Yes!" I exclaim, excitedly. I remember that very play. I was in the stands at the game, which was played, for whatever reason, at the pristine baseball diamond at CSUN. "It wasn't a throw that should have been possible," Lou recalls. "Coach Stroh said that Sean Brown had the best arm of any baseball player in Los Angeles, including all the players on the Dodgers and Angels!"

And Lou remembers another story that involves Sean Brown. One of his friends had dropped out of the Permits-With-Transportation pro-gram to return to his inner-city, neighborhood school. (This could be Jeff, I think but don't say.) Coach Johnson, Lou declares, had asked Sean why he decided to remain at Granada Hills rather than return with this buddy to his neighborhood school. "I'm not that kind of kid," Sean had tersely, and somewhat cryptically, told Johnson. Interesting that Coach John-son had found this comment significant enough to relay to his assistant coach, and that Lou remembers the story twenty years later. What kind of kid *was* Sean's friend? What kind of kids attended inner-city schools? Drug-dealers? Gang-bangers? That was the stereotype, which contained, no doubt, a kernel of truth. Gang violence between the Bloods (who wore red) and the Crips (who wore blue) was prevalent in the inner city during the 1980s. While gangs hadn't yet infiltrated Granada Hills—while my school probably did represent refuge to a certain extent—it should probably be noted that my Valley school wasn't exactly immune to crime, either. Police narcs, in fact, infiltrated an elaborate network at Granada Hills my junior year and made a major drug bust involving cocaine. One of my white classmates in chemistry, among several other students, was arrested and never returned.

"Whatever happened to Terrell?" I ask Lou. Terrell had been our starting point guard, lightning quick with an outrageous vertical leap. He possessed a reliable "handle," to boot. Rarely did he turn the ball over. His on-court demeanor was confident, even cocky. "You could work out all night every night, Andy," I remember him trash-talking me, "and I could just go home and eat Mickey D's every night, but come morning I'd still whup you all up and down the court." We had just completed practice, having endured our "suicides," a grueling sprinting exercise, referred to these days by a more innocuous name. I had remained behind to work on my jump shot—and probably to curry favor rather artlessly with the coaches—which is what provoked Terrell's comment, deployed flippantly with a backward glance as he headed off to the locker room. I don't remember thinking that Terrell's quip was very funny at the time. But Coach Lou and I laugh it off now. "That sounds like Terrell," he says, chuckling. "Just like him."

"Terrell lived in Granada Hills you know," Lou says. "He wasn't bused in."

"Really?" I ask. The disclosure takes me utterly by surprise. I had just assumed that Terrell, like the rest of my African American teammates, lived over the hill, that he was bused in from the inner city. I was his teammate for two years. How could I not have known that Terrell lived in the Valley, just like me? How narrow my vision must have been.

I don't quite have time to process this news—to ponder its significance at the time to Terrell or to our black teammates—for Lou reveals another surprise that truly rocks me.

"Terrell played great during the city championship season."

"City championship?" I ask, nonplussed.

Lou had assumed that I knew. The year after I graduated, apparently, my team had won the city championship, beating Birmingham in the Los Angeles Sports Arena in the spring of '87.

I hadn't the foggiest idea.

I marvel, speechless, at the news. How completely and utterly I had pulled up stakes and fled! The Sports Arena had seemed hallowed ground to me that senior year. I remember attending the 4A city championships as a spectator with Sam that year, witnessing an outrageous gravity-defying slam dunk by Crenshaw High's Stevie Thompson, who would go on to play for Jim Boeheim's Syracuse University Orangemen. We had hoped to make it to the Sports Arena ourselves, but we didn't make the 3A city championships my senior season. We might have. Rather, we should have. Given our talent pool (from both the Valley and over the hill), we would have been a moderately successful 4A team. Instead, we were a 3A powerhouse, having gone undefeated in the regular season.

But we underachieved in the playoffs. Jefferson High, an inner-city school, handed us our first and final loss of the season in the second round of the city playoffs on February 26, 1986. How do I recall the date? The game program, designed and printed by journalism students at Granada, had somehow survived in my parents' files through four moves. "Here," my mother declared to me in the kitchen of her latest Boca Raton home, brandishing the yellowing program. "Take this." Apparently, four moves represented a cap, after which she could no longer be expected to store her son's high school detritus. I gazed down, dazedly, at the brochure, a sixteen-by-twenty-two sheet of paper of indeterminate bond, folded at the center to make four eight-by-eleven pages. A color illustration, which smacks of a 1970s rather than 1980s artistic sensibility, graces the cover page. Two players, one black and one white, emerge chest-high from the bottom border against a fantastical yellow and orange backdrop. They lunge skyward toward the center of the frame, competing for a loose ball just above with outstretched arms, splayed fingers. The white player seems to have the upper hand. The price of the program is printed in bold black typescript on the black player's white jersey—25 c.

We should have won that game. We were one point down, with only a second or two on the clock. Gary Gray, a reliable free-throw shooter, was at the line to shoot a one-and-one. (I, predictably, was on the bench.) *Just hit one,* I remember myself thinking. Jefferson had stuck around doggedly, but we were the better team. We'd take them in overtime. Gary, however, missed the front end, which clanged off the right side of the rim; a Jefferson player rebounded the ball. Our season was over.

I can still remember the sight of Gary, just after the buzzer mercilessly sounded, lifting both his palms to cover his anguished face, then the awkward collapse of his hefty, six-foot-eight frame to the hardwood floor. He had a boyish face back then, and vestiges still of what seemed like baby fat around his middle. A Jefferson player approached to console him and tried to lift him to his feet. But Gary, enormous Gary, wouldn't budge. *Leave him alone,* I remember thinking. It was a shocking, and devastating, loss. Couldn't Gary just *be* devastated for a few moments?

Gary and the boys, I learn only now, had achieved retribution in 1987. What a difference a year makes! Gary's jersey, Lou tells me, is retired in our old gym. I should be elated, of course, upon hearing this news of the team's triumph. I should be happy for Gary and for all my other old teammates—Sam, Terrell, Sean, Todd—who had stayed on to achieve glory in '87. So why this queasy feeling in my gut? Instead of elation, I feel . . . what? Envy, it occurs to me. Can any of my accomplishments since high school stack up to the Los Angeles City Championship?

It always seemed to me that *I* had gone on to the fruitful future on the east coast, that *I* had enjoyed a seamless escape from the provincial, smog-choked Valley. Now, however, it seems that I've had it all wrong. Gary and the others had been the ones to go on to glory. *I* was the one more truly left behind . . .

I don't have much time to wallow in self-pity, as Lou continues his ruthless barrage of information.

"Terrell's *still* a fantastic player," he emphasizes. "He plays pretty regularly in the alumni games."

"Alumni games?" I ask.

We still hold them every year, Lou tells me. On Monday or Tuesday, the week of Thanksgiving. Do I ever make it out to L.A.? he asks. No, I tell him. Not really. My brother now lives in Santa Monica, but he and his family usually come east to visit us. I haven't been to the Valley in nearly twenty years.

"How about this year? You can play in the game," Lou proposes, brightly.

Yes, I'd like to play this year, I hear myself tell him, brightening myself, my interest piqued. "Terrific," he says. Suddenly, it's all planned. I'm flying to the Valley. In mere weeks. Lou will try to get in touch with some of my old teammates. He'll track down some telephone numbers. He'll get back to me on the precise date and time of the alumni game.

I feel lightheaded by the time I hang up the phone. It's all happening so fast, this reunion. What have I gotten myself into? Do I have any idea what I'm doing? At various random moments over the next several weeks, my thoughts drift to the upcoming trip across the country—the alumni game, visits with some of my old teammates, coaches, and neighbors— and a cold sweat breaks out on my forehead. It would be so very easy *not* to go through with any of this. I've earned tenure; I've been promoted to full professor; I've written a couple of well-received scholarly books, a somewhat less well-received novel, but a novel nonetheless. In short, I've worked hard over the past ten years. It should be smooth sailing from here on out. My university, on the whole, expects fairly little of me. I need only keep my nose clean, teach my courses, and attend diligently to the administrative duties of my middle-management station as department chair. On the research front, I need only remain "active." A few articles and reviews from time to time, another book only if I feel the urge. Why tax myself with this particular undertaking?

"You're trying to validate your existence," my father answers my question at the community pool of his gated Boca Raton development. My ever utilitarian father only refers here to the research portion of my academic assignment. For a Jew, he possesses a Protestant work ethic that would warm Martin Luther's cockles. "I don't quite understand tenure," he admitted to me one day. "Doesn't earning tenure only encourage laziness?" Although he would probably deny it, my professor gig—the relatively few courses I teach, those long afternoons of reading-in-repose I call work—has always seemed to my father a suspect way to earn a living.

This last phrase summarizes perfectly both my parents' essential take on life. You must "earn" your "living," your life, through hard work. This arduous project of mine, my father feels, is the least I can do to justify my salary at the university, not to mention the generous benefits package. This is all that he means.

You're trying to validate your existence. As if through osmosis, I share my father's essential take on matters. No one gets a free ride. An existence, a life, must be earned on a daily basis. Not frittered away. One earns one's share of the earth's atmosphere through hard work and good old-fashioned stick-to-it-ness. If our views diverge, it is only in how we define productive work. Plain old sitting and thinking—what some might dismiss as idle time—has always seemed to me a vital component of my business here. What's more, I've been fortunate enough to carve out a workplace niche that doesn't wholly discourage protracted stretches of unapologetic introspection.

Which may be why I can't help pondering the more philosophical implications of my father's comment. Is his observation more insightful than he realizes? I might pursue any number of scholarly or creative enterprises if mere "production" were the goal—if, at issue, was simply validating my share of the Florida Atlantic University payroll. So why *this* project? Do I mean to justify my existence in more essential terms? My actual existence, that is. The rather privileged contours of my *hereness?* Having fled the Valley, does it feel somehow incumbent upon me to return to the scene of the crime, to survey the damage, to report back from the front? What do I hope to learn from my former white neighbors, coaches, and schoolmates? That the forced busing episode was a disaster? That my parents were right to withdraw me from the system? And what do I hope to gain from tracking down some teammates from over the hill? What do I hope to find? That they are okay? That the voluntary PWT program worked wonders for them and was a sufficient desegregation program in and of itself? Or do I hope to expose the opposite so that I might shine a light upon the horrors visited upon the children of the inner city? Is this why I've dusted off these long-forgotten court cases? It's tough, in either case, in *any* case, not to feel that a deep reservoir of guilt fuels this entire endeavor. Ah, guilt. That much-maligned white liberal streak. But perhaps that's unfair. I come from a culture, after all, that doesn't so readily dismiss the utility and appropriateness of guilt as a motivating influence. If guilt is what inspires me, perhaps it is okay. At least for now.

Training

THERE'S A CERTAIN SOUND to a basketball gymnasium—or sounds, rather, that practically all gymnasiums share. It's a controlled, if not hermetically sealed, environment. The ceilings above the lacquered hardwood floor are unusually high, both to accommodate the loft of desperate, long-range shots and to ensure a reasonably capacious stack of bleacher seating. The cavernous space, framed by hard surfaces, creates a unique acoustical effect. I suppose I could only appreciate this strange music after leaving the game for a time, for the sound is the first thing I notice upon reentering the gymnasium at Boca Raton High School after my extended hiatus.

For a long while in south Florida, my athleticism on the wane, I had played in two local leagues and, more significantly, I had played "pick-up" each Saturday morning at 7:00 A.M. in this gym, and in its earlier dilapidated incarnation before the school's recent renovation. This pick-up game had been, and continues to be, from what I understand, ultra-competitive yet good-spirited. Most of the players are superb athletes, African Americans, old friends from Atlantic High School in Delray Beach, one town to the north. Anthony, the vice-principal of Boca High, who happens to have an outrageous vertical leap, for years has reliably opened up the gym for his old friends, for some of his recently graduated students, and for newer friends like me.

Still, after a string of dispiriting performances, I had decided once and for all to give up basketball about six months ago. The adult team I had played on had just been unceremoniously dispatched in the first round of playoffs in the local recreation center league. Basketball, a sport of quick bursts, is notoriously unkind to aging legs. Generally speaking, one's basketball fitness declines precipitously at or before age thirty. To remain competitive into my mid-thirties, I had been forced to develop a fairly reliable three-point shot. But it was growing increasingly clear that my accuracy from beyond the arc could no longer compensate for those manifold creeping deficiencies plaguing my game. Quickness is all-important for a 2-guard (more so than for a post-player), and quickness had been my greatest weapon. Although I had never been much of a leaper, the combination of my lateral agility and hand speed had made me a pretty effective defender in my prime; at the offensive end, I was fleet-of-foot enough that my first step almost invariably shed most opponents. Unfortunately, my quickness had been fairly ravaged by time.

The team that had just schooled us was far younger and stronger. Their players jumped higher, sprinted faster, and defended more aggressively than us weary, Advil-popping veterans; they beat us to every loose ball and fairly cleaned up the boards. (Besides these factors, we had the clear advantage!) What particularly infuriated me about this loss was that our opponents weren't truly hoops players. You could tell by the awkward manner with which they laid the ball up or cocked it back behind their heads, elbows akimbo, for an outside shot. A couple of them, during foul shots, scarcely knew where to stand around the key. They were just athletes. Football players, perhaps, in high school, only a couple years back for them. Worse, they were punks, who exhibited not the least bit of basketball etiquette. "Get that shit outta here!" a particularly burly opponent exclaimed after stuffing my lay-up in the paint. While a certain amount of trash-talking is permissible (if never my way), you can generally count upon restraint when the opposing team is up by twenty-five points or so. No, these weren't ballers. They were adolescent morons, against whom our team would have put on a clinic had our legs been closer to thirty than forty years old. I knew immediately after the game—my face hot and red from some admixture of rage and exhaustion—that I couldn't bear another such loss.

To be sure, many peers in similar circumstances pursue options other than giving up the game. Less competitive leagues and pick-up games abound. The knee-brace circuit, as it were. I wouldn't deny my friends any pleasure they glean from such outlets. But for whatever reason, something inside me wouldn't permit me to continue on in this fashion. My game had dissipated from its former modest prowess to a level at which the sport ceased to provide its heady pleasures. What's more, continuing on artlessly (as I gauged my performance) seemed somehow disrespectful of the sport. In short, I had had enough.

Yet, having committed myself to the upcoming alumni game at my old high school, it occurred to me that I'd better set about restoring my fitness to a level at least approximating game shape. So here I am. A bit late. The first game of the morning is already underway. No one has noticed my arrival, so I sit quietly on the sideline, lace up my high-tops, and listen for a moment to the rhythmic *squeak* of rubber soles during a half-court set, the solid and somehow reassuring *thud* of the leather ball as it's dribbled rhythmically against the hardwood (*thud . . . thud . . . thud-thud*), its *kiss* off the glass backboard upon a shot attempt, the *scuffle* and *squeak* of sneakers once again as players jockey for rebounding position, the *thwack* of a palm against its prize. I wonder: have I missed these sounds, themselves, or just what these sounds represent? This healthful morning reprieve from all anxiety, domestic and workplace. This ninety-four-by-fifty-foot space inside the lines where the rules are simple and fair and I succeed or fail upon my own efforts. This increasingly rare, and rewarding, social space of uncomplicated male camaraderie.

I haven't seen any of these guys, or spoken with them, even, since I hung up the high-tops. It might seem strange that I haven't kept in better touch—or *any* touch, really—with my basketball friends. It seems a bit strange to *me*. But friendships I have developed on the court have always pretty much remained there. On the court. Part of me must feel that it represents something of a personal failing that these relationships (with players both black and white) have rarely traveled beyond the baselines and sidelines of the gym. Why else do I find myself scouring the Internet to restore contact with my long-lost teammates from L.A.? Yet as I've grown older, as my domestic and work life becomes ever more complicated, another part of me has come to appreciate these highly localized relationships uncluttered by the hurly-burly of the external realm, these friendships that flourish exclusively within proscribed boundaries: the

neighborhood, the university, the basketball court. I count these friendships among the most fruitful and functional relationships in my life.

A new player, apparently, has joined our ranks at the Boca Raton
High School gymnasium: the eight-time NFL pro-bowl wide receiver
Cris Carter. I recognize that hawkish face of his immediately, probably on
account of his role on the current HBO program *Inside the NFL*. Interesting. I had heard that Carter lived in the area, that he runs some sort of
speed-training camp for elite athletes, so I'm not completely surprised by
his presence.

"Andy Furman!" Anthony shouts from the court, having finally spotted me. My name booms against the metal rafters. *Andy Furmannnn*. The
game comes to a halt as Anthony and five or six of the others, the guys
I know best, strut over to greet me on the sideline. I must confess that it
feels uncommonly good to receive such a welcoming, one I hadn't really
expected. I've known some of these guys for ten years, so I suppose that
the brief interruption is in order. We share that choreographed combination handshake and half-hug with which all hoops players are eminently
familiar. In about thirty seconds we're all caught up on essential details.
Anthony has been promoted to principal of a middle school in West Boca,
but can still open the high school gym; Dante still works at the Boy's
Club in Delray Beach; Pat's still the foreman at some opulent Manalapan
mansion-in-progress; Manny finally graduated from FAU and works as
an accountant for a large bank (that was his Range Rover outside); James,
well, James still seems to have any number of alleged irons in the fire. The
game resumes as I stretch stubborn hamstrings, calves, and quads and
await my turn on the floor.

It's a pretty nice moment, this reunion. But things pretty much go
downhill from here, once I take to the floor. It's not so much that my basketball fitness has declined (although it has, somewhat) as that I'm out of
synch. My timing is all off. I feel the way I imagine classical musicians
must feel after returning to a piece they haven't played in years. Full-court
basketball, like music, has its rhythm, and this rhythm seems wholly to
elude me the first few times up and down the court. I attempt an inlet pass
a second too late to a teammate posting-up in the key, which his defender
steals with a practiced swipe of his hand; I take a couple of mid-range

shots, which feel okay, but which fly ludicrously above the rim to the other side of the court. I can't quite "find the range." Basketball isn't generally seen as a precision sport, like golf, say, or tennis. Yet this is only because we take for granted the well-honed finesse, the kinesthetic intelligence, of its finest players. A slight hesitation here, a bit too much muscle there, means the difference between a successful pass or shot and a turnover or "brick."

After my third rushed shot, I admonish myself to slow down, to play within myself, to let the game come to me. And things begin to improve. I spot up at the foul line on offense, receive a pass from Anthony, and remember to square up to the basket before shooting. I release the ball upon following through with my index and middle finger, my "touch" fingers. The ball, mercifully, falls through the hoop. I exhale, volubly. *Phew!* Funny, it's only basketball, only a game, but it feels as if an enormous load has been lifted from my shoulders. Suddenly, I'm back in the swing of things. I make a three-pointer. I gather a rebound. I complete a successful entry pass to James at the bottom of the key. All in all, it turns out to be a good first day back. I win a couple of games. I lose a couple of games. I don't injure myself. Things could have gone a lot worse.

I'll see them all next Saturday, I tell them after our last game. They seem mostly to believe me, but take extra time bidding me farewell, just in case.

"You're gonna do just fine in your alumni game," Pat assures me, the last to slap my hand.

In the meantime, I set about making contact with my former teammates. Coach Lou has given me telephone numbers right off the bat for our starting center, Gary Gray, and for Terrell Smith, our starting point guard. Gary's number proves immediately fruitful. He answers after only one ring. "This is going to come as a surprise," I warn the familiar voice. "It's Andy Furman. Your old teammate. Do you remember me?"

"Andy Furman," he nearly sings. "Sure. You were a lefty."

"Well, no," I correct him.

"Really?" he says, audibly addled. I can almost see him lifting his enormous hand to scratch his head in Las Vegas.

"I did have a really *good* left hand," I assure him, which is true enough, and which may be why he remembers me for it.

Use your off-hand and you'll be twice the player, Coach Johnson would routinely exhort. He wouldn't tolerate right-handed lay-ups from the left side of the field goal and penalized any such infraction during practice by sending the perpetrator off on immediate laps. It was a lesson I took to heart. I worked constantly, before and after practice, on my left-handed dribbling, my lay-ups, and even on across-the-key left-handed shots (or runners). Coach Johnson was right. It *did* make me twice the player. It *has* made me twice the player (I can't quite reconcile myself to the pastness of my basketball days), even if this sum total has never quite added up to very much.

Was it a good time to talk? I ask Gary. He assures me that it is. He was just sitting in the reception area of his auto mechanic's shop in Las Vegas, waiting for an oil change. We spend about twenty minutes reminiscing and quickly move on to more recent history. Yes, he affirms Lou's news. He enjoyed a long professional career in Europe, having only retired a few years ago. He now sells basketball gymnasium flooring for a large company, headquartered out of Las Vegas. If the Florida Atlantic University gym needed a new floor, he alerts me, suddenly shifting to salesman mode, I'd have to be sure to give the Athletic Department his number. "Oh definitely," I say, and I mean it. I'll give the folks I know over there a call later today.

Like me, Gary is married now. Like me, he has two young children. Unlike me, Coach Johnson and Lou both attended his wedding. I feel a reflexive pang in my stomach not unlike the one I felt upon hearing the news that my old team had won the city championship in the Sports Arena the year after I graduated. It's silly, this feeling. My wife and I pretty much eloped ten year ago. *No one,* not even our parents, came to our wedding. Still, that our old coaches attended Gary's wedding, and not mine, makes me slightly envious. Again, this feeling that *I* had somehow been left behind.

We talk for a while longer. Gary's parents still live in the Valley, and he returns from time to time, mostly, he jokes, to make sure that his jersey is still retired in our gym. I alert him to this year's alumni game. The Tuesday evening before Thanksgiving. Can he play?

"It'll have to be a last-minute thing," he says. "I never know when I'm going to have to travel for my job. If there's a lead on a gym that needs a floor, I gotta go after it."

I tell him I understand. "I just wanted to put a bug in your ear," I say. "I'll check in closer to the date."

I'm encouraged by the conversation with Gary, but I pretty much hit the wall immediately thereafter. Terrell's number, the one Lou had provided, is disconnected. Lou had asked his fellow Granada Hills coach, Donald Puathasnanon, to tell his brother Sam to contact him but, for whatever reason, Lou hasn't heard from Sam, and I have no way of reaching him. I've located my own telephone number for a Sam Puathasnanon in L.A. (how many can there be?), but my messages go unanswered. I try any number of online search engines for other players, even come up with several hopeful leads, but to no avail. Possible telephone numbers for Jeff Inzar, Thomas McBride, Dennis Bishop, Kevin Cross, and the others lead to nowhere.

I'm especially interested in locating Jeff Inzar. Among the bused-in teammates, Jeff had been my closest friend. A talented starter, he had been particularly generous with me on the court, feeding me assists for midrange shots and lay-ups he could just as well have taken for himself. Going into the season, I had pretty much made my peace with the probability that I wouldn't receive any "quality" game time, only "charity" time. It was a powerhouse squad and I was just happy to be along for the ride. Fortunately, I made the most of the time I did receive. After the starters had pulled out to a large lead against Canoga Park High School in the second half, Coach Johnson put in most of his reserve players, including me. I surprised pretty much everyone on the team, not least of all myself, by scoring a flurry of eleven points to emerge as the second leading scorer of the game, after Gary Gray. I can still remember glancing over at Coach Johnson in the midst of my performance, making certain that he was catching all of it. I could see him shaking his head slowly, incredulously, his mouth agape, leaning forward in his chair, his elbows resting on both knees. On account of my performance in the Canoga Park game, Coach Johnson began to point down the bench toward me more often, offering me two- and three-minute snatches of quality time. This didn't sit well with some of the other players, whom I had leapfrogged. To add some fraternal levity to our marginal status on the squad, Kevin Cross, Dan Meyer, and I referred to ourselves as the "Pine Brothers." But it was understood that I rode the pine farther down than the two of them. I remember Kevin, specifically, whipping his towel down to the glossy hardwood floor in disgust after Coach Johnson rose from his chair and pointed down the bench toward me, instead of Kevin, during our contest against Monroe High School. I wasn't quite the standout this game (my Canoga Park performance would represent the zenith of my on-court accomplishments), but I did score a couple of fast-break lay-ups upon Jeff Inzar assists. Coach Johnson would present me with the Coach's Award at our end of the season banquet, the award granted historically to players who had demonstrated the following qualities in varying proportions: outsized effort, marginal talent, and solid sportsmanship.

"I got you Fur-dog," I remember Jeff saying after delivering one of his assists against Monroe High, pointing my way as we hustled back on "D." It probably ranks fairly low on the scale of generous acts, a couple of assists to a lesser player so that he might see himself in the box scores the next morning. But it meant something to me at the time, and it means something to me today. There's something giant in these most modest childhood gestures of kindness.

While I search in vain for Jeff, I decide to call my old across-the-street neighbors, the Bloomfields, not so much because I feel that they can be of any help in this endeavor, but because I'm coming to the Valley and should arrange a visit with them. I've been particularly lazy over the past twenty years about keeping in touch with them. While they haven't made particularly strenuous efforts to do so with me, it feels that the greater responsibility has rested on my shoulders. They took me in, after all, allowing me to live under their roof for three months, my final months in the Valley. My parents, along with my sister, had moved to Philadelphia earlier during my senior high school year. My brother was already in Philadelphia as a University of Pennsylvania sophomore. But I wasn't quite ready to leave the Valley. I wanted to complete my senior year at Granada. And so the Bloomfields, mustering a generosity of spirit I took wholly for granted at the time, volunteered to take me in. I could sleep on the bottom bunk in Joey's room.

I still remember saying goodbye to Mrs. Bloomfield in their Formica kitchen shortly after my graduation. My white Toyota Celica was all packed and ready to go on the sloped, concrete driveway. Joey and another neighborhood friend, Michael, would be making the trip with me. "Good luck, Andy," a berobed Mrs. Bloomfield said (it must have been early morning), and then she kissed me straight on the lips. The gesture surprised me, utterly. She was always pleasant with me, Mrs. Bloomfield, but her natural demeanor was stern and somehow remote. I never imagined that she would kiss me good-bye, much less on the lips. Perhaps she knew, more so than I did, that this was pretty much the last she'd see of Andy Furman.

When I ask my mother for the Bloomfield's phone number she needs only her memory to retrieve it. She rattles it off without skipping a beat. "Wait," I say, "I have to get a pen." How easy it would have been to keep in better touch. They still live in the same house with the same telephone number. I call the Bloomfields immediately, early enough in the morning, Pacific time, to rouse poor Buddy Bloomfield from bed. Buddy's voice sounds familiar, if somewhat frail, broken in phrases. He must be in his seventies by now, or nearly so.

"Jeanette's still not married," Joanne Bloomfield blurts out not long after taking the phone from her husband. "And her biological clock is ticking," she adds, ominously.

"Oh, well . . . that's . . . too bad," I respond, lamely. "It's tough out there." Jeannette. She was lean and athletic (especially lithesome in a bikini) with crystal blue eyes and straight dark hair. I endured, in those days, any number of secret crushes. Jeannette had been the primary focus of my unexpressed, but probably transparent, ardor when I was fifteen and she was fourteen.

"She's in great shape," Joanne summons a list of inexplicable variables. "She does yoga, she keeps herself busy, she gets out there . . ."

"Dana just got married a year or so ago," I interject brightly, hoping that news of my sister's late nuptials might offer some encouragement.

We move on to other family members. It takes some time catching ourselves up on the last twenty years. There's a lot to say, but not as much as one might think. Conversations like this—I've now discovered after undertaking a few—have impressed upon me how little about our lives actually seems significant at the end of the day. *I am married. We have children. A boy and a girl. They are healthy. My parents and my siblings are in good health, too. They live here now. In Florida. All is well.*

"Jeannette was the only one of the kids threatened by busing," Buddy Bloomfield, who's picked up the other line, tells me when I get around to revealing the primary purpose of my trip. *Threatened.* His choice of words betrays, rather precisely, how so many Valley parents, including my own, viewed the forced busing component of the school integration plan. "We sent Jeannette to a private school for a few years, Mrs. Paula's."

I hadn't remembered.

I tell the Bloomfields that I'm interested in hearing the perspectives of my black teammates on these matters, too, but that I've had a devil of a time tracking them down. I should call Joey, they advise. He would be able to help me. Of course. Joey was a sterling athlete at Granada, the star quarterback on the Bee squad and a fine second baseman on the varsity baseball team. He would have kept in touch with some teammates from over the hill. He lives in San Diego now, Buddy tells me, and has three daughters. His wife is a successful attorney. "He's Mr. Mom," Buddy announces.

I call Joey immediately after hanging up the phone with his parents.

"Do you remember me?" I ask my old friend. Although unscripted, it seems to be the rather clumsy way I initiate most of these conversations with long-lost neighbors, friends, coaches, and teammates. Perhaps this is all I hope to affirm through this project—that my time in the Valley, at the very least, left something of an impression. That I am remembered.

"Do I remember you?" Joey replies. "You mean my neighbor for fifteen years, the guy who lived in my house for three months?" His voice sounds more nasal than I remember it, but it's clearly Joey. He's been playing a lot of golf, he tells me. He's on the way to play nine holes now, as a matter of fact, having just dropped the girls off at school. Joey promises that he can find Jeff Inzar's number. He still keeps in touch with an inner-city classmate. A woman, he tells me, who still lives in her childhood home with her parents. My hopes are buoyed. Yet weeks go by and I hear nothing.

October gives way to November. The game is only weeks away.

I focus upon factors within my control, my basketball game, fore-most. My confidence on the court grows each Saturday morning. Every-where on the court, that is, but inside the key. For whatever reason, I can't quite shake the last vestige of timidity that keeps me from scrapping for rebounds inside the paint and from driving full-force to the hoop during opportune moments. What am I so scared of? That I'll get out-muscled for a "board"? That I'll have my shot stuffed? That I'll flub a lay-up? *Who cares?* I chastise myself.

Cris Carter, oddly enough, is the one who finally draws me out of my shell. During my clumsy attempt to corral a loose ball near the baseline, he shoves me in the back with his forearm (mildly, I'll allow). Bobbling the ball out of bounds, I call what I feel is an obvious foul on the former Viking. The foul, unfortunately, doesn't seem so obvious to Carter. He challenges the call.

"What?" he cries, falsetto. "Foul? You crazy!" And suddenly I find myself in an argument.

"Yeah. Foul," I exclaim. "You shoved me out of bounds!" I add, indignantly.

"Yeah, he did!" my teammate Manny bolsters my case.

"You telling me you would have saved that ball if I didn't hit you?" Carter poses the question.

"Probably. Who knows? That's the whole point!"

He dismisses my logic, swiping the air with one of his frying pan–sized hands.

"Next time I'll *really* hit you!" he threatens, which ought properly to frighten me. After all, if Cris Carter *really* hit me, my modest scaffolding would surely collapse under the insult. For a former wide receiver, he is surprisingly broad-chested and burly.

Still, on the hoops court there's only one way to respond to such a remark.

"I'm shaking."

I think that I carry off the utterance semi-convincingly, puffing up my chest. Per court etiquette, the players respect my call, and we "check" the ball from the top of the key. The episode restores my competitive fire.

It feels good—oddly enough—to have it out like this on the court. Full-throated. To be in the fray.

All the same, my performance is lackluster for the remainder of the game, forcing a three-pointer, which clangs off the back of the rim, turning the ball over off my dribble, sloppily. We lose the game. But no matter. I know I won't hesitate to mix it up inside the key next time. Perhaps that was all I needed. This first 'bow in back.

Later this evening, I stumble across Carter's visage on HBO, a previously taped show. I notice that he fails to conjugate his adverbs. "Bill Belichick of the New England Patriots played the game 'conservative,'" Carter says, a grammatical gaffe which stupidly cheers me.

With only a couple of weeks remaining before the alumni game, my wife suggests that I hire a private investigator. For some reason—a reason beyond the obvious financial one—I can't bring myself to take this step. It seems, somehow, impersonal and inappropriate. I should succeed or fail in this endeavor, it seems to me, on the basis of my own energies. All the same, the utter thwarting of my efforts leaves me paralyzed, given the serendipitous ease of my initial contact with Coach Lou and Gary.

There doesn't seem to be much I can do at the moment, other than work on my hoops game. I redirect my energies to the workaday details of my academic job, while I consider my next step. I hem and I haw. And then, one morning at home, I receive a curious call.

"Are you Mr. Andrew Furman?" The standard lead-in, of course, for any number of annoying telemarketing solicitations, but something about the voice tells me that this isn't a telemarketer. It's a female voice. Young-ish, perhaps seventeen or eighteen, and inflected with the sweetness of a southern state I can't quite place.

"Yes," I tell the voice. "I'm Andrew Furman."

"Did you go to high school in Little Rock, Arkansas?"

"No, I'm afraid not. I went to high school in the San Fernando Valley of Los Angeles."

"Are you sure?" she asks, giving me another chance.

"I'm afraid so," I tell her.

"Oh, bummer," she says, the pitch of her voice having abruptly descended. "I'm sorry, sir," she continues, "for having bothered you." I can tell that she's about to hang up the phone but, for whatever reason, I don't want her to hang up the phone. Not quite yet.

"Wait. Hold on a sec," I say. "You're not bothering me. I'm curious. Who's this Andrew Furman, the one who went to high school in Little Rock, Arkansas?"

"My biological father," she answers. The disclosure strikes me like a blow, leaving my throat thick.

"Well, good luck to you, dear," I say, as if I were a much older person or the caller were a much younger girl. "I hope you find your father."

The girl thanks me and hangs up the phone. I feel humbled, even somewhat ashamed, by the encounter, which throws my own project of retrieval in sharp relief. How shabbily my project compares to this young girl's more essential undertaking. How did she find my number, anyway? Most likely, it occurs to me, through some of the same Internet search engines that I have relied upon, to little avail. We have never been more contactable, it seems. We're all connected, somehow, through the World Wide Web. And so children search for lost parents. Parents search for their lost children. Siblings search for lost siblings. And here I am, clogging up the telephone and Internet lines with efforts I fear may be trivial and self-indulgent. What had my father said?

You're trying to validate your existence.

There seems little I can do but sit and wait for Joey to do what he has assured me he would do. In the meantime, there is one number I do have in my possession, which I have been reluctant to call. It's Coach Bob Johnson's number. Unlike Lou, Johnson had never been particularly approachable. There was something austere about his presence. Frosty, even. I was afraid of him. The power of his station, I'm sure, largely accounted for the powerful effect he had over me. But I'm a grown man now! Screwing up my courage, I finally decide to break down and call my old head coach. I am relieved (ridiculously) when an automated, disembodied voice—one of those androgynously anonymous voices—offers to receive a message for someone I can only trust is Coach Johnson. I leave a rather flustered (where to begin?) and overlong account of myself, which would have been longer had the answering service not mercilessly cut me off with an abrupt and extended *beeeeep.*

A day later, I receive a message on my own home answering machine from a preternaturally young-sounding Bob Johnson. The call cheers me, and I immediately return it.

"Coach?" I inquire upon hearing the familiar male voice on the other end of the line. I thank him, profusely, for having called me back. It may be a sign of my inferiority complex that I rarely expect people to call me back and am always surprised when they take the time to do so.

"Do you remember me?" I ask my old coach.

"Now what number were you?" he inquires, noncommital.

"Oh I don't know," I blurt out reflexively (how could I have remembered my number?), but then I summon the number to my consciousness upon a mere moment of contemplation. "Wait, come to think of it, I *do* remember," I say. "I was number forty."

"Yep," he says. "Yes you were. I'm looking at you right now."

"Huh."

"I'm standing in my garage. I have photos up on the walls of every varsity team I coached from 1979 to 1992. I started at Granada in '68 with the Bee team."

How lucky for Coach Johnson, I reflect, that he can step into his garage and gaze up at the young people whose lives he influenced over his long career. How rare this privilege, to possess such a tangible album of one's hard work over the span of a long career. What will remain of my efforts? A stack of articles tucked away in a file? A few slim volumes nestled shoulder-to-shoulder in the corner of a bookshelf? It seems a meager record, by comparison. Small succor.

I must see this wall in Coach Johnson's garage. As luck would have it, he will be in town during my visit. He and his wife don't travel during the football season. They are die-hard USC fans, something of which I was unaware twenty years ago. We arrange for a visit. He lives south of the city now, in, San Clemente, somewhere south of Irvine. They sold the house in Northridge, fortuitously, just a year before the big earthquake. The commute isn't a problem, I assure him. I'm renting a car. I tell him what I'm working on, the sort of issues that most concern me, the racial make-up of our team, the way the various school integration programs affected the dynamics of his teams over the years. I merely want to give my old coach a heads-up, get those memory juices flowing in advance of my arrival. Apparently, however, he doesn't need any such lead time.

"I never approved of that busing business," he declares, "bringing those kids into the school. And you know, it's worse now in the Valley," he adds, ominously. Coach Johnson's sudden loquaciousness surprises me. "It was bad for the communities, bad for the—"

"Well, listen," I hear myself interrupt my old coach. "We'll have plenty of time to talk about all this stuff when I get into town. I should really get directions now."

What kind of investigative journalist was I? Here I had a subject who had a lot to say about precisely what I presumed to explore, and I had stopped him from speaking. Why? It wasn't because I wasn't prepared to take notes, or that I wanted to script a more cinematic conversation on these matters in Coach Johnson's shrine of a garage, or anything like that. Rather, I had reflexively interrupted him, it occurs to me only after we hang up the phone, because I was afraid to hear what it seemed he was about to say. I had always assumed that Coach Johnson favored the busing program that brought inner-city kids to Granada, if not for egalitarian reasons then at least for recruitment purposes. Surely, the added talent from over the hill ensured more victories for his Highlander basketball squads, including the city championship victory in 1987. Where would that team have been without my old teammate, Sean Brown? But here was Coach Johnson, about to say . . . what? That these black kids from over the hill had no business being at Granada? That they should have stayed in their own disheveled neighborhood schools? And what did he mean that it was worse in the Valley now? Was the place now overrun with the unwashed? Is that why he had moved southward, over the hill and beyond, clear past Anaheim? If these were the thoughts that my old coach was about to express, I wasn't quite prepared to hear them from his lips. At least not yet.

The alumni game is suddenly a week away. My writing director, Barclay, who perhaps has grown tired of his sad sack of a chair darkening his doorway, urges me to let one of our more talented research assistants take a stab at finding Jeff Inzar. "What do you have to lose?" he asks. It's tough to argue with such logic. So I relent, offer up my list of missing persons, which he passes along to our *über*-researcher, Paul. Within an hour—a mere hour!—as I busily bat back disputatious e-mails regarding the proposed time and format of a PhD examination, Barclay and Paul reappear in my office, wearing coy expressions.

"Does this guy look familiar?" Barclay asks, handing me a sheet of computer paper. My eyes immediately dart to the small black-and-white digital photograph at the upper left. Upon the briefest glance, hot pin-pricks race up and down my forearms. Jeff Inzar! He looks different, Jeff, but it's clearly him. Whereas his head and face were fairly clean-shaven while we were teammates, save for a slight tuft at the nape, the Jeff in the digital photo sports a goatee and tightly coiled dreadlocks flowing forward over both shoulders. A floppy Rasta hat tames the shock. The cap bears a winged insignia with lettering I can't quite make out. He doesn't so much smile toward the camera as stare pleasantly toward it. A white girl posing beside Jeff *is* smiling. She wears a baseball cap tilted dramatically sideward in hip-hop mode. I can't help wondering (on account of Jeff's semidazed stare? his dreadlocks?) whether he might be stoned in the photograph.

Jeff, apparently, works as a DJ in L.A., goes by the moniker, Brotha Benji, and specializes in reggaeton, a fusion of reggae and hip-hop. "It's real popular on the hip-hop scene right now," Paul tells me, "so it makes sense." I can't help smiling at this nugget of information. Our young research assistant is white (nearly translucent, frankly), diminutive, prematurely balding, and painfully shy. That Paul has his finger on the pulse of the hip-hop scene throws me for something of a loop. He located my old teammate on MySpace, he reveals, an Internet site I had only vaguely heard of and had associated, in any case, with a much younger demographic. You need an account, evidently, to send a message to someone on the site. And so Paul, who must have a MySpace account (and whom I'm learning more about by the minute), offers to send Jeff a message on my behalf.

Over the next few days, while I wait for Jeff to read Paul's message and, I hope, contact me, I find myself staring down at the black-and-white digital photo of my former teammate and comparing it side-by-side to that older team photograph of Jeff in our yearbook. He stands immediately beside me to my right in the team photo, this photo that had been recomposed to effect racial harmony. He wears a thin gold chain that rests just above the scoop of his tank top. I marvel at these two Jeffs, studying the photos as if they were a puzzle I hope to solve. Jeff, like me, had invented himself as an athlete in high school. At some point after graduating, he had invented himself anew as Brotha Benji. I shouldn't be terribly surprised. Jeff had been seriously interested in rap when we were in high school. He had even learned to use his mouth as a bass instrument, of sorts, manipulating his lips, his tongue, his inhalations and exhalations, aided sometimes by the acoustical cavern of conjoined hands, to effect a veritable beat-box score. I can see him now, waiting in line during our three-man weave drill, running through his repertoire of vocalizations. Still, the visual transition from Jeff-the-athlete to reggaeton-Jeff seems significant and makes me wonder, above all else, how many inventions of ourselves Jeff and I still have left in store. Will Jeff be wearing his dreadlocks and Rasta hat ten years from now? Will I still be wearing my crumpled khakis and oxford cloth shirts, the uniform of the Florida professorate? And, finally, does an essential, immutable Jeff-and-Andy, a Jeff-and-Andy we might both still recognize, lay somewhere beneath these occasional wardrobe changes? I hope so.

It's tough to tell, however, from our first telephone conversation. (Jeff hadn't checked his MySpace page, but his girlfriend had done so and passed along his phone number to Paul's e-mail address.) Time is short, so I release the students in my evening class early and call Jeff's number. When a mellow, male voice at the other end of the line answers, I ask him if he is Jeff Inzar. He says yes, and asks somewhat testily (as I would), who I am. I present my name to him, neutrally, as if it were an offering he might take or leave. "Andy Furman," Jeff repeats the name, summoning his memory. "Granada Hills High." *Phew!* He remembers me after only a moment's hesitation, which is something of a relief. "Yeah, we were cool," Jeff recalls, his way of acknowledging that we had been friends. We spend some time catching up. He wasn't only a DJ but had actually put out a rap album, which, he admits, "didn't do too well." His humility prompts me to offer my own disclosure. I published a novel a year ago. It didn't do too well, either.

I tell him about my upcoming visit, just days away, the alumni game, my larger project, which he thinks sounds cool. Jeff had played ball with Dennis Bishop a few times after high school, but he wasn't sure what had happened to him or to the rest of our team, except for Thomas McBride. He's still in touch with TMac, who has a few kids and is doing well. "Real good," Jeff says. They both still live in the city, even though TMac lives a bit further south. He'll talk to TMac, see if they both can make the game this Tuesday. We'll all "hook up," regardless, when I'm in town, Jeff assures me. We decide to firm things up in a couple of days. All in all, it's a good conversation. But unlike the other long-lost voices I've heard over the past few months, I can't say that I actually recognize Jeff's voice at the other end of the line. Or, more, I can't say that I recognize that patina of Jeff-ness I had hoped to recognize. What will this reunion hold in store? I wonder. I'll know soon enough.

I receive an e-mail message the next morning from Coach Lou, just a few days before my flight:

Its already time to play! I have the oxygen ready :-).
    Lou

The Valley Revisited, via Santa Monica

IT'S AN INTERESTING ENVIRONMENT for contemplation, the coach-class cabin of a passenger jet. This human stew-pot. South Florida is a uniquely diverse region, and it's impossible for me (perhaps on account of my itinerary) not to reflect upon the diversity on ample display in these cramped quarters. On the first leg of the trip, I sit beside a distinguished black couple in their sixties or so. The man I presume to be the husband of the woman beside him wears a starched oxford cloth shirt, the sleeves rolled to reveal a gleaming metal watch. His hair at some point seems to have nearly completed its transition from salt and pepper to salt. A younger black woman sits just in front of me, sporting a painstakingly lacquered do; small, disciplined waves lap up at the air like so many tongues. For pretty much the entire trip, she carries on a spirited conversation with the elderly white woman beside her. Across the aisle, a hulking white man with a down-home dialect and buzz cut opens a glossy magazine to a page featuring various hunting rifles. Behind him, one row back, a young black man wearing a designer sweat suit bobs his head to whatever's playing on his iPod and fiddles with what appears to be a high-end PDA, while, behind him, two Latinos (a young woman and an older man) carry on a loud conversation in Spanish.

I'm under no illusion that this brief moment of forced integration betrays an actualized, amicable integration in South Florida. On the whole, our traffic with one another will dissipate dramatically once we return to our South Florida neighborhoods and workplaces. All the same, the dis-integration of South Florida has never seemed as dramatic to me as that of Los Angeles. That I teach at an increasingly diverse state university may account, in part, for this impression. *Diverse Issues in Higher Education* ranked FAU ninth nationally in the number of bachelor's degrees awarded to African Americans in 2007, and *US News & World Report* recently ranked FAU twenty-seventh nationally in overall student-body diversity.[1] But the starkly contrastive geographies of South Florida and Los Angeles, I suspect, influence relations between races in these locales. Greater Los Angeles, its basin and beyond, is capacious, sprawling, divided here and there by mountains and valleys and canyons. The Southern California topography flaunts its bursting personality as we make our descent. In South Florida, by contrast, we all occupy more or less the same meager swatch of real estate, stranded as we are on a coastal ridge at the eastern-most toe-tip of the state, hemmed in by the uninhabitable Everglades to the west and the Atlantic Ocean to the east, with absolutely no topography to shield one community from the other. The very reason that gated com-munities proliferate in South Florida, I suspect, is that we lack not only the sheer acreage of Greater L.A., but also the natural, geological barriers that might be of use. Once we step outside of our homes, we have little choice but to put up with one another.

"Well, folks, it's another miserable day in Los Angeles," our L.A.-based pilot informs us facetiously over the loudspeaker. "Clear, sunny skies, and a temperature of just about 78 degrees." I smile, reflexively. It's always struck me as an amusing curiosity, the way Angelenos boast of their weather, as if it's all part of some organized public relations campaign. (By con-trast, all the people I've met from Seattle tend to overplay the inclemency of their region, the incessant precipitation, perhaps to keep their liveable city from being overrun by L.A. transplants.) The much-touted Southern California climate, I've come to believe, represents a crucial element of the L.A. ethos. They put up with a lot, Angelenos: exorbitant real estate prices, earthquakes, mud slides, raging wildfires that send homeowners scurry-ing atop their cedar-shingle roofs with garden hoses, bumper-to-bumper traffic at any given hour on the complex web of cruelly named "freeways." It seems churlish to deprive them their energetic claim to the best weather in the country. All the same, I grew up in L.A., so I know what the weather is like, and while it's lovely for much of the time, it's not "all that," either, as my students would put it. It's not always sunny, for one thing. In addition to torrential downpours, blankets of fog often refuse to recede until late into the day. And while Angelenos boast of their dry, Mediterranean warmth—implicitly or explicitly alluding to oppressively muggy South Florida—the dramatic fluctuations between the hot days and frigid nights on the left coast can be a downright hassle from a wardrobe standpoint. Still, there's no denying the splendor of this particular November day in Los Angeles. Even the airport terminal wears a pleasant unharried expression, bathed in the waning light of midafternoon.

I'll be spending the Thanksgiving week with my brother and his family in Santa Monica, splitting my time between filial and research pursuits. My nephew and niece are nine and seven, respectively, and I've spent woefully little time with them. I'd like to know them, and I'd like them to know me—well enough, at least, to develop an informed opinion about their uncle, for better or for worse.

Santa Monica. After eluding the obligatory chicanery of the rental-car agent, it takes only twenty minutes or so to reach my brother's verdant neighborhood. Thick muscled pines and date palms canopy the quiet streets and the immaculate, multihued front-yard gardens. The impressive arboreal specimens seem to have outgrown their residential environs, looming as they do over several of the charming Spanish tile rooftops, their powerful roots buckling the cement sidewalk here and there. This isn't *my* L.A. If this were my L.A., if Richard still lived at the far northwest quadrant of the San Fernando Valley, it would take an additional half-hour, at the very least, to reach his home. But there was never any question that if my brother returned to the West Coast after college, he wouldn't settle for a Valley address.

The provincial, middle-class Valley could never hold my brother. As soon as he was able to drive, he would pack up his golf clubs any chance he got and head south over the 405 to Brentwood Country Club, one of L.A.'s "Jewish" clubs. Our father's Big-Eight accounting firm paid the dues for our family's membership. It was a key element of the package offered to my father to encourage his westward transfer from the New York office. My brother developed an immediate passion for golf as a youngster and demonstrated great prowess. By contrast, I never felt particularly comfortable on the golf course. My middling aptitude aside, the meticulous rules of etiquette governing the sport seemed ever to elude me. I would commit any number of inexcusable gaffes the few times I braved the course, under the strict supervision of my father and brother. I'd hit the ball when I should have deferred, or defer when I should have hit, holding up the works; I'd stand in the wrong place on the green while a member of our foursome attempted a putt; I'd walk across someone's lie; or, most egregiously, I'd blurt something out at an inopportune moment—during someone's back-swing, say. It was tough to take the endless string of chastisements. Consequently, I stuck to the more conventional boyhood sports, basketball foremost. While my brother needed to leave the Valley to pursue golf, there was no need to leave the Valley to play basketball. One could argue that our contrasting athletic pursuits set my brother and me on starkly contrastive trajectories.

Golf afforded Richard access to an entirely separate sphere, a more affluent, and almost exclusively Jewish, realm. The only people of color at Brentwood were the Mexican American maintenance men and the impeccably polite black waiters in the clubhouse. While it was always impressed upon me that Brentwood represented a Jewish haven of sorts—our well-deserved warren of leisure to combat our exclusion from the host of tonier Gentile clubs—there was always something discomfiting to me about our recapitulation of these essential terms. Although I lacked the language to think about racial matters at Brentwood in these precise terms, I was nonetheless sensitive (perhaps overly so) to the not-quite-rightness of things, which is another reason I pretty much stayed clear of Brentwood. Richard developed an entirely separate network of friends at the club, sons of wealthier Jewish parents, who lived in Brentwood, Pacific Palisades, and Santa Monica. Many of them attended elite private schools, like Brentwood Academy. My brother seemed to disappear almost altogether from our Valley home, especially over the summer. He may have slept most nights in his room at the far end of hall, but even when he was home in the Valley he never truly seemed present. His sights were always elsewhere, southward, beyond our smog-choked Valley basin toward the upscale childhood he more truly deserved and would surely carve out for his own progeny.

Richard lives within walking distance of Brentwood now, just a couple of blocks off picturesque San Vincente Boulevard, where ultra-fit locals run at all hours of the day beneath the canopy of coral trees on the boulevard's broad center island. Walking distance to Brentwood! It's tough not to admire my brother's moxie as I pull up to the house beneath one of the street's towering pines. Richard is someone who seems always to have know what he wanted—in short, a solid step or two up the socioeconomic ladder—and who worked hard to achieve exactly that and no less. After graduating from Penn, he attended law school at UCLA and is now a tax attorney and partner at a firm in nearby Westwood.

I take a deep breath before exiting the car. While Richard and I enjoy a peaceable fraternal relationship as adults (helped along, no doubt, by our cross-continent addresses), we were never particularly close growing up. He was always intense, my brother, and not particularly communicative. And so it often seemed that he was angry with me for some reason or another, although it was never easy to be sure until I provoked one of his small rages by committing some prosaic brotherly transgression, like crossing the hostile border into his bedroom without permission. I was afraid of Richard. Foolishly, I continue to be afraid of him, even though he hasn't spoken a harsh word to me in years. He simply sets the bar so high—in every area of endeavor—that it's difficult not to feel that anything I might do or say on this trip is bound to disappoint him in one way or another.

We shake hands when he opens the door. He's not effusive, my brother, and I suppose neither am I. But he seems genuinely happy to see me. He mentions some prospective activities for the week: swimming at the club, a visit to my nephew's private elementary school in Bel-Air, a sushi lunch in Westwood if I have time, maybe the new James Bond movie. "Unfortunately," he says, "UCLA doesn't have a home basketball game this week, so we can't do that." He has devoted some thought to my rare visit; he wishes to spend some time with his little brother, which cheers me. "Also," he continues, "I'm sorry about this, but Leila and I are stuck with this charity dinner we have to go to tonight. This is the only night we have something," he promises. It's not a problem, I tell him. I can spend some quality time with the kids.

My sister-in-law's parents are in town, as well, so we'll share child duty this evening. Stalwart, lifetime New Yorkers, my brother's in-laws are nonetheless wealthy enough to have bought a third home in my brother's Santa Monica neighborhood. The three of us plan on taking Daniel and Ruth to dinner, but the kids can't agree upon a restaurant. Of course, we adults should probably make an executive decision, but, not really knowing the area and not wanting to favor one child over the other, we hem and haw amateurishly, all the while trying, in vain, to persuade one of the children to relent. They, of course, refuse. And so I suggest that we divide and conquer. I'll take Ruth to El Cholo, her favorite Mexican restaurant.

This first night turns out to be a great success for me. Not only do I manage not to lose my niece, but we enjoy each other's company at the restaurant, uninterrupted by the extraneous noise of the usual domestic machinery. We play several games of tic-tac-toe on the children's menu—designed to proffer such constructive distractions—and she fairly dazzles me with her prowess once we move on to the word scramble. As tomorrow is a school day, I bathe her when we return home and comb out her tangled hair. My own daughter squeals and squirms through such treatment, so I marvel at Ruthie's patience, her uninterrupted affability, as I clumsily perform this necessary exercise. My sister-in-law, once she returns from the charity dinner, is fairly blown away by my usefulness, as I pretty much knew she would be, and which, in all honesty, partly motivated my energetic efforts vis à vis Ruth. It wouldn't be a bad idea, I figured, to ingratiate myself to Leila. I'll be sleeping on her family room couch for a week, after all.

"Uncle Andy's the golden boy," Leila announces the next morning over breakfast, offering me my proper due to Daniel and to Ruth. Ruth chortles at my title between bites of her peanut butter toast. "You're the golden boy," she tastes the phrase on her lips, affirming her mother's judgment. It's a nice start to the trip, although I'll lose and reclaim this title of distinction, in Ruth's eyes, on various occasions during the week.

The alumni game isn't until tomorrow night. I'll be visiting my head coach in San Clemente, about halfway to San Diego, on Wednesday. Some time

later in the week I'll (I hope) visit with two of my African American former teammates, Jeff Inzar and Thomas McBride. Today, I hope only to
visit the Valley, explore the new demographics firsthand, check out the
old neighborhood and a few other relevant childhood haunts. There's no
reason to rush. I sit at the kitchen bar next to my niece and, over coffee,
scan the front page of the *New York Times.* The title of a story on the front
page, above the fold, immediately captures my attention. SCHOOLS SLOW IN
CLOSING GAPS BETWEEN RACES.

How current the struggle remains that had provoked the *Brown* case,
the *Jackson* case, the *Crawford* case! The article amounts to a rather scathing
critique of President Bush's No Child Left Behind program, designed to
close the achievement gap between the races by requiring states, districts,
and schools to administer and report annual test results for all racial and
ethnic groups. Schools must demonstrate annual improvements for each
group, based upon designated targets, or suffer rather harsh sanctions.
Evidently, at least a half-dozen recent studies suggest that the achievement
gap persists, despite the tough policies of No Child Left Behind. "Despite
concerted efforts by educators," Sam Dillon reports, "the test-score gaps
are so large that, on average, African American and Hispanic students in
high school can read and do arithmetic at only the average level of whites
in junior high school."[2] One comprehensive study notes pithily that, "For
each score level at each grade in each subject, minority students grew less
than European-Americans, and students from poor schools grew less than
those from wealthier ones."[3] In California, specifically, the achievement
gap seems to grow only wider, according to a study conducted jointly by
researchers at the University of California and Stanford.[4]

The studies cited in the article offer various strategies that might be
pursued to close the achievement gap more effectively. We might increase
public financing for early education programs; we might implement additional tutoring at low-income and minority schools; we might institute
more rigorous provisions to recruit and retain quality teachers at these
mostly urban institutions. Curiously, that we might undertake more rigorous efforts to promote the integration of our public schools is the one
possible strategy for closing the achievement gap that is not broached in
the article. This ship, it increasingly seems to me, has already sailed. To

narrow the achievement gap, the focus at the national and local levels seems to have shifted almost entirely from integrating our schools to improving the quality of education in low-income, minority school zones. A recent *New York Times Magazine* article, for example, "What It Takes to Make a Student," examines one of the more successful inner-city charter school programs, the Knowledge Is Power Program founded in Houston in 1994 by David Levin and Michael Feinberg.[5] And again, neither the journalist of the article nor anyone he interviews even broaches the topic of school integration. In an increasingly polarized culture, improving minority schools themselves seems to be the only strategy that parents and politicians on both the right and left of the political spectrum can rally behind.

These days, even those scattered initiatives designed to promote voluntary (rather than forced) school integration face increased public and judicial scrutiny. As I write these lines, the United States Supreme Court prepares to hear two such cases brought by conservative plaintiff groups against school districts in Seattle, Washington, and Louisville, Kentucky. (In both districts, students currently are offered a choice of schools, but to achieve a reasonable racial balance the boards consider race as one of several factors in granting or denying admission.) When I call the integration office of the LAUSD to inquire about its current student integration programs, I'm immediately transferred to a lawyer in their General Counsel office. The sensitivity surprises me, somewhat, until the genial lawyer at the LAUSD informs me that a suit, similar in spirit to the Seattle and Louisville cases, has, in fact, recently been filed in the Los Angeles Superior Court against Los Angeles Unified. At issue, primarily, are the modest, voluntary integration programs still offered by the district: its magnet program and its much diminished PWT program, the program that enabled my former teammates to attend Granada. Such programs, according to the plaintiffs, violate California's controversial Proposition 209, passed in 1996, which "Prohibits the state, local governments, districts, public universities, colleges, and schools, and other government instrumentalities from discriminating against or giving preferential treatment to any individual or group in public employment, public education, or public contracting on the basis of race, sex, color, ethnicity, or national origin."[6]

Some fifty-odd years after the landmark *Brown* decision—a decision unanimously lauded by conservative and liberal justices alike—we still find ourselves wrangling over its precise terms, parsing its language to mete out the constitutionally appropriate applications of its principles. And the pendulum, based upon the very terms of the current litigation (whatever the outcome), increasingly swings like a wrecking ball against the crumbling bulwarks of our remaining school integration programs. Given the zeitgeist, it's hard to imagine any collective fervor that might develop to enhance or invigorate diversity initiatives in our public schools. In Los Angeles, the tumultuous efforts to reverse de facto segregation of the public schools in the 1960s and 1970s—in the wake of the *Brown*, *Jackson*, and *Crawford* cases—exacted a great emotional toll. Few seem to have the stomach even to revisit those sweeping integration initiatives. In preparation for my westward trip, I had contacted several retired teachers, who had served in the LAUSD during the era of forced busing. One of these teachers from the Valley was willing to speak with me about these tumultuous times—when both students and teachers, to reverse years of de facto segregation, were assigned to schools far beyond their immediate zones—but she experienced great difficulty in coaxing her former colleagues to join us. An e-mail she forwarded to me from one of these former colleagues aptly illustrates how raw and freighted the emotions remain some thirty years later among those who were deep in the fray.

In the e-mail, this former teacher claims that most of his thoughts about those years would be negative, and that he fears saying something in haste that would be quoted in a book. He had gotten himself into some trouble by opening up his mouth during contentious parent-teacher meetings and would rather not revisit these unpleasant memories. While he mentions that a lot of the bused-in kids were great, the sum of the whole thing still leaves a bad taste in his mouth. So he passes on the opportunity to participate in the discussion and closes his e-mail with a brief mention of his pleasant recent vacation to France and the Mediterranean coast.

Taking the measure of the institutionalized racism of the nineteenth century, still close at hand, W. E. B. Du Bois famously predicted in *The Souls of Black Folk* (1903) that "the problem of the Twentieth Century is the problem of the color-line."[7] Race, Du Bois knew, would be *the* national issue among Americans in the new century. The tumultuous Civil Rights movement of the 1950s and 1960s would bear out his contention. Yet it only takes my first morning in L.A.—and months before the political rise of one Barack Obama—to suggest to me that race will persist as our national issue well into the twenty-first century, whether we care to talk about it or not.

After mulling over the aforementioned *Times* article on the stubborn achievement gap between the races, I hop into my rental car to make my commute into the Valley and immediately hear the breaking news over the radio. Michael Richards, one of the former stars of the *Seinfeld* television sitcom, has managed to get himself into trouble by unleashing a blistering barrage of racial epithets at an African American heckler during his stand-up routine at a local comedy club. Minutes later, before I even reach the 405 on-ramp on Sunset Boulevard to head south over the Santa Monica Mountains into the Valley, another story breaks. Rupert Murdoch, chairman of Fox News Corporation, has decided, after facing considerable public pressure, to pull the plug on the forthcoming O. J. Simpson book and television special, *If I Did It,* in which the former African American football star was to describe how he *would* have murdered his white ex-wife and her friend *if* he did it.

Is it just me, I wonder? Has the purpose for my visit to L.A. sensitized me to these particular media headlines, or does our race problem continue to permeate our felt lives, our collective consciousness, to the degree that it appears? Racially charged episodes continue to dog us, as anxious as we are to close the book on this chapter of the American experience. Could it be that the strident clamoring, among an increasing cohort, for "race-neutral" policies and a "colorblind" society originates in the visceral urge for simple relief from these pitched battles? Haven't we already been through the war, so to speak? Must we visit and revisit the ongoing legacy of our tortured racial history? How much easier it would be to talk about our trip to France and the Mediterranean coast—to talk about *anything*—instead!

The Valley basin wears its finest colors to receive me on this morning. The view from the crest of the 405 is, in a word, breathtaking. The admixture of smog and fog, which famously settles along the Valley basin, more often than not precludes such crystal-clear vistas of my sprawling hometown region. Peering to the far northwest—while taking care not to ram into the slowing car on its descent in front of me—I almost feel that I can see my old neighborhood miles off in the distance. I recognize instantly, at any rate, the distinct contours of the Santa Susana Mountains looming above those few suburban blocks. The view disappears in an instant once I reach Ventura Boulevard and the Valley floor. The Valley doesn't look so special anymore, just an asphalt and cement grid, peppered with strip-malls. Reaching Roscoe Boulevard, I roll down the windows and take in the yeasty aroma, instantly familiar, of the Anheuser-Busch plant. I can almost taste the chili-cheeseburger of Tommy's, just across the street from the plant. I exit at Nordhoff and head west toward Northridge, marveling at the familiar street names I had all but forgotten: Hayvenhurst, Etiwanda, Woodley, Louise, Encino, White Oak! My forehead breaks out in a cold sweat; my hands tremble on the steering wheel. I suddenly feel nauseated and take deep breaths, chastising myself for this outsized, visceral response. *Get a grip, Furman.* It's been a long time, I suppose. I'm overwrought, not on account of any particular painful childhood memory. It's just something of a sensory overload, experiencing once again these manifold sights and smells of childhood. Even the forgotten, but instantly familiar, radio advertisements conspire to put me in a different place, that vulnerable childhood place: *Oh, you won't get a lemon, from Toyota of Orange (I wouldn't have got a lemon?) No, you won't get a lemon (I wouldn't have got a lemon . . .).*

My first stop is the Northridge Fashion Center, the mall where, like most suburban teens, I spent hours loitering with my friends. Where better to capture a glimpse of the Valley's demographic sea change than a local mall? According to the latest census, the population of my hometown has dramatically altered. In the 1960s, nine out of ten Valley residents were white. As late as 1975, according to the LAUSD's Racial and Ethnic Survey, my public high school, Granada Hills High, boasted a gargantuan populace of 3,579 students, 94 percent of whom were white. But that has all changed. Between 1990 and 2000, Northridge saw a modest overall population increase of 5 percent, but its African American population increased by almost 80 percent, its Latino population increased by almost

50 percent, and its Asian American/Pacific Islander population increased by almost 45 percent. Meanwhile, the white population declined by 15 percent. White students constituted only 39 percent of the student body at Granada Hills High in 2005 (though still over four times greater than the white enrollment in LAUSD schools, generally, in 2005), while Hispanic students represented 27 percent and Asian students 22 percent of the gargantuan 3,468 student body populace. Curiously, African American students represented only 6 percent of the student body at Granada in 2005, roughly half that of the general African American enrollment in LAUSD schools in 2005, and dramatically down, also, from the 13 percent of my 1986 graduating year. I'll pursue the causes for this proportional dip when I visit the school tomorrow for the alumni game. For now I can only wonder what role the dramatic rise in the Asian American and Latino/a populations at Granada plays in all of this—whether, that is, the perceived need for African American student recruitment from the inner city has waned as these two other minority American groups have swelled the student body ranks, enhancing the overall diversity of the school.

The Northridge Fashion Center was pretty much leveled by the 1994 earthquake. The mall was closed for renovations for nearly two years. I was a graduate student at Penn State at the time, and I can still remember glimpsing the pervasive television images of the collapsed three-story parking garage at this former childhood haunt of mine, my mouth agape. The mall is downright posh in its new incarnation, resplendent with marble floors and vaulted glass ceilings. Save for the general layout, I scarcely recognize the place. I knew that the mall had been reconstructed, so I suppose that I should have anticipated its American-Mall-Circa-2000 Splendor. But I hadn't. I sit on a bench near the See's Candies franchise and watch the people. It's pretty early in the day for shopping, even for an American suburb during the holiday season, so the place isn't exactly overrun. Still, the people I do see—Latina and Asian American mothers, primarily, strolling their babies, their toddlers in tow—pretty much confirm the census reports. And it occurs to me, shamefully, that my awareness of the new demographics accounted, significantly at least, for my low expectations of my hometown's state of repair. Northridge was never particularly affluent or upscale, and I had pretty much presumed further dilapidation on account of the immigrant surge. This preconception was reinforced, perhaps, by Coach Lou, who over the phone cited somewhat nebulous reasons for moving with his family to Simi Valley, further west: "It's like the San Fernando Valley *used* to be," he noted, wistfully. My hometown, I suspected—this white, middle-class refuge from inner-city blight—had gone to seed.

But the Valley, at least the areas I traverse upon leaving the mall, heading the few blocks up Tampa Avenue, then across Vanalden to my old neighborhood, seems pretty much unaltered, save for a few additional tracts of stucco homes. It seems nicer, even. Nearly verdant. It is a lovely day, so this might have something to do with my overall impression, but not much. The distinctive, beige masonry walls have all been repaired since the earthquake. The homes on my block all seem well-maintained, replete with fresh coats of paint and fastidiously manicured lawns and gardens. Wood shingle roofs have mostly all been replaced at some point by concrete tile, rather than the cheap asphalt shingle common in my Florida neighborhood.

It's a cliché, I realize, but everything really does look smaller when you return to your childhood home: the distance between Nobel Junior High School (now called Nobel Middle, a sixth-to-eighth-grade rather than a seventh-to-ninth-grade institution) and my block, the distance between Mayall Avenue at the bottom end of my block and Tuba Street at the top, where my old corner house sits, the width of the streets and driveways. The only thing that doesn't seem smaller is my childhood home itself, which wraps around the corner and seems enormous, as if it has struggled to keep pace with its two gargantuan shade trees, the branches of which I used to climb and recline upon with a book, the roots of which now buckle the sidewalk. I scarcely recognize the house. It seems to have been wholly remodeled, its exterior skinned and resurfaced. Gone is the tacky white rock siding. Gone is the enormous rubber tree in the front. The birches still remain, and these seem, oddly, not to have grown an inch since we had left. Perhaps these are new plantings. I used to snatch down the dry, caterpillar-shaped seed pods and roll them between the pads of my thumb and forefinger, disintegrating them, scattering the seed flakes to the Santa Ana winds.

I finally ring the Bloomfield's bell, and Mrs. Bloomfield, wearing overalls, receives me warmly. "I don't remember you being this tall," Buddy Bloomfield tells me, looming in the background of the foyer. Maybe I grew a little bit, I admit, but I was always tall, I remind them. During the few months I lived in their house, completing my senior year of high school before heading east to join my family, it used to drive Mrs. Bloomfield crazy the way I left the bathroom walls soaking wet after my shower. "I figured it out," I can remember her charitable interpretation after a few weeks of tolerating the soaked bathroom. "You're so tall that the water bounces off your head and flies over the curtain."

They look well, the Bloomfields, having aged at a pace commensurate to the years that have passed. "Here's your old room," Joanne tells me, opening her palm to the small bedroom. I used to sleep on the bottom level of the heavy wooden bunk bed, nowhere to be seen. "We moved the bunk bed to Jeannette's room," Joanne mentions, as if reading my thoughts. "That's where our grandchildren mostly stay when they visit."

We sit on the cushiony leather sofa in the family room, the only room of the house that seems utterly untouched over the past twenty years, right down to the seventies-era shag carpet and Formica bar, complete with its padded, vinyl-upholstered edges. We reminisce a bit on the sofa as they scan, and squabble over, the photos of my family I've brought to share. They've never seen photos of my wife and kids. After talking for a while, after depleting my store of photos, I grow restless. I'd like to take in the neighborhood a bit more fully, so I suggest a walk around the block. Buddy declines. He takes it easy these days, he says. Both of them do, Joanne adds, somewhat proudly. They now pay for a cleaning "girl," a pool man, and a gardener. All this paid help at the Bloomfield estate shouldn't surprise me, given their age and the dearth of available child labor now that their kids have grown and departed. But it somehow does surprise me, as self-sufficient an enterprise as the Bloomfield home used to be. The house, quiet now, ever seemed a blur of frenetic domestic activity, as if their modest Valley home were a small farm. The boys, Jerry and Joey, seemed always to be mowing a stretch of lawn or trimming a tree or large shrub with a treacherous-looking, gas-powered implement. The girls, Jeannette and Julie, seemed to spend hours at the dining-room table sewing their own clothes, or preparing a meal in the kitchen, or doing the laundry. Buddy, the paterfamilias, dressed in one of his ubiquitous white undershirts, spent hours working on the engines of his many American-made automobiles or his boat, a white and red can of Budweiser beer within arm's reach. He displayed daily a virtual catalog of predilections I associated, even as a child, with *goyische-ness,* which probably accounted for my great surprise upon learning only as a teenager that the Bloomfields were, in fact, Jewish.

Our first stop around the block is my former backyard, just across the street. The current residents, the same couple who bought the house from my parents twenty years ago, won't mind, Joanne assures me. We open the gate beside the three-car garage and stand on the patch of lawn where my rickety pigeon coop used to stand. The yard looks smaller, and greener, than I remember. It had seemed pretty rugged to me growing up, countryish, lots of bare dusty ground beneath our veritable orange orchard. At least three or four of the orange trees have been removed and replaced with a disciplined carpet of lawn. The iron pool fence has also been removed, giving the area a more open feel. The diving board, at some point, had been moved from the far corner of the pool to the more proper middle of the far wall.

"We can go inside," Joanne proposes, brightly. "If they're not home, I have a key. They won't mind."

"No," I hear myself say, surprising myself with the conviction in my voice. "I don't want to go in."

This brief moment in my old backyard summons a childhood memory, but not a memory of L.A. My mother and I are walking down Arthur Avenue in Scranton, Pennsylvania, with my mother's Aunt Shirley, still unstooped—tall, dark, and striking. Shirley still lives on Arthur Avenue, three doors down from where my mother was raised. My grandfather, Shirley's brother, had died of lung cancer by this time, having rushed too quickly to join my grandmother, who had succumbed to breast cancer at the age of fifty-nine, just a few years earlier.

"We should go in," my Aunt Shirley proposes to my mother as we approach the red brick front walkway of my grandparents' former home. I always used to pluck a few fine strands of the grass that grew between these bricks as a memento of Scranton, just before heading to the airport to return to L.A. from one of our extended summer visits.

"I don't think so," my mother answers.

"But they've done a wonderful job with the place," Shirley presses on. "It's just beautiful inside. You should see it. It'll make you feel better."

"No, I don't think so," my mother holds firm.

I couldn't understand why my mother didn't want to go inside. *I* certainly wanted to go inside and was disappointed by her refusal, which may be why I remember the episode so vividly. But standing here in my own childhood backyard in the Valley, I think I understand now why my mother declined the invitation. It's good to see the house from the outside, to stand in the backyard and take the measure of the place. But there's a limit to how aggressively one ought to court the past.

"We better get going," I say.

Joanne and I leave my old backyard and walk around the block. She points to houses here and there, documenting their status. "The Changs still live here . . . the Haineys moved out awhile ago . . . the Weinzimmers still live there."

"Do you remember the few years of forced busing?" I blurt out, finally broaching the question I had been waiting to ask. I knew that like my parents they had pulled Jeannette out of the system and enrolled her in private school to wait out the storm. But what did she remember of these days?

"Sure, I remember," Joanne answers, laconically.

"Did you and Buddy attend any of the school board or PTA meetings?"

"Oh, yes," she replies. "Of course."

But Mrs. Bloomfield, apparently, doesn't have too much else to say about these faraway, fractious days. "Now, the Levines still live here," she changes the subject, drawing my attention to the Levines' home.

The more I talk to my parents, and to their friends, about the embattled era of forced busing, the more it seems to me that it's a subject that if not altogether taboo is one they'd simply rather not talk about. It was an episode during which their generally egalitarian and humane principles warred against those more instinctive impulses to protect their own. What had my mother told me? *We didn't have anything against blacks coming to* your *school.* This was probably true, for the most part, but my parents and most of their friends weren't so enamored of integration that they would send their children on a bus to a faraway inner-city neighborhood to achieve it. They would resist such efforts, while simultaneously not feeling too good about it.

My parents' best friends from the Valley, Carol and Cecil (who owned a meat-packing plant downtown), were one of the few families we knew who acceded to the LAUSD's plans to bus their child to faraway Griffin Avenue. Carol, in fact, rode the bus along with her son, Jason, and volunteered for a time at the Griffin Avenue school library.

"I wanted to see what it was all about," Carol declared to me over phone, just before my trip to the Valley. "All this talk about integration. I wanted to see if it was all it was cracked up to be." I could tell by the tenor of her voice that she had been disappointed by the outcome of her efforts.

"And it wasn't?" I asked

"Not in my humble opinion," she answered. She would elaborate later via e-mail:

> You have a hand full of students being transported an hour each way to school. They are unable to stay for after school activities or go to a friends home because they must get back on the bus. When they return home, all their friends are already involved in their activities. If the point was to equalize the education standards, it failed. It did accomplish to miss place the children at both ends.

While the English professor in me bristled at most of the grammatical gaffes (perfectly normal for an e-mail communication), I found myself pondering the significance of "miss place." Perhaps this was the perfect phrase to evoke the forced busing experience for many Valley and city children, no matter where we ended up. Given the contentious circumstances, how many of us would miss our true place, or feel somehow that we might have?

Upon leaving the Bloomfields, I drive the short distance down the modest slope to Topeka Drive Elementary, which seems no worse for the wear. I drive past the brushed metal bars of the front gate, the gate before which the yellow buses must have arrived and departed to and from

Griffin Avenue Elementary in East L.A. during the late 1970s. I distinctly remember the unique look of this gate, not so imposing now, through which I used to enter the school in the morning after walking the few blocks from home. It must be recess when I arrive, for the expansive asphalt grounds beside the low-lying buildings are abuzz with multi-ethnic schoolchildren at play, reflecting the current demographics. Compared to its 84 percent white student body in 1977—the year before the buses rolled between Griffin Avenue and Topeka—my Valley elementary school now boasts a 27 percent Hispanic population and a 23 percent Asian population (if only a 5 percent African American population) to complement its 40 percent white student body. The children, apparently, still play handball with the same red rubber balls that were popular in my day at Topeka.

There's one more, out-of-the-way stop I'd like to make today before heading back to Santa Monica. Clutching the folded sheet of MapQuest directions in my grip at the steering wheel, I make my way the 28.59 miles toward 2025 Griffin Avenue. For whatever reason, I'm curious about this commute, as impossible as it is to duplicate its precise contours.

I realize that this little journey may smack entirely of self-indulgence. At least I realize that now. Blissfully ebullient about my little homecoming, I had initially planned on visiting with one of the Griffin Avenue school administrators. I had even called the front office, hoping to secure an appointment with someone or another. Might a teacher or administrator be willing to speak with me about those long-ago days, their short-lived partnership with Topeka? There weren't any teachers still around from those years, an administrative assistant remarked. Her name was Martha. The new principal, in fact, had only been at Griffin Avenue for a few months. Besides which, Martha couldn't see what business I had visiting her school, though didn't put it quite so bluntly.

"I don't understand," she confessed, "You never attended Griffin Avenue?"

"Well, no," I admitted.

"You opted *out* of the system rather than be bused here?"

"Well, my parents pulled me out of the system," I retorted, defensive suddenly. "I was only ten years old."

"Okay, your parents pulled you from the system," Martha conceded. "But not having gone here, I still don't know why you'd want to visit the school now."

I think I managed to utter a few reasonably credible research goals, but it was a good question. What, in truth, did I truly hope to achieve, at this late date, through speaking with a Griffin Avenue teacher or administrator? Absolution? I thanked Martha for her time and hung up the phone.

It has been nearly thirty years since the short-lived forced busing program shuttled Mexican American students briefly from Griffin Avenue to Topeka in the northwest San Fernando Valley, and shuttled white students briefly from Topeka to Griffin Avenue in East L.A. While minorities have increasingly settled in the Valley, integrating Topeka and other Valley schools, inner-city schools like Griffin Avenue would never retrieve a significant population of white students. (The two white students enrolled at Griffin Avenue in 2005 represented only .3 percent of the student body.) Small wonder, given this dynamic, that an administrative assistant at Griffin Avenue would have little patience with the likes of me. Sitting by myself in my large department chair's office in Boca Raton, Florida, I felt that I could hear my own voice for an instant through Martha's ears. Who did this guy think he was? This man who had grown up in the lily-white Valley of the 1970s, wanting only now to grace us with his presence for a half hour or so?

Had I simply been a reporter from the East, someone *not* from L.A., someone without my particular past, Martha might have received me warmly. It wouldn't take much subterfuge, I knew, to gain entry. I glimpsed the prospect for an instant, yet quickly dismissed it. I have little interest in slipping my skin. There's a limit to what sorts of visitations I might appropriately pursue. It makes sense for me to visit inner-city L.A. to see my old teammates, Jeff Inzar and Thomas McBride. We had been friends during our two years on the junior varsity and then varsity squads at Granada Hills High School. But Griffin Avenue Elementary in East L.A. was never my school. I have little business there.

Still, I'm curious enough to make the commute, at least, even if I'm not so hungry for verisimilitude that I'll attempt it during the morning rush hour. The midday traffic is fairly light on the surface roads east to the I-5. Although my father routinely commuted to downtown L.A. on the I-5, the rest of us only braved this particular freeway on those rare occasions we visited the Los Angeles Zoo or attended a Dodger's game. It looks wholly unfamiliar to me, and I feel my grip tighten on the steering wheel, crinkling the MapQuest sheet, as I negotiate the increased congestion, weaving my way downtown. Here's another difference between L.A. and South Florida. While the I-95 in South Florida rivals L.A. freeways in terms of its congestion and its many lanes, the Florida highway is primarily a straight shot, while the freeways in L.A. were designed intentionally to include several curves and bends. The goal was to provide enough of a recreational diversion to keep its drivers on their toes. But these engineers in the 1940s and 1950s couldn't have anticipated the inharmonious mix of blazing speeds and choked congestion that defines these roadways today. Having gotten used to the I-95, there's something altogether unnerving about these twisting and turning freeways in L.A., the competitive, vaguely NASCAR feel of my commute along with these hell-bent hordes speeding seventy miles per hour one instant, then braking hard the next instant to avoid a collision with the slowing traffic ahead.

It takes over a half-hour to reach the exit. A far haul, to be sure, although I make it here, exit 136, Main Street, without incident. It's still clearly a working-class, Mexican American neighborhood. The storefronts advertise their presence in Spanish. The *carniceria* (butcher shop), painted in multicolored florescent hues, particularly stands out against the otherwise drab, urban environs. The houses adjacent to the school are small and squat. The windows are barred. The campus itself seems to be roughly three times smaller than the Topeka campus. I stop the car and peer behind the chain-link fence at the multistory brick building, which looks not unlike a penitentiary. Rows of modular classrooms sit on the edge of the small asphalt playground. Having just glimpsed the more expansive grounds of Topeka, having taken in its less institutionalized low-lying classroom buildings and exterior halls, it's easy to imagine how superior court judge Alfred Gitelson affirmed in his 1970 *Crawford* case ruling that the physical plant at minority segregated schools in the Los Angeles district was "of poorer quality than the plant . . . at its predominantly white schools." I can't imagine how I might have reacted to this journey as a ten-year-old, or to the alien school, to my new schoolmates and teachers, and vice versa. Nor can I imagine how or even whether the experience might have shaped a somewhat different adult me. So I don't pursue these ruminations. It's enough that I see the school as a real place, finally. I fire the ignition and head west, toward the leafier environs of Santa Monica.

Game Time

THE SCHOOL I VISIT the next morning couldn't contrast more markedly from Griffin Avenue, or from Topeka for that matter. It's the day of my alumni basketball game, but, as my morning is free, I drive my nephew with my sister-in-law to his elite private school in the Bel-Air hills, accented with dusky patches of chaparral, where he attends third grade. We park amid a sea of gleaming, high-end SUVs, which dwarf the narrow street. The first thing I notice as we walk onto the grounds is the view, or, rather, the blanket of white where the view downward toward the Pacific Ocean ought to be. It's a typically foggy morning up in the canyon.

"Yesterday," my nephew boasts, "we could see all the way to Catalina Island."

The school grounds are, predictably, immaculate. A meticulously edged and trimmed carpet of lawn—a tender variety I associate with golf courses—lay just outside the doors to the classrooms. The weight of my stride leaves an imprint. The interior walls of my nephew's classroom are festooned with constructive, multicolored projects. The young, pretty teacher's aide receives me warmly, even solicitously. She's someone, it appears, who is used to frequent spirited interaction with parents and other family members. She received her B.A. from Berkeley, she tells me after I inquire, and works now toward her M.A. at a local state university. It's one of the great things about Daniel's school, she informs me. They provide funding for their teachers and teacher's aides to pursue advanced degrees in education. "You have to stay for the salutation," she suggests. "It's pretty inspiring." Not knowing the young woman, I can't quite tell to what extent, or even whether, she speaks facetiously. Playing it safe, I tell her that I do plan on staying, that I've heard all about it, which is true.

In the meantime, Leila decides to show me the original two-story schoolhouse adjacent to Daniel's classroom, which now holds the administrative offices. It looks not unlike a ski lodge, what with its vaulted dark wooden ceilings and its large fireplace at the far wall of the ground floor.

"It's not a particularly Jewish school," Leila declares, as if to explain the large oil painting that has captured my attention, a blond-haired child astride an enormous painted horse. "That's the founder's son," she elaborates. I'm not surprised to see on display this somewhat crude painting of the founder's blond-haired child astride his horse, or to hear about the demographics of the place. The campus—from its rugged immediate environs to its few buildings—has an upscale, ranchy feel I associate with monied gentility, sort of Gene Autry meets Ralph Lauren (née Lifschitz).

We head outside to hear the morning salutation. All the fair-skinned children stand just outside their classrooms on the immaculate green, facing the flagpost and the foggy backdrop down the canyon. I try to take my nephew's photograph during the pledge of allegiance, but he'll have none of it; he holds his palm toward the camera, smiling with the delight that petulance tends to bring to a nine year-old. After the pledge, the students segue directly into "The Salutation of the Dawn," a prayer, of sorts, written by the Classical Sanskrit poet, Kalidasa:

> Listen to the Exhortation of the Dawn!
> Look to this Day!
> For it is life, the very life of life.
> In its brief course lie all the verities
> And realities of your existence:
> The glory of action,
> The bliss of growth,
> The splendor of beauty,
> For yesterday is just a dream,
> And tomorrow is only a vision;
> But today well lived, makes
> Every yesterday a dream of happiness

And every tomorrow a vision of hope.

Look well, therefore, to this Day!

Such is the Salutation of the Dawn.

There's something oddly bracing, even fatalistic, about the salutation, this philosophical outlook that amounts to buck-up-and-make-the-most-of-the-day-within-your-grasp. These are children, after all, mostly blessed with golden pasts, presents, *and* futures. Luckily for them, they've been given every material advantage over the children from Griffin Avenue, and from Topeka as well. In addition to exorbitant matriculation fees, the school also conducts a yearly, semivoluntary capital campaign, publishing the contributions in a glossy mailing. I perused the mailing on my brother's kitchen counter and was fairly dumbstruck by the staggering wealth on display. These are children, indeed, who will not want for anything material. And while money may not mean everything, I find myself reflecting upon the oft-spoken mantra of one of my college professors as Leila and I make our way back down the canyon. "Money won't buy you happiness," he used to exclaim, "but if you're unhappy, it sure helps."

It's time to visit Granada Hills High School. The game isn't until this evening, but with the help of Coach Lou, I've set up an appointment with Carolyn Gunny, the co-chair of the Physical Education program at Granada. Ms. Gunny has been at Granada since 1973 and so I figure she's seen it all when it comes to the various efforts to integrate my old high school. I vaguely remember her as one of the phys ed teachers, whom I mostly avoided through playing junior varsity and varsity basketball, instead.

The campus on Zelzah Avenue looks pretty much the same from the outside, save for the fancy new sign at the entrance of the main parking lot, complete with a scrolling electronic display I associate with professional sports venues. G-HOUSE! a green and black banner reads just inside the iron bars. I sign in at the security desk at the administration building and walk toward the main office to check in more formally and receive my visitor sticker. I pass a young white girl (a student?) strolling her baby down the hall. I'm a few minutes early, so a kindly receptionist advises that I wait there before proceeding to the gym. I notice the large old-fashioned Seth Thomas clock on the wall and smile as I observe its familiar movement—the long hand inching backwards slightly before lurching forward upon each passing minute. I remember studying these clocks diligently during the classes I found most boring, pleading with the long hand to move faster. Two knit rugs of Scotsmen dancing a jig decorate the walls of the main office. Our mascot, evidently, dances on, despite his anachronistic presence at Granada. This dancing Scot seemed out of place at Granada even in my day.

When the time comes, I walk slowly down the campus toward my appointment with Ms. Gunny, taking in the new banners that hang from the ceilings above the exterior halls, coaxing constructive behavior: REACHING EXCELLENCE ONE STEP AT A TIME, one reads. KNOWLEDGE IS POWER, reads another. RESPECT YOURSELF, RESPECT OTHERS, RESPECT YOUR SCHOOL, reads still another. A rose garden in the quad, just before the sheltered dining area, also seems new. The pines between the rows of single-story classroom buildings have grown much taller. But, on the whole, the campus seems to have changed little over the past twenty years.

I reach the high chain-link fence that separates the classroom buildings from the athletic grounds (the asphalt courts, the gym, the new artificially turfed John Elway Football Stadium) just before the bell. A security guard mans the closed gate, behind which a placid mob of multiethnic students await their release from phys ed. I wait on the other side and am nearly stampeded once the bell sounds and the students are released for lunch. I had noticed a separate security guard, his polo shirt and cap advertising his station, patrolling the exterior classroom halls on my way across campus. This is something new, these apparently outsourced security guards, even though the fierce regimentation on display—this mass of students awaiting the bell behind a closed gate—seems familiar.

I'm somewhat disappointed in myself that I don't quite recognize Carolyn Gunny when she flags me down from afar, having spotted my strange presence on the asphalt playground on the way to her office. She welcomes me into the large room she shares with her co-chair. Tattered papers and all kinds of athletic detritus clutter the broad desks and linoleum floor, which seems fitting for a bustling operation like this one. We're interrupted on several occasions during our meeting by student-athletes, who assail Ms. Gunny with questions or who simply wish to pass through the office to some undisclosed interior locale. "They're water-polo players," she explains after the fourth or fifth interruption. "They have an event this evening."

Physically, Carolyn Gunny is the antithesis of the stereotypical female gym teacher. By which I mean to say, primarily, that she is slim and looks fit. Pretty too, at fifty-five or so, I speculate, with lively bright eyes and a shock of longish, wispy hair, easily tamed in a youthful ponytail. Her tanned, somewhat leathery skin is the only visible sign that she has worked mostly outdoors for a long career as a physical education teacher and athletic coach.

"I've been at Granada since the fall of '73," Ms. Gunny tells me from her wooden chair behind her desk. She raises a sneakered heel and lifts it onto the edge of her seat as she speaks, bracing her upraised leg between interlocked arms. It's the carefree pose of a much younger person. "I began my career at Jeff, in the city, for a few years," she continues.

"Jefferson?" I seek clarification, my interest piqued. Jefferson was the team that knocked my varsity squad out of the city playoffs in the second round in 1986.

"Yeah. From 1970 to '73." I silently do the math, barely managing a rough calculation. Yes, Ms. Gunny must be in her mid-50s or so. She knows the bare bones of my interests and needs little encouragement to reflect upon Granada's experiences with desegregation. I mostly sit back and listen. "We never had forced *student* busing from Granada," she recalls (correctly). "We did have forced teacher transfers for those few years," she adds, "and that didn't go over very well." The district, Ms. Gunny explains, endeavored to integrate its faculty and administrative ranks among its schools, as well. They implemented a lottery, based upon birthdays. Coach Stroh, Granada's famously imperious baseball and football coach, was forced to transfer to a minority school for those few years before making his way back to Granada.

"Some of the teachers here were worried about the volunteer student busing *into* Granada, bringing kids here from the city." Here she refers to the PWT program. "They were, umm"—she pauses, choosing her next word carefully—"sensitive about the whole race thing. They were intimidated by the black students. But I'd already been at Jeff for a few years. It wasn't a big deal for me. I'd broken up plenty of fights before." She waves an insouciant hand before her face, dismissing her prima donna peers. She's clearly proud of her inner-city bona fides.

"Were there already gangs back then, in the seventies?" I inquire.

"Oh yeah. The Crips. The Ace/Deuce. That was before they broke off into the 86th Street Crips and so on. All that subdividing started in the eighties, when you were here. Teachers and parents were mostly concerned about that part. Bringing all the city problems to the Valley. The gangs and the drugs. But we already had the drugs."

I tell her about the drug bust at Granada that I remember, about the white, youthful-looking undercover police officer who had infiltrated the cocaine ring. She tells me that the police still send undercover narcotics officers into the class, that the teachers don't even know who they are, that they still make a big bust now and again.

"Now the gang activity did come here with some of the bused-in kids, but the violence, for the most part"—she unlocks her arms from around her upraised knee so that she can gesticulate—"wasn't black against white, so much. The fights were mostly black against black, or white against white." She pauses here and squints upward toward the harsh, florescent lights. She seems to be mulling over the portrait she has just drawn, as if unsatisfied with its contours.

"You know, most of the kids with PWTs are good kids," she continues. "You know what the PWTs are, right?" I nod. Most of my African American teammates, of course, had attended Granada by virtue of the Permits With Transportation program. It was a much larger program in my day, I learn from the Integration Office at the LAUSD, with roughly twenty-five thousand students in the district participating in the mid-1980s, compared to just over three thousand today. "The principal reason" for this decline, an attorney at the LAUSD writes, "is that the number of Integration Receiver Schools . . . have gradually reduced in number as well."

"For most of them," Gunny reflects upon her remaining PWT students, "Granada's a safer atmosphere. They're better off here, they *want* to be here, and they do fine. We've always had a healthy portion of PWT kids on our sports teams, and we haven't really had any racial incidents. Now the Cap-receiving program is a different story."

"Cap-receiving?" I inquire. I hadn't yet heard of this program. She goes on to explain that certain schools in the Valley are designated Cap-receiving ("though you'll have to check on the exact terminology," she warns), which means they receive overflow students from inner-city schools until they reach their own enrollment cap.

"And those students aren't as strong as the PWT students?" I inquire.

"Well, the overcrowded schools in the city aren't supposed to send you their worst students, and they wouldn't admit to it. But that's what they do," Ms. Gunny notes, with a sort of wink-wink, nudge-nudge glint in her eye, like someone who's been around long enough to know the score.

She goes on to say, however, that some of the athletics coaches in the Valley appreciate the Cap-receiving program, as it allows them to recruit more talent from the inner city on the sly. It's something of a point of controversy, she elaborates, between coaches at Cap-receiving and non-Cap-receiving schools. "We don't even get very many PWTs, anymore," she says. "But it's okay. We fill up with students in our own zone and we're plenty diverse. Now that we're a charter we have about 95 percent autonomy from the district." Here she affirms what I had suspected, that the shrinking proportion of African American students at Granada (down from the 13 percent of my day to just 6 percent in 2005) can be at least partially attributed to heady growth of the Latino/a and Asian American student percentages, minorities living now primarily within the school zone of this dramatically altered Valley, a demographic shift which, perhaps, has precluded the perceived need to pursue additional PWTs for inner-city students, most of whom had historically been African Americans, like my teammates Jeff, TMac, Sean, and Dennis.

"I'm not sure I've helped you any," Ms. Gunny says after our conversation winds down. It's curious that she seems to feel that she hasn't said very much. Having worked within the system for so long, it may be that she has grown inured to the various integration programs that have cycled through Granada from its days in the early 1970s, when it still an essentially all-white school in an essentially all-white stretch of Valley, to its current incarnation as an increasingly diverse (though with low African

American enrollment) charter high school in an increasingly diverse Valley. PWTs, forced teacher transfers, Cap-receiving. I didn't think much, or at all, while I was a high school student about the particular programs in place that had integrated my basketball team. My school simply *was*. But a particular program, one of many that the district would implement over the years, and one that might *not* have been implemented, had created a particular high school environment for me—a demographic sea change from the affluent private junior high school I had attended—with a uniquely integrated high school basketball team, an odd conglomerate of white, Asian, and black kids from the Valley and the city. The strange experience has served as a touchstone of sorts ever since, affecting my sensibilities, my responses even to the most prosaic episodes of day-to-day life (a certain news story, a casual quip from a colleague) in ways of which I don't think I've been fully aware. I'm hoping that my upcoming visits with my coaches, and especially with Jeff and TMac, might help bring things into greater focus.

"Don't be silly," I tell Ms. Gunny. "You've been a great help."

I still have a few hours until the alumni game, and I don't quite know what to do with myself. All I know is that I don't feel particularly well. I've been fighting a cold ever since I got off the airplane a few days ago, struggling not to give in to its ever more unignorable presence. In addition to a sore throat and runny nose, I find myself feeling achy now, too, and a sudden queasiness seizes my insides. I'm nervous, it occurs to me, which explains these exacerbated symptoms—nervous about the alumni game and my upcoming performance. I haven't seen Coach Lou, or been in the old gym, for twenty years. I worry that I'll make a fool of myself out there on the court, that I'll trip over my feet en route to a free lay-up off a break (as I did once during a JV game). *Get a hold of yourself for God's sake,* I chastise myself. *You're nearly forty years old, for crying out loud. It's only a basketball game.*

I figure that I'll go to the old Northridge Public Library, get my head off the game and into some reading, as I make my way back across campus toward my rental car. But, suddenly, I receive a call from a restricted number on my cell phone. It's Eric, an old friend of mine from the Valley. Earlier in the year, Eric had contacted me out of the blue, just after I had received the formal invitation to our class reunion.

"Is this Andy Furman?" the vaguely familiar voice had asked on the other end of the line. "Yes," I answered, warily. "The Andy Furman who grew up on Wystone Avenue in the Valley?" the caller pressed. By this point, I had recognized the voice, even though I hadn't heard it in nearly twenty years.

"This is Eric, isn't it?"

He affirmed that it was. We exchanged a few more sentences, over-assuring ourselves of our Eric-from-the-Valley and Andy-from-the-Valley bona fides. "Damn," he finally uttered, stretching the word rakishly into two syllables just as he used to do, "you sound, like, totally the same. It's friggin' weird, man."

If I were to have remained in touch with anyone, it probably should have been Eric. He was one of my best friends. Yet I think we both knew as soon as I loaded up my Toyota Celica after graduation to head east that we wouldn't be staying in touch. We had bonded over our affinity for sarcastic witticisms at someone else's expense and blow-out dance keggers held at random Valley properties until the ubiquitous LAPD helicopters and squad cars broke things up. Both activities were all the rage in those days but flimsy stuff upon which to maintain a long-distance friendship. Eric and I had very little in common, otherwise. Academics were never his bag. I was headed off to college while he had decided to pursue a career as a Hollywood stunt man, last I heard.

That we had even less in common as adults nearing middle age became clear soon into our phone conversation, which I'm fairly certain was every bit as awkward for him as it was for me. Despite all the time that had passed, all that had surely *happened* in both our lives over the long interregnum, we had startlingly little to say to each other. We stuck to basics. We asked about each other's parents and siblings. I told him about my career, my family, trying not to sound boastful one instant, then chastising myself the next instant for fatuously believing that such news would seem impressive to Eric, or to 95 percent of the populace for that matter. When I asked Eric what he did for a living now, he revealed without a trace of embarrassment that he managed a sizeable assortment of pornographic Web sites with apocryphal-sounding addresses like mommy-loves-cock. com and yank-my-crank.com. I can't say that I was particularly surprised by the revelation. The San Fernando Valley, after all, is the reigning capitol of the porn industry, and Eric had ever been something of an operator, receptive back in high school to any number of dubious get-rich-quick schemes. Yes, Internet pornography seemed just the thing that Eric would get himself mixed up in, while managing somehow to squander any profits the business might realize. As unfazed as I was by the news, I wasn't quite sure how to respond. "Oh," I think I uttered. "Internet pornography. That's . . . something."

Would I be making it out west to the reunion? Eric finally asked. It would be cool to see me. I told him that I was thinking about it, which was true enough. Even if I couldn't make it, he followed up, we should stay in touch. "Yes, yes, definitely," I agreed. "We should." I'm sure that the perfunctory tenor of my response wasn't lost upon him, and I immediately felt shitty that I couldn't feign a modicum of enthusiasm for the prospect of keeping in touch with my old friend, who had assuredly gone through a certain amount of trouble in locating me. I glimpsed myself, at that moment, just as I'm sure my friend glimpsed me, or should have: haughty and remote.

Since that initial conversation, I had spoken to Eric once or twice. He, like Joey, had thought that he could secure some phone numbers for me, but to no avail. Then his cell phone number stopped working, and I had no way of reaching him.

I had, frankly, given up hope of seeing him on this trip.

"Can I call you back in a second?" I ask him now. I'm still in the center of campus walking the exterior concrete halls, slick from the heavy traffic of sneakered feet. I'm unsure of the cell-phone protocol at Granada. Something about the institutional, nearly lock-down quality of the place suggests to me that cell phones are probably banned, and I'd rather not cause trouble. Outside the gates, I call him back and we agree to meet at Northridge Park, where I used to play basketball. My family would occasionally play tennis there on the outside courts, as well, and I can even remember, as a younger child, playing on the sandy playground, equipped back in the day with a treacherous metal merry-go-round and heavy wooden seesaws, the likes of which you don't see in playgrounds anymore, and probably for good reason. In any case, Northridge Park is the first place that springs to mind.

I park the car in the lot beside the playground and immediately recognize the mural painted on the park office wall, facing the playground, that vaguely Native American motif. I approach the mural and scan its bottom corner for a date. At the bottom it reads '73, the year my family moved to Northridge from New Jersey. There aren't very many people about, just a couple of kids shooting hoops on the outdoor court. Random, solo joggers emerge and then just as quickly disappear on their way. When a large dark Mercedes speeds into the lot, I pretty much know that it must be Eric, and so I approach the car. I smile, reflexively, nervously, as he exits. "Hey Fur-ball," he greets me, and we hug, in that abbreviated, masculine fashion. I can barely wrap my arms about his expanded torso. He had been an athlete too, Eric, a cornerback on our varsity football squad. So I'm surprised by his weight. I hadn't thought that I had developed a stereotyped notion of pornographers, so I am surprised a second time when it surfaces to my consciousness that my old friend *looks* like a pornographer, from his outsized girth (unsuccessfully concealed by an even more outsized, untucked shirt) to his sparse, gelled remnants of receding hair.

We walk the expansive grounds of the park as we talk, making our way across the broad lawn of the athletic fields up to the gymnasium, where I played in the youth basketball league for a few years. I want to check it out, I tell him. We reminisce along the way, share random memories about this and that. I ask about his parents and his three brothers, two of whom have struggled with drug addiction, one of whom is now serving a life sentence. He had been in jail, last I heard, but was set to be released soon, so I'm surprised and disappointed to hear that he got himself mixed up in drugs and crime again so soon after receiving parole. Eric switches the topic to my brother, volunteering that he (like me) was intimidated by Richard's air of aloof intelligence. "You just didn't go back there to his room," he remembers. "Gary, boy," he alludes to one of our mutual friends (not the Gary from my basketball team), "used to try to go back there, and Richard'd just diss him. Like, vicious."

Eric's cell phone interrupts us on several occasions as we walk. He apologizes as he takes the calls. I can only overhear one end of these conversations, which somehow enhances the comic effect:

"Yeah, Frank, we finished the orgy shot—"

"It's fine. I just dubbed it. The ass-slaps are all in sync. It's real good—"

"The club scenes . . . yeah, yeah . . . I still gotta reshoot some of those. We're set for tomorrow—"

It seems almost like a parody, an act, these conversations about orgy scenes and ass-slaps, and I wonder for a moment whether I'm being had. But I suppose that this is, in fact, what pornographers must talk about.

We reach the small, concrete gym and walk inside. If a certain sound permeates a basketball gym, at least some of them emit a particular smell, too, because it's the first thing I recognize about the place, this not-unpleasant indoor smell, an admixture of sweat and whatever cleanser they must still use on the wood floors. It's dimly lit, the gym. Four kids about middle-school age play four-on-four, unskilled, at the far end. Eric and I stand there for a moment, taking the place in, then just as quickly leave to head back across the field toward the picnic benches near the playground. We sit across from each other and reminisce some more, interrupted from time to time as Eric points out random women jogging by who he's either filmed or knows have been filmed by other pornographers.

"She's in the business," he says flatly, nodding toward one woman running by somewhat unathletically, her arms flailing, pulling by leash an enormous dog of indeterminate breeding. "Her name's Roxy. She does stills."

It seems, after awhile, as if every third woman in the Valley is in the porn industry, and I wonder again for a moment whether Eric is just putting me on. Finally, he tells me about his experiences during forced busing in the 1970s. I didn't know Eric then. His family had moved from the Chicago area to a house only a block away from Topeka a year or so before the buses rolled to Griffin Avenue. Private school wasn't really an option for Eric's parents, who weren't particularly well off. And so Eric rode the buses to Griffin Avenue for two years, and then to San Fernando Junior High for half a year, before Prop 1 put an end to forced busing, altogether.

"I'll tell you one thing," Eric says, "I did a lot better, academically, when I was bused. It was intimidating, the new school, all the Mexicans, so I didn't screw around. I just put my head down and worked."

"Was it really intimidating?" I inquire. "Physically, I mean? Even in fifth grade?"

"Oh yeah. Sure. You had to get in with the right guy. That's what I did, boy. I even remember his name. Paco. A big, fat kid. If you were in with Paco, you were okay. Gary, though, he got his *ass* kicked," Eric remembers, stretching out the word "ass" in that familiar, rakish way of his.

"Really?"

"Yeah, he got punked a lot at San Fernando in seventh grade. You know Gary. He had such a fuckin' wise-ass mouth."

Eric exhales and gazes absently toward the dirt ground somewhere beyond my left shoulder. A slight smile surfaces on his face, still somewhat scarred by the adolescent acne that plagued him. Just before I can ask him what he's thinking about, he tells me:

"You know there was one cool thing about being bused for those few years. Later, when we played San Fernando High during football games, I knew all those guys. We hadn't seen each other in five or six years, but we remembered each other. Lots of guys on our team were intimidated by the Mexicans and black kids at San Fernando, or just looked down on them. Especially at the Mexicans. The beaners. But it was cool for me shaking hands after the game with all these guys I knew. I used to feel like I could go in any neighborhood in the east Valley or the city and I'd be okay, 'cause I knew so many guys, either from Griffin or San Fernando, or the ones bused in to Granada from the 'hood."

I sit silently, taking this in for a moment. "Access" is the buzzword that surfaces across my mental screen, perhaps because it's a word so liberally sprinkled across the paragraphs of my public university's mission statement. To be sure, the school integration programs in L.A. weren't implemented, primarily, to offer Eric and other Valley children access to minority schools and neighborhoods. The converse was the primary impetus. Yet as Eric reflects upon his postgame, hand-shaking rituals at San Fernando High and other minority schools, it seems clear to me that his participation in the forced busing program of the late 1970s had offered him access to a broader L.A. than I had experienced. Those few years at Griffin Avenue and San Fernando Junior High hadn't exactly made Eric a model citizen. Yet his L.A. was larger than mine, and his access to this larger community was clearly something that he still valued some twenty-odd years later.

We talk for a bit more, but once we exhaust our memories from our Granada days we really don't have much else to say. We've gone off in entirely different directions since high school. The increasing evening chill and our clumsy, protracted silences tell me that it's time to go. Eric asks me if I have any plans Friday night. He'd like to take me to a high school football game. There's a great one coming up, he says, citing a couple of schools whose names I don't recognize. "I tape all their games," he says, referring to one of the teams. "Then I give the real good athletes copies of the tapes to give to college recruiters."

"Cool," I say. And I mean it. It's nice of him to do this. I can't imagine the school pays him much for his efforts.

"I do it all for free," Eric adds, as if reading my thoughts. "It's what I do to make myself feel better for being such a fuckin' scumbag." He says this only half-facetiously. I don't know what else to do but smile, awkwardly. It's good to see Eric. Truly it is. But I won't be able to make the Friday night game, I tell him. It'll be my last night in L.A., and I should really spend it with my niece and nephew. Eric understands. He promises to drop in at the alumni game tonight. After that, we'll probably never see each other or speak with each other again. And perhaps that's okay. He's not sure if he'll be able to stay for the entire game, he says, "so we better say good-bye now." Neither of us make any pretense about staying in touch. All we have together is a shared past, one thankfully lacking great tumult. Just an ordinary Valley childhood and adolescence, spent in family rooms before the TV, in front-yards playing two-hand touch, and, later, at those Valley keggers during the height of the break-dance and "popping" craze.

But it's still something, anyway. We hug good-bye (a clumsy embrace, on account of Eric's girth) and head to our cars.

I arrive early at the old gym, which looks exactly the same, right down to the Granada Hills High School seal painted in black and green at center court, and the HOME OF THE HIGHLANDERS logo painted in the same colors high on the wall behind the glass backboard. I sit high in the bleachers and watch the end of what I deduce must be the women's alumni game. Looking across the court, I spot Lou immediately, energetically coaching his girls' team, rolling his wheelchair up and down the sideline, exhorting his players, mostly white and Asian American girls. He was always a bit hefty in his wheelchair, Lou, but I'm pleased to see that, unlike my friend Eric, my old assistant coach has managed roughly to maintain his weight over the past twenty years. Only his thinning curly hair and eyeglasses, from this distance, reveals his now middle-aged status. That and his snappy blue sweater vest, anyway.

I sit back and try to relax before the big game, trying to ignore my increasingly sore throat and intestinal queasiness—symptoms that spring forth from some curious combination of silly nervousness and genuine illness. The girls' game only half-occupies my attention, vying as it does with the spirited canoodling of a skinny white high school boy and his Asian American girlfriend a couple of rows down. Ah, high school!

After the game concludes (the varsity girls pretty much trounce the alumni), I weave my way through the crowd and greet my old assistant coach, who chuckles upon seeing me, as if he weren't quite sure I'd actually make it all the way from Florida. "Are you gonna play?" Lou asks, offering me his strong, meaty paw. I suppose it's a fair question, as I haven't yet changed into my game shorts and high-tops.

"That's what I'm here for," I tell him. He points toward the boy's locker room, in case I've forgotten its precise locale.

Lou hands me a jersey when I return and directs me toward the lay-up line. It's somewhat deflating to see that there must be twenty of us or so who have suited up to play, and that most of my teammates look like they graduated within the past five years. It doesn't look like I'll be getting much playing time, which is probably why all the former teammates Lou and I have managed to track down have, evidently, passed on the opportunity to play tonight. Jeff told me that he, TMac, and Terrell played in the alumni game for a few years after we all graduated but hadn't played in it lately. We're all a bit long in the tooth at this point.

Most of the youthful players on our alumni squad seem to know one another, and they chat amiably in the lay-up line as they wait their turn. By contrast, I don't know or recognize any of these guys, so I appreciate it when one of them, a tall and muscular white player, approaches me in line and asks me my name.

"Andy," I tell him. "What's yours?"

"Eddie?" he asks, speaking from the back of his throat in that somewhat constricted manner that betrays a hearing impairment. He focuses his gaze upon my mouth in anticipation of my next utterance, so I'm not quite sure whether it makes sense to speak more loudly or simply work my lips more demonstrably around the syllables. I try doing both.

"NO. . . . A N D Y," I say.

"Eddie," he declares more than asks this time, as if seeking confirmation.

"Yeah," I say. "Eddie." What the hell's the difference?

"I'm Adam," he volunteers. "I graduated in '96."

"I graduated in '86," I say—clearly, loudly, enunciating each syllable— proud suddenly of my advanced age. He smiles at this, just before receiving the brisk pass for his lay-up, either impressed or simply amused by my geriatric status. I'm surprised, glancing into the stands, that a decent crowd has turned out for this inconsequential game. I see Eric, my brother, and another childhood friend of mine, Michael. I give them an abashed wave.

A buzzer sounds and Lou calls us into a huddle. We lean over his wheelchair in a tight circle and he begins to speak, half-shouting over the ambient noise of our lively high school gym: "Thanks all of you for coming out. It's great to see you guys. We have players here from three separate decades, which is fantastic. I know that some of you have gone on to college ball, and that's great too. Now, I'm not gonna even pretend that I can give you all as much playing time as you probably want. It might be that some of you don't get in the game at all. I'll tell you one thing, though. You play defense, you'll play more." We utter a mild, collective chuckle at this.

"I'll tell you one thing about this varsity team," Lou continues more stridently now, screwing himself up in his chair with his powerful forearms, "these kids just love to sit back and shoot the three." He flicks a few meaty fingers beside his ear, a mocking, effeminate parody of a long-range shot. He's shifted into coaching mode, his prefatory welcome and disclaimer out of the way. It's a beautiful thing to watch, really. The focus and passion of a coach, coaching. All of us crouch over him, our attention rapt. (All of us except for Adam, who focuses half an eye on the young woman standing at the periphery, who signs Lou's words so that Adam can understand.) We may no longer be in high school, but Lou's still our high school coach. And there's something godlike about a high school coach.

"Now, people can say what they want about the three, but I've always thought that the game is won or lost in the paint." Lou gestures with both his muscled arms to the hardwood floor beneath him. "This might not seem like a big game to people in the stands, or even to some of you. But I want to *win* this game!" Lou exhorts, slapping his clipboard against his lap.

"Yeahhhh!" we all cheer.

"Now bring it in!" We raise our arms toward the middle, canopying Lou inside our makeshift tent. "'Alumni' on three," Lou instructs. "One-two-three—"

"ALUMNI!"

The game itself is scarcely worth mentioning.

We win, out-muscling the varsity in the paint (as Lou had urged), and I'm pleased to see that my new friend, Adam, is one of our better players. He snatches down a few rebounds and scores several points, mostly from inside the key.

"You're playing great!" I say to him once he returns to the bench after his first burst of playing time. He slaps my thigh with the back of his hand in appreciation. After all is said and done, I'm thankful to get a few minutes of playing time. I take one shot, which I miss, but it's a respectable attempt. I snatch a loose ball, diving to the floor to retrieve it. (I've come all the way from Florida, after all.) My performance pretty much boils down to what I manage *not* to do. I don't commit a sloppy turnover; I don't shoot a ridiculous brick; I don't commit any artless fouls; I don't injure myself or anyone else.

I had hoped, certainly, for more playing time, to play long enough, that is, to work up a sweat and be something of a factor in this effort. But sitting on the bench as the seconds wind down, I'm not terribly deflated. It's enough simply to be here once more, suited up in the old gym. To see Lou and watch him coach us to victory. To play this familiar, minor role in this team effort with this diverse bunch of ordinary guys.

With only a minute or so remaining, our victory secured, Lou sends me back into the game with four others for some charity time.

"Okay, we better not screw this up now," one of my teammates utters as the buzzer sounds, ushering us onto the court. The five of us share a laugh. Yes, it's good to be here in the old gym. I finish out the game, then pose for a photograph with Coach Lou. I thank him for having been my coach, and say good-bye.

I return to my brother's home in Santa Monica, stopping along the way at Tommy's on Roscoe, a caloric splurge I haven't quite earned through my modest caloric expenditure on the court. I don't expect the chili double cheeseburger or the chili fries to be as delectable as I remember. How could they be? But the food, complemented by the yeasty smell of the Anheuser-Busch plant across the street, surprises me with its familiar deliciousness.

Only my brother remains awake in the downstairs family room by the time I finally make it to Santa Monica, flipping through channels on his TV, his feet up on the sofa, his ankles crossed casually. I sit not far from him, the television an ambient distraction.

"Sorry you had to go all that way," I hear myself apologizing. "I thought I'd play a bit more."

"Don't worry about it," Richard says. "It was cool to see the gym again." Something about my brother's posture, the way he nods his head in contemplation, tells me that something else is on his mind. "You never really got that much playing time back in high school, did you?" he inquires, neutrally. He had been at Wharton in Philadelphia during my junior and senior high school years.

2. Assistant coach Lou Cicciari at the alumni game.

"No," I admit. "I was pretty much a bench-warmer."

He takes this in silently, pensively, as Richard tends to take a lot of things in. But I know what he's thinking, this perfectionist brother of mine, who still plays golf with a five handicap. If I wasn't the *best* player on the team, or at least a starter, or at least someone who received quality minutes, why did I bother playing at all? Wouldn't my time have been better spent doing something else, anything else?

To his credit, Richard finally comes around to asking me these questions, though not quite in these brutal terms. I manage a credible response, I think, citing the fun of the practices, the exercise, the thrill of simply *being* on the varsity. All of which is true to an appreciable extent. But what

I wish I had thought to tell my brother was that there was, and remains, something inherent to the sport—from the rules and conventional etiquette governing the game to the sensibilities of its players and coaches—that defines the basketball gym as a truer place, somehow, than the other outposts I daily navigate. It's tough to explain. There was something sheltered, provincial and unreal about my L.A., just as there seems something vaguely counterfeit about the professional and primary social realms I occupy in Florida. The basketball court, by contrast, has always been a *real* place, above all, which attracts the most real people, white and minority, I have ever encountered. It's a simple place where good honest effort and teamwork usually pay off in the end. Of course, episodes of discord and even ugliness occur. But, on the whole, I've found the basketball gym to be a site of uncomplicated, uncommon human grace. It's a more cryptic explanation, of course, than what I managed to utter to my brother. But I think it's a truer explanation, nonetheless.

Coach

"NOT TOO MANY PLAYERS CALL," Bob Johnson had told me during our single long-distance phone conversation, weeks ago. It struck me as sad, this comment. My former head coach now lives in San Clemente, about a two-hour drive south from L.A. I'm on my way there on the 405 and have ample time to mull over our upcoming reunion, as the traffic on the freeway just south of LAX suddenly comes to an utter halt. Ah, L.A. I flip through channels on the radio until a station informs me that the 405 has been shut down just a mile or so south of my current location. Apparently, tanker trucks carry the chemical acetone, and at least one of these trucks has crashed and overturned up ahead, creating a situation hazardous enough to shut down the freeway. I have no idea how I might navigate around this obstruction. By some stroke of luck, my sister-in-law is home, and I reach her, somewhat frantically, on the cell. Consulting a Web site that monitors traffic patterns on L.A. roadways in real time, Leila manages to chart an elaborate, and sterling, detour. After a two-hour delay, I finally reach the 405 well south of the incident, frazzled but back on track. That Angelenos like my sister-in-law must consult such Web sites to negotiate L.A. traffic sufficiently quashes any nostalgic yearnings for the SoCal lifestyle.

"Boy, *you* look familiar," I exclaim to Coach Johnson as I approach him on his small driveway, where he greets me. It's my lame way, I suppose, of breaking the ice. All the same, it's the truth. He does look familiar as we shake hands and smile at each other. He has aged, of course. His hair, a scrupulously lacquered shock of golden blond twenty years ago, is now completely white and trimmed short in military fashion. His eyes (perhaps on account of his white hair) appear more strikingly blue than I remember. More liquid, too, though, which betrays his advanced age.

"Well, thanks for coming down," Johnson fairly sings. "I'm glad you made it." I can't help smiling at the familiar undulations of his voice, rising and dipping as if he were a game-show host. A certain gentility had always permeated Coach Johnson's affect. Even moments of intensity on the sideline were held in disciplined check. His trademark fist-pumps after a strong play, I recall, adhered to a tight arc across his chest, his elbow hinged to his waist. I suppose I had plenty of time to observe my coach, seated as I was on the bench most of the time while the game was being played. In addition to the fist-pump, there was a restrained little clap he'd perform after an unfortunate turn of events, sort of sliding one palm across the other at the final instant to lessen the violence of the palm-to-palm collision. And it's here that I remember something else, too, something I'm not so pleased to remember—that while I respected Coach Johnson, even held him in that reverence typical of high school boys for their athletic coaches, I simultaneously (and in contrast to my feelings for Coach Lou) didn't care much for him at the time. I was raised by parents who showered my siblings and me with extravagant glottals. Their shouts weren't always, or even mostly, shouts of praise, but I always knew how my parents were feeling about me. More, I always knew that my parents *were* feeling something about me. By contrast, Johnson's cool, disciplined demeanor had always struck me as strange and standoffish.

"Here's the garage you've wanted to see," Johnson declares, leading me from the driveway into his small open garage, toward the wall of team photographs. My first glimpse of his garage, the garage I've come all this way to see, doesn't exactly warm me to my former coach. The first thing I notice is the large red, white, and blue campaign sign posted on the rear wall. BUSH CHENEY, the placard reads. While I've never been a particularly active or engaged member of the Democratic Party, I must confess my visceral reaction upon seeing such a sign posted proudly in my former coach's garage in late 2006, in the midst of a deceptively sold and thoroughly botched military effort, during which, in lieu of even a token sacrifice, most of our citizenry have been called upon only to pay

3. Head coach Robert Johnson.

fewer taxes, shop more, and visit Disney World. In short, a wave of nausea sweeps over me before I can even speculate uncharitably upon the intellectual or moral indolence of my former coach. It's an outsized and thoroughly tendentious reaction, I realize, but there you are.

"Let's get a photo of you in front of all your teams before I forget," I suggest, mostly to jar myself out of my sudden and silly funk. The large framed photographs, fifteen of them or so, hang on the adjacent wall to the right, beside what appears to be Johnson's vintage MG. He gamely complies as I raise my camera, posing before his wall of team photos. Almost instinctively, I find myself composing the photograph so that the BUSH CHENEY sign lies outside the frame. It shouldn't be there, it seems to me. It doesn't fit amid this multicultural tableau. Then, before snapping the photo, I reconsider. It *is* there, this campaign sign. And so it *should* be there. I widen the angle of the lens—"say cheese"—and snap the photo.

"Let's find you," he says.

"Yes," I reply. "Let's find me." I join him at the wall and spot myself instantly.

"There you are," he says, before I think to point myself out to him. It's the same familiar team photo from the yearbook, much enlarged, though, and in color. Somehow, I look much younger, impossibly young, in this larger full-color reproduction, those last remnants of baby fat in the cheeks lending my expression a pouty cast, rather than that intimidating expression I was clearly shooting for. "Look at that little *pisher*," I hear myself say. I ask Johnson if he remembers the story of this photograph, the way in which we had initially arranged ourselves, all our black teammates to one side, our white teammates and Sam to the other side. He shakes his head, which makes me wonder for a moment whether I've imagined the whole episode. But no. It happened. I remember.

I ask Johnson if he remembers cutting me (he doesn't); if he remembers our conversation when I practically begged him for my spot back on the team (again, he doesn't); if he remembers my single, stand-out performance against what was probably the weakest team in our league, Canoga Park High, or if he remembers granting me the Coach's Award at the end of the season (ditto, ditto). I'm suddenly grateful that we at least have this team portrait before us to validate my identity. Only common decency stops me from asking my old coach whether he remembers me at all. All this ought properly to depress me. Somehow, though, it doesn't. Rather, there's something downright liberating about *not* being remembered, those most lugubrious and self-indulgent preoccupations with myself having been thrown against a sharp, clarifying relief. It's not really me that I'm interested in, anyway. I'm curious about these other players on the wall.

"Lots of photos," I observe, banally, taking them all in now. The framed photos on the wall, Johnson tells me, represent every team from 1979, when he took over the varsity, until 1993, when he retired. Johnson began at Granada as the Bee coach in 1968. (John Elway, I learn, after playing on the Bee team for a season, did play on the varsity for a week or so before hurting his knee and calling it quits, which I'm sure the Denver Broncos appreciated.) One team photo, the one from 1991, captures my attention because only six players appear. I ask my former coach about it.

"Those were pretty bad years for us," he recalls, "the early nineties." He grows silent for a moment, studying the photo. I don't interrupt his reflection with chatter. I've been teaching long enough to know that such moments of protracted silence should be greeted with a certain amount of patience. "All the schools in the city had moved to a year-round calendar," Johnson continues. "The schools in the inner city were so overcrowded that they needed to. Now, we didn't need to do this at Granada. We weren't overcrowded. But"—here Johnson pauses—"well, I probably shouldn't say this, but some black members of the school board insisted that if the inner-city kids had to rotate through the twelve-month cycle, then out of fairness *all* the kids at all the schools in the district should have to do the same." I don't quite understand how the twelve-month school calendar alleviated the overcrowding, and so Johnson explains. Students, apparently, rotated throughout the year through separate quarters, with each student having one quarter off. As Granada wasn't overcrowded, the school simply emptied out during one of the quarters, which might as well have been during the summer but, for whatever reason, was timed during the heart of the basketball season. The players only had to come in for practices and games. Most of them lost interest and quit, especially the PWT students who rode the bus all the way from the city. Johnson sighs ruefully, recalling this difficult stretch. "I suppose that I lost interest at that point, too," he utters. "That's one of the reasons I retired a bit early. We sold the house in '93, just a few months before the Northridge earthquake, as luck would have it."

I'm not sure exactly how baldly to pursue the issue of race. But how can I not broach the issue, given these team photos, given the subject at hand? Plus, he's the one who brought up the black school board members. I couch the question as vaguely as possible: how would he describe his experiences with his white and black players over the years?

"It depended on the kid," Johnson replies, but he makes a rather dramatic segue. "Now, true, your black player goes about things differently from the typical white player. A white player takes the ball out of bounds, works it up the court, looks inside for the open man, then makes a pass inside, maybe works it around the key." Johnson's cadence as he says all this emulates the methodical patience of his typical white player. He even dribbles an imaginary ball slowly on his immaculate garage floor. "The black player doesn't do that. He barrels down and wants to score right away."

I'm fairly shocked to hear such a reductive take on the proclivities of white and black players, despite our initial phone conversation, which might have prepared me for the moment, despite my impressions of the BUSH CHENEY campaign sign in Johnson's garage. But Johnson has a larger point to make. I keep quiet and listen. "So what I did"—here he points to one of the black players from the '91 team—"is I'd have this kid drive the ball full court hard to the hoop every time, then either go for the dunk or dish it out for a three if the defense plugged the lane."

"Interesting," I say.

"Well, it stopped working after a while," Johnson admits. He continues to describe some of the differences between black and white players (e.g., white players tend to cry when they're cut; black players tended to "lash out" in anger) in ways that surprise me, but probably shouldn't surprise me. Although I've experienced only rare moments of racial tension or strife on the basketball court, it's been naïve of me, even willfully blind of me, to overlook the prejudice and stereotypes that persist. My now legendary Division III college coach, I recall with some associative embarrassment, would place a white chalk-mark next to the names of each of the black players on the opposing team during our pregame preparation in the locker room. He must have felt at least some discomfiture over this routine of his, because he once explained his rationale. "Now I put that dot there for a reason," he declared, gripping the chalk as if one of us had challenged the practice. "The black players tend to be more athletic, quicker. And they usually jump higher." The basketball squad at my small Pennsylvania college was far less integrated than my high school team. Indeed, only a few black players populated the rosters of any of the liberal arts colleges we played, nestled mostly amid pastoral swatches of Pennsylvania and Maryland farmland. Our team only had one black player, Charles, a soft-spoken and talented player, who went by the nickname Chez. Who knew what Chez thought of our coach's pregame prep ritual? He was so quiet, Chez. Inscrutably so. Unapproachably so. I didn't dare ask him. The teams at my former college are now populated by an increasing number of African American players, as my former college coach continues to pile on the wins. He must have jettisoned the white-chalk-mark routine long ago.

But Greater L.A. was hardly rural Lancaster, Pennsylvania. Coach Johnson's teams had pretty much always been integrated. So what to make of his clumsy comments about these young black players on the wall staring down on us in his garage? The black players hassled him when they were cut or didn't receive more playing time; they bridled against his disciplined approach to the game and only wanted to take it to the hole. Is this all that his experiences with the PWT student-athletes amounted to?

While I think these churlish thoughts, wondering about what to say next, I notice my former coach concentrating upon one of the team photographs from the early 1990s. His eyes seem fixed particularly upon a player kneeling on the bottom row.

"Some of those kids had it really rough," he utters flatly, at a lower register. No trace of the game-show host now. "This kid," he points at the black player in the team photograph. "What was his name?" He lifts his fingertips to his lowered forehead, as if hoping to pluck the name from his skull. "Well, I'm drawing a blank, but he was a fine player. A point guard. He was selected as one of the Area Players of the Year by the *Los Angeles Times*. They held a banquet each year to honor these players. His parents were supposed to take him, but he asked me if I could drive him. He claimed that they'd be coming later to the banquet." Johnson sighs here, the kind of sigh one makes just before the lamentable portion of a story. "So I picked him up downtown. He was waiting at the curb. I took him to the banquet."

"His parents?" I ask, even though I know the answer to the question.

"Oh, they never showed up. He knew they wouldn't. He was embarrassed about the whole thing. Poor kid."

"This other kid," Johnson taps a knuckle at the glass before a black player in a different team photo. "I remember one afternoon coming across him waiting by himself at the curb at Granada for the late bus home. Now, it was a half-day at school and we didn't have practice, so he should have just taken the first bus, around lunchtime. When I asked him why he was taking the last bus . . . well, he just hung his head and said, 'Coach, I don't wanna go home.' You see, it was better for him to sit on the curb for three hours than go home. It was a tough neighborhood. There was gang pressure on him. On lots of them." Johnson nods silently, pensively, at the photo for a moment. "That was a good kid. Most of the kids were good kids," Johnson reflects.

Perhaps I had been all too anxious to see the worst in my former coach, the coach I frankly thought had paid short shrift to my abilities. Hadn't I practically set him up for his early, clumsy disclosures? *I'm* the one, after all, who encouraged him to reflect upon the differences between his black and white players; *I'm* the one obsessed with race, the one who has cultivated these overly sensitive receptors when it comes to race matters.

Coach Johnson, to be sure, was no exemplar of interracial outreach or understanding. He was probably never ambitious enough or arrogant enough to see himself in this role. He was simply a high school basketball coach in a public school district grappling with a complicated racial legacy. His chosen vocation had, by dint of circumstance, thrust him before a curious multicultural mix of student-athletes for some of the more impressionable years of their lives. His charge, as he understood it, was to hold tryouts, to retain the most talented players—whomever they happened to be—and to teach all of us the finer points of a game that he loved. Whatever else one might say about Johnson—whatever else, that is, I've already said about my former head coach—he taught us the game to the best of his abilities, modeling qualities of utmost professionalism and discipline. To be sure, there was never anything lackadaisical or half-assed about his approach to the game. He did his best for his players during the brief time we flitted into his sphere. What else was required?

Johnson invites me inside to a small family room bathed copiously in natural light from westward facing windows. I had traversed a modest, winding incline to reach his small home, but I hadn't anticipated this breathtaking view of the Pacific Ocean, tiny chops glinting below in the waning afternoon sunlight. We sit at a small table and Johnson, from out of nowhere, brandishes a stuffed manila folder. "Here," he says. "You can keep this." I look down at the stapled sheets of paper. He has granted me a series of his practice plans, hand-written in fine-tipped black marker, which no doubt contained several of the very plans he had used during my own team's practices in the Granada Hills High School gymnasium. I shuffle briefly through the stack. I recognize the hand from the carefully prepared stat sheets Johnson posted in the quad after each game. The hand is neat, in print rather than cursive, and all caps.

Interesting that these hand-written practice plans, like his team photos, survived Johnson's uprooting from what was certainly his larger Valley home, and that these carefully transcribed notes are what he wishes to bequeath to me. Clearly, he takes great pride in his scrupulous practice preparations. After shuffling through the sheaf, I take a longer moment to read through the top plan. "Manhandler," I declare, wistfully. It was an exercise, in my experience, unique to my high school team. I remember its contours only dimly, which I confess to my former coach. He smiles, struggling himself to recall the precise choreography of the drill.

"What I really liked to work on was the fundamentals," he tells me.

"Yes," I say. "I remember all those left-handed lay-ups. All the free throws." Johnson smiles at this.

We spend some time talking about the younger players on my team—Gary, Sam, Terrell, Sean—particularly their more victorious season in 1987, the year after Jeff, TMac, and I had graduated. Early in the 1987 season, Johnson had been given a last-minute option to play a regular season game against San Fernando at the Sports Arena. It wasn't an easy decision, Johnson recalls, as it was originally scheduled as a home game. But he had remembered a newspaper blurb attributed to one of the star players from Cleveland High, who had played in a recent city championship game at the Sports Arena. "'I ain't never played in no gym with no walls before,'" Johnson utters. "Just like that he said it." And so Johnson figured that the initiation might come in handy, should they make it, as expected, to the city championship game later in the season. "We ended up losing that regular season game to San Fernando,"

GRANADA HILLS HIGH SCHOOL
BASKETBALL PRACTICE

EVERYONE TOGETHER

1. ANNOUNCEMENTS
2. JUMPING JACKS PUSH UPS AND JUMP ROPE
3. FULL COURT LAY-UPS
4. CROSSOVER DRIBBLE FULL COURT
5. REVERSE PIVOT DRIBBLE FULL COURT
6. SUICIDES
7. DEFENSIVE SLIDING

IN GROUPS OF FOUR

8. TEN JUMPS WITH BOTH HANDS TO BOARDS
9. PASSING DRILLS
   A. PASS + RUN TO END OF LINE (USING ALL PASSES)
   B. FOUR CORNERS
   C. MAN IN MIDDLE — SIX HALF AROUND (TWO BASKET~~BALLS~~
10. SHOOTING DRILLS
    A. ONE MINUTE LAY-UPS STRAIGHT + REVERSE
    B. ONE MINUTE 10' JUMPER WITH FOLLOW UP
    C. ONE ON ONE CONTEST TO BASKET (FAKE + GO)
    D. SHOOTING - BACK TO BASKET AND ACCROSS FREE
         THROW LINE (FIVE TIMES EACH SIDE)
    E. OUTSIDE SHOOTING WITH REBOUNDER
    F. 21 GAME
    G. FREE THROW SHOOTING (NEXT UP RUNS)
    H. PRESSURE FREE THROWS
11. SET BALL UP EACH SIDE OF BASKET THEN TIPS
12. DEFENSIVE - OFFENSIVE DRILLS
    A. LANES DRILL FOR QUICKNESS
    B. DENIAL ACCROSS LANE

4. Coach Johnson's practice plan.

12. CONTINUED
    C. BOX OUT
    D. REBOUNDING DRILL
    E. FORWARD REVERSE
    F. POST PLAY GAME
    G. TWO ON ONE TO BASKET
    H. ONE ON ONE TEAM GAME
        EVERYONE TOGETHER

13. FULL COURT FAST BREAK DRILLS
    A. WEAVE
    B. MANHANDLER
    C. OFFENSE AFTER BASKET (OTHER TEAM NOT PRESSING)
    D. FAST BREAK AFTER REBOUND

14. PRESS PRACTICE
    A. GREEN PRESS   1-2-1-1
    B. WHITE PRESS   2-2-1
    C. BLACK PRESS   MAN TO MAN
    D. ½ COURT PRESS

15. DEFENSE
    A. MAN-TO-MAN (WHEN TO PRESSURE + SAG)
    B. ZONES   2-1-2   1-2-2   1-3-1   DIAMOND AND ONE
            BOX AND ONE

16. OFFENSE
    A. MAN-TO-MAN
    B. ZONE

17. OUT OF BOUNDS PLAYS

18. SCRIMMAGE
    A. HALF COURT
    B. FULL COURT

19. FOUR CORNER OFFENSE

20. FREE THROW SHOOTING

Johnson continues. "But it sure was a good decision to play that game in the Sports Arena."

"Well, you won your city championship," I declare, brightly. "Congratulations, coach." We've been talking for a while now. The light is fading. It's time for me to leave.

"We really beat those guys," Johnson recalls, staring somewhat dazedly over my shoulder, beyond the ocean, toward the place, I suppose, where good memories lay.

The 'Hood, via Sherman Oaks

THERE ARE ANY NUMBER of jokes about Jews and money, several of which are funny. My favorite in this veritable subgenre is the one about the three Jews who chance upon a poster in front of a church as they walk down the road together. $1,000 TO ANY JEW WHO CONVERTS, the sign reads, OFFER GOOD UNTIL SUNDAY. Two of the Jews, Shlomo and Moishe, dismiss the enticement, but Chaim cannot. His business has been failing, he confesses to his friends. There are six hungry mouths to feed at home. What is he to do? Chaim's friends listen, sympathetically. The three men part ways for a couple of weeks and then meet each other by chance walking down the same street. "Well, did you convert?" Shlomo asks Chaim. "Yep, I sure did," Chaim responds. "I'm a Christian now." "And did they give you the money?" Moishe inquires. And here's Chaim's rim-shot: "Is that all you Jews think about is the money?"

The joke is funny on a number of levels, of course (e.g., the very invocation of three Jews walking down the road, bearing decidedly ethnic names, priming us for the shtetl humor to follow; the absurdity of the proposition, which pokes fun at the proselytizing earnestness of Christianity; the mockery of facile Christian stereotypes about Jews and money, deployed through Chaim's instantaneous and utter enlistment). But what I find most interesting about the joke is the way in which it implicitly answers Chaim's question. The answer, at least to a certain extent, is *yes*: we Jews *do* think about money quite a bit (witness this in-joke and the many others created by Jews and shared among Jews about the subject). Yet we don't think about money in the way that Chaim implies, the way that anti-Semites—both casual anti-Semites and the ones who take their bigotry more seriously—presume that Jews think about money. Jews, at least those in my sphere, worry far less about accumulating money than they do about their ethical relationship with money and, more specifically, how this relationship might be perceived by non-Jews. Subject of and to the pernicious imaginings of non-Jews on the issue, how could thoughtful Jews *not* contemplate each and every move that touches upon the pecuniary?

I offer this digression on the subject of Jews and money as a somewhat clumsy way of broaching my Thanksgiving day in Los Angeles, which at once seems altogether extraneous to the story at hand and inescapably pertinent. I had hoped to spend a quiet Thanksgiving at my brother's home, a day of relief from my busy agenda. Perhaps I would help prepare the stuffing, or usefully distract my niece and nephew with a game of catch in the backyard. But my brother has other plans for me. Instead of a simple family affair at home, we have all been invited to enjoy a Thanksgiving meal at a rather lavish Sherman Oaks estate, the home of longtime friends of my brother's in-laws. The man of the house, I'm informed ahead of time, is a successful Hollywood producer, the executive producer, most notably, of a rather famous television series that had been set in outer space. One of the semifamous stars from the show, in fact, will be in attendance, along with an accomplished Hollywood screenwriter or two.

Jewish wealth has always made me uncomfortable. (Other groups, of course, must reckon with their own stereotypes; one thinks, for example, of the anxiety that descends upon Ralph Ellison's eponymous invisible man when he finds himself hankering for a yam on a bustling city street.) Even though, by any reasonable standard, I've enjoyed my own share of material success, and even though there's something admittedly self-hating and dysfunctional about depriving myself and other members of the tribe any hard-fought gains in this regard, material plenty has always seemed to me the proper province of the Gentiles and a dangerous, corruptible influence upon Jews in America. Call it nostalgia based on stereotype, but *Jewish* to me is braininess, bookishness, nagging disenfranchisement, progressive politics, tragedy-sopped humor, and cholesterol-laden comfort food. I'll cede the nouvelle cuisine and the summer cottage at the Cape to the Gentiles.

All of which I hope explains, if not justifies, my visceral recoil upon pulling up to the gabled, slate-roofed magnificence of this Jewish home in Sherman Oaks, located in the tonier southern rim of the Valley. I'll be visiting the more hardscrabble city housing of my former teammates tomorrow, and knowing this, thinking this, surely amplifies my response. Still, there seems to me something inappropriate, even vaguely shameful, about such a home, this ostentatious display of wealth. Ingrate that I am (a tagalong guest who ought to appreciate the invitation and stop thinking so darn much), I'm thoroughly prepared not to like this famous Hollywood producer and his family. Glimpsing the stadium-sized kitchen off the foyer, I don't so much wonder about the food (fast forward: the chestnut ravioli appetizer is scrumptious; perhaps I'm not so willing to cede the nouvelle cuisine) as I wonder about the labor conditions of the hired help. Are they unionized? Have they been afforded proper benefits? Health insurance, long-term disability and the like?

I can't quite sustain such sanctimony—despite the unignorable, Johannesburg-sized diamond rings on the fingers of practically all the female guests—which begins to fade before I even finish my first lime-shpritzed Bombay Sapphire and tonic. For one thing, my hosts are impossibly welcoming and kind, the accomplished man of the house having insisted upon preparing my drink. For another, it's folly to dissociate myself utterly from this social circle. I may be a tagalong guest, this may not be *my* social circle, quite, but it's not so far removed as I would like to think. My private junior high school, after all, that refuge from the threat of forced busing nearly thirty years ago, is only a few miles away, just on the other side of Ventura Boulevard. Further, I'm captivated by the sheer verve of the pre-dinner conversation in the family room. As a professor, I'm usually called upon to do my share of the talking, so it's a special treat simply to sit back on the sofa and listen in on these Hollywood insiders squabbling over the relative merits of "Spiely's" latest effort, to hear them parse the narrative arc of an entire season of HBO's *The Wire* and excoriate the weaknesses of the more ballyhooed recent movies—the ones, apparently, that they hadn't written or appeared in. "I'm sorry," the semifamous actor declares, "but *Million Dollar Baby* to me was just another *Every Which Way But Loose*, except the chimp dies." Isn't this obvious? he seems to inquire through the nonplussed tenor of his observation. The Michael Richards scandal emerges as a topic of conversation as well, particularly his poor effort a night or two ago to rehabilitate himself on *The David Letterman Show*. "Had he just said, 'Listen, I'm an improvisational comic. I was going for something and it just didn't work,' he would have been okay," the semifamous actor opines. Others weigh in. The word "shmuck" is invoked more than once, vis à vis the former *Seinfeld* star. While not all the guests in the room are Jewish, it's the kind of spunky kaffee klatsch that I associate with Jewish circles. It's one of the qualities of the tribe that I especially appreciate, this fondness for energetic verbal exchange, for dialogue and dissent, no matter the issue at hand—this love, at the very root, for language. Even though I have little (well, nothing) to contribute to this crackling discussion, I can't deny the strong affinity I suddenly feel for these people.

The progressive politics of the host family soon emerges, which only further complicates those impulses I have to distance myself from these monied Angelenos. Two of the hosts' children attend UC Berkeley (no dearth of Jewish braininess here) and steer the conversation from the movie industry to the recent Democratic landslide victories in the national elections. "It would be criminal for us [the Democrats] *not* to pursue Congressional hearings on the Iraq debacle," the affable, bearishly built older son declares. "My brother worked for the Democratic campaign," the younger brother informs me. He sports a wispy red beard, this more slender son, and wears a floppy Rasta hat to contain his uncombed, yet undreadable, locks. As he speaks, my eyes drift beyond his shoulder, up toward a statue on the mantle. "Is that an Emmy?" I inquire, unable to neuter my sudden and silly star-struckedness. The slender shaggy son glances over toward the mantle, as if to confirm my sighting. "Yeah," he tells me, "it was a special diversity award Dad won." He says this matter-of-factly, mildly abashed, it seems, at the prominent display. But why should he be? His father's television show set in outer space, come to think of it, did feature an unusually diverse cast, an oft-noted trailblazer in this regard. This *is* something to be proud of.

Even so, it's tough for me to reckon great wealth, so amply on display here, with progressive politics. A certain cognitive dissonance plagues me. All of which comes to a head during the after-dinner entertainment. We retreat to the more formally upholstered living room to listen to some live music. My brother's father-in-law (the inheritor of great wealth in his own right) has brought along his steel guitar. He sets it on his lap, frets up, and plies the instrument for a few riffs in twangy slide fashion. Accompanied by the slender son on his more traditional acoustic guitar, the two perform an impressive set of bluesy, folk songs:

Oxford Town, Oxford Town
Ev'rybody's got their heads bowed down
The Sun don't shine above the ground
Ain't a-goin' down to Oxford Town . . .

I try to relax and enjoy the music. Really I do. I'm as liquored up by this point as any of the fifteen or so people still here, so this shouldn't be too difficult. But somehow it *is* difficult. Trained as a close reader, I can't resist subjecting nearly every experience to my unrelenting, party-crashing scrutiny. And so . . . is it just me, I wonder, or is there something risible about this scene, this tableau of wealthy Jews in this lavishly appointed living room, swaying back and forth, some of us even singing along, to these tunes decrying racism and economic disenfranchisement? Are we entitled, anymore, to these lusty outraged tracks, or have we forfeited our bona fides by snuggling up to the fat gods? Talk all you want about those Jewish musicians and songwriters who crafted many of these tunes (including the lyrics of that most profound antiracist song, "Strange Fruit"), or about the transcendent nature of art, which cuts across racial, gender, and class lines. The question remains: amid an economic landscape predicated stubbornly upon racial disenfranchisement, can those recently embraced by Caucasia enjoy outsized material comfort extricated from the complications of complicity? *I'll take the second house in the Hamptons, please. Hold the guilt!* "Sometimes," my wife tells me, "you have to just turn it off, for crying out loud," by which she means my hypercritical sensibilities. But come on!

He went down to Oxford Town
Guns and clubs followed him down

All because his face was brown
Better get away from Oxford Town . . .

I'm more nervous the next day than I've been on any previous day of my extended reunion. It's time for me to visit Jeff Inzar and TMac, two of my teammates, whom I haven't seen in twenty years. We had been friends during those two high school years, our junior year together on the JV and our senior year on the varsity. But we had gone our separate ways immediately after the team banquet, a muted affair tinged with the disappointment of our surprising second-round playoff loss on our home court to Jefferson High School. What must they think of this bizarre overture? *I'm coming to town over Thanksgiving. I'd like to meet with you. See how you've been doing. Talk about your experiences in the school district when we were kids.* We had never talked about the Permits With Transportation busing program when we were teammates—why they, or their parents, had decided to take advantage of this voluntary busing program so that they could attend public schools in the Valley rather than in the city. Nor did we talk much at all about their families or neighborhoods. The only occasional references to inner-city L.A. I can recall consisted primarily of their ominous warnings against my possible visitation. "If you *do* get lost and find yourself in the 'hood," I recall TMac cautioning me, "don't ever stop your car if you think you just run someone over. Don't worry about no hit-and-run charge. You just keep on driving if you don't wanna get shot." Apparently, the mock pedestrian collision was a commonplace ruse of certain gang-bangers intent upon stealing a car. TMac's warning struck me as so much bluster at the time, the flaunting of his street cred, not unlike his pregame threat to swing open the doors in the Los Angeles High School locker room so that he might take on those hoodlums the school administrator had sternly warned us about. Yet I wasn't so entirely dismissive of his warning that I ever dared venture over the hill toward the inner city.

Perhaps these simple visits lay at the root of this entire project, which would explain my trepidation. Jeff and TMac, Sean and Dennis ventured daily over the hill to my neighborhood. We'd hang out at Mickey D's, or at my house, or at the house of one of our other Valley teammates, whiling away the long afternoons before our evening games. We'd see each other also on the weekends from time to time at those Valley blow-out dance keggers. It just seems, twenty years later, somehow not quite right (if not reparable in a single day, either) that I'd never visited them in *their* neighborhoods, at their homes, that I can only summon to my mental screen the most shadowy, ill-informed contours of their lived experiences, then and now, off the bus. Yet what does it mean that I am moved only now (entitled might be another way of putting it) to pursue these ruminations, to seek on terms of my own choosing the reunion I hope to achieve? I'm not sure that there's a way around this complicated problem of agency.

The drive to Jeff's house downtown from my brother's Santa Monica neighborhood is remarkably short, much shorter than Jeff's erstwhile commute to my former Valley neighborhood. It's just a few eastward exits, really, down the Santa Monica Freeway away from the picturesque coast, past street names that sound familiar but that I had never traversed as a youngster: La Cienega, Fairfax, La Brea, Crenshaw. I take the Arlington off-ramp and drive what amounts to a long city block, looping me back around to Jeff's street, a street of duplexes facing an enormous concrete wall, shielding the neighborhood somewhat from the roar of the freeway I had just exited. So *this* is the 'hood, I think to myself as I make my way slowly down Jeff's street. My next thought: it doesn't look so bad, which probably says more about my meager expectations than it does about the actual condition of the neighborhood. The large duplexes don't look dilapidated, per se, as much as they simply look bleak. A layer of soot, probably from the freeway exhaust just over the concrete wall, seems to coat the dull brick and siding exteriors. The front yards are small. Concrete patios and weed-encroached rock gardens mostly stand in for the cultivated greenery of most Valley frontage. The overcast day probably doesn't help matters, but gray seems to be the monochromatic color scheme of the neighborhood.

I had, for whatever reason, expected more vibrant, or at least visible, street life of some sort, but I spot nary a soul outside these homes. The whole place seems oddly deserted, which I'd take more time to contemplate were I not looking so hard to spot Jeff's home. Only sporadic numbering mark the addresses of random properties, as if most residents aren't so keen on being located. I spot Jeff before I spot his house, or the back of the person I presume to be Jeff, leaning over the open hood of his car, a slim figure in shabby sweatpants and a soccer shirt, dreadlocks bursting the borders of a black visor. I park the car and approach. He glances toward me and flashes an immediate smile of recognition, just before placing the dip stick into its slot. It's a distinctive, light-up-the-sky smile, to my relief, that pierces the strangeness of the dreadlocks, immediately marking this person as the Jeff I know from high school.

"Fur-dog," he greets me, tersely.

"Jeff Inzar," I say, as if I weren't too convinced, until this very moment, that I would actually find him.

We share that chest-bump, quasi-hug greeting. "How you doin', big man?" I inquire, hearing my vernacular shift, instinctively, to the current frequency.

"*You're* the big man," Jeff corrects me. "Look at you?" He stands up straight beside me, prompting me to do the same. "You were never taller than me back in school. Damn." I do seem about a half inch or so taller now than Jeff. Perhaps I had continued to grow an inch or two in college. Interesting.

We catch up some on the driveway while Jeff finishes attending to his car. I tell him about my family, my two kids, my job at the university. A small photo of my children summons again that broad, instantly recognizable smile to his face. "Your son looks exactly like you, boy. Look at those curls." Returning the photo, he tells me that he got close to getting married once, but doesn't elaborate. He seems mellower, Jeff, mellower than the Jeff I knew in high school. More laconic, too. I find myself doing most of the talking, nervous blather mostly, feeling, for whatever reason, uncomfortable with our intermittent silences as Jeff pours motor oil and windshield fluid into the proper receptacles. I suppose I should take it as a compliment, of sorts, that Jeff seems utterly unfazed by my presence— "hand me that rag, would you?"—as if it's perfectly normal that his old high school basketball teammate happened to drop in to say "hey" twenty years after graduation.

The street remains desolate for these ten minutes or so, which is why, I suppose, I take special note of the small car that approaches and parks across the street, just behind my rental. Two black men, roughly our age, exit the vehicle. Holy shit, I think to myself. Jeff Mays? It surprises me that I recognize him immediately upon his approach, especially as he doesn't appear in the team yearbook photo I've studied on and off over the past several months. Jeff Mays. A reflexive smile blooms across my face, a smile reciprocated by Mays' grin as he spots me, acknowledging me with the mildest nod of his head. *Give me the rock!* Jeff Mays. Audacious, hysterical, talented Jeff Mays. The last player to make the varsity squad before mysteriously leaving Granada, bequeathing me his spot on the team.

"Look at *you*, Fur-dog," Mays greets me, giving me that street hug. "You grown, man."

"That seems to be the consensus," I answer, words that sound stiff and standoffish to my own ears. How to explain the odd shifts in my diction and tone, from *how you doin', big man* to *that seems to be the consensus?* I don't care to be anything that I'm not with my former teammates. It's important to me that, at the very least, I present an honest version of myself during this brief reunion, that I show my old friends the real me. But who is this me? Can it be the person who utters both *how you doin', big man* and, in the next breath, *that seems to be the consensus?* The person staying with his brother in Santa Monica, enjoying Thanksgiving in a Sherman Oaks mansion, and visiting high school teammates in the 'hood the next day?

Unlike Inzar, Mays seems to have put on twenty pounds or so, most of which show in his protruding belly and fuller cheeks, bursting with unkempt stubble. But it's unmistakably him. Mays's brother, I learn, is Jeff's roommate. Jeff told Mays that I'd be stopping by so Mays figured he'd come over to see me, as well. While more chipper than Jeff, he doesn't exactly exude healthfulness, Mays. In addition to his paunch, the sclera of his eyes seems yellowed, jaundiced. His friend, Terence, to whom I'm introduced, is slightly built, wears dreadlocks (more fastidiously maintained than Jeff's) and fashionable, plastic-framed eyeglasses. Wearing a button-down, collared shirt, he seems neater, altogether, than the two Jeffs. Neater than me, too.

"Terence teaches English at Canoga Park High," Mays informs me. A Valley school. The site of my surprising, double-digit performance on the court.

"Oh," I utter enthusiastically, perhaps too enthusiastically. "Cool." Why should it surprise me that my former teammates count an English teacher among their friends?

Jeff closes the hood of the car, and the four of us head inside through a steel-reinforced screen door, which Jeff bolts behind us. How to describe the space? It's dimly lit with dark wooden floors. Clutter lay everywhere: plastic crates holding vinyl record albums, stray socks and sweats on a card table, towels and junk-mail strewn across the floor. The seating, such as it is, consists of a few vinyl-covered, steel bar stools, perched a few feet away from a tiny color television set, propped precariously eye-level upon a couple of cardboard boxes, themselves propped upon a flimsy tray table. I spot an unmade twin bed, which I presume to be Jeff's, through an open door to an adjacent room. We all sit, positioning ourselves around the LSU-Arkansas football game on the tube more than around each other. I'm grateful for the game, actually, which alleviates some of the social pressure. We can watch the game and converse casually as topics of interest arise.

Overall, the place brings to mind the disheveled, not-quite-squalor of a fraternity house. Except there are more books. Books, I'm pleased to see, lay here and there as well, some of them leaning lazily, like the albums, in their own makeshift plastic crate shelving.

"I see you have a copy of the Bible," I observe, apropos of nothing.

"Uh-huh," Jeff says, "I try to read a chapter a day."

"Does that work its way into your music?" I inquire, glancing toward the two turntables that occupy a large swath of floor space beyond the television. Ever since reading his MySpace page, I've been curious about Jeff's music, the specific mode of hip-hop he sees himself working in, which may or may not be reggaeton.

"Mmm-hmm," Jeff answers. Again, he seems more mellow, more reticent than the Jeff I remember from high school, if not quite withdrawn. I have to press him to describe his brand of music. "It's like . . . Conscious Rap," he elaborates, identifying a subgenre I hadn't known existed. "Most of the stuff out there"—he shrugs, disapprovingly—"it's all about the bling. My stuff's not like that."

He rises and strides a few steps toward a beat-box on the floor. After checking to see the CD in the tray, he presses a button and, suddenly,

I hear Jeff's voice, mellow like the accompanying music, the cadence almost hypnotic:

> Run come come,
> ya betta run come
> come, run come
> come ya betta
> run . . .

"You smoke?" Jeff inquires as he returns to his seat, offering me a blunt he seems to have brandished from thin air. He doesn't specifically name the psychotropic substance to which he refers. No need, given the pungent, herbal aroma suddenly wafting about. All this goes some way, perhaps, toward explaining his languor, this new, mellower, more laconic Jeff. I shouldn't be particularly surprised by the offer, I guess, but somehow I *am* surprised. Jeff might have smoked every once in a while back in high school, but he certainly wasn't as . . . well . . . good at it. I consider my options for a moment before answering. It might be fruitful to take Jeff up on the offer, a gesture of camaraderie. Yet I can't quite go there. It seems folly, above all else, to partake of a midday joint. To pretend that this is me.

"No," I answer. "I don't smoke. I mean, not really."

"Cool," Jeff answers, unperturbed, leaning back in his chair. Mays and Jeff share the blunt. For whatever reason, it pleases me to see that Terence, who remains rather quiet throughout, doesn't partake, either. Between exciting football plays on the small screen, Mays and Jeff tell me about their experiences in the voluntary busing program.

Mays had urged his parents in junior high to let him take the buses to a Valley school. "I wanted to see what it was like out there," he tells me. "There was a commercial on TV they played all the time"—here he taps Jeff on the shoulder with the back of a hand—"what was it for, Sears or something?" Jeff shrugs, noncommittal. "Everything just seemed so nice out there. Peaceful, you know?" I nod, silently, contemplating Mays's reflections. *Out there.* It speaks either to my comparative privilege or my impoverished imagination that I had never imagined a better, more peaceful life "out there" during childhood. More, I had never imagined any "out there." For me there was only the Valley. Northridge, specifically. My here sufficed.

"You gotta be lookin' over your head all the time goin' to school here," Mays continues. "It's tough to concentrate. The Valley was a more peaceful environment." He articulates this last phrase, peaceful environment, in a slower, more deliberate cadence, wrapping his mouth around the syllables. It's the key phrase, his intonations imply. "I liked hangin' out there with you fellas. The cool houses, the swimming pools, the food—"

"The food?" I inquire. I'm not quite sure what he means.

Mays smiles as he contemplates the question, recalling a fond memory, it seems. "I ain't *never* seen so much food in a refrigerator than at your houses in the Valley!" He says this demonstratively, humorously, smacking his thigh with a hand, deploying that old Jeff Mays charisma. "You know what I'm talking about, right Jeff?"

Jeff nods, issues a mild chuckle, which transitions into a mild cough from the smoke. "Oh, yeah," he adds in his mellow timbre, "that was something different than living here."

Food, I contemplate. My book research for this undertaking suggested that children residing in segregated, low-income attendance zones often lacked the basic nutrition required for healthfulness, not to mention academic prowess. For whatever reason, however, I hadn't imagined—then, or even now—that my teammates, friends in my hemisphere, wanted for such essentials. Food.

"And it was good to get that exposure to other cultures," Mays picks up the thread. "That's the world, man. That's *life,*" he exhorts, wide-eyed. All this energy. It occurs to me that Mays would make a good teacher. Or minister. But then another thought occurs to me.

"So wait," I say to Mays, "if you liked it out there in the Valley so much, then why did you quit the team?"

"I didn't quit," Mays corrects me. "I was kicked out of Granada for a little scuffle I was involved in," he coyly admits, a glint in his eye. "But I stayed in the Valley. I was transferred to Birmingham. Then I wasn't getting much time on the squad, so I transferred to El Camino. That's where I finished up." Apparently, both Jeffs jumped into a fight at Granada to help one of their friends. "The fight wasn't with a white kid," Jeff interjects midway through Mays's story, as if I had inquired. "They were both from the bus." Exacerbating matters, Mays accidentally punched a teacher who was trying to break things up. We all chuckle a bit at this. The principal at Granada allowed Inzar to stay, as it was his senior year and he had never been in trouble before. But she gave Mays the boot. Funny that I had no idea about this fight, the precise circumstances of Mays's departure. I had assumed that he had quit, that he had returned to his neighborhood school. Isn't that what Coach Lou had told me? I suppose the dust had settled by the time I rejoined the team. As thankful as I was simply to be on the squad, I probably never inquired why, exactly, Mays had left. But more, I didn't care, it occurs to me. This sudden realization fills me with something close to shame.

I ask Jeff Inzar about his own experiences in the PWT program. My casual allusion to the acronym jars his memory. "Permits With Transportation," Jeff intones the phrase for his ears, as if it were a familiar phrase, but one he hadn't thought of in quite a while. "Yeah," he says. "That's what it was called. Permits With Transportation." Jeff leans forward here, taps off the ash of his joint into a plastic cup. "My mother got Ned and me to do it. Like Mays says, she saw the Valley as a safer place for us to go to school. She worked as a teller at a bank here for a while when I was young. When I was, like, six or seven some cat pulled a gun on her, robbed her . . ." here Jeff exhales an audible burst of pent-up air. "It messed her up good, man. She volunteers now at the senior center nearby, but she never could work after that. Anyway, I started taking the buses way back then, in elementary school."

"I'm sorry," I say. Even though this was all a long time ago, I'm sorry seems like the right thing to say. "I didn't know about your mom."

Yet another thing that I didn't know.

I ask them about their classroom experiences at Valley schools, whether they ever felt any hostility, or simple disapproval, from the teachers, or from some of their fellow students. It surprises me somewhat to hear that they always felt perfectly at home at Granada, and at the other Valley schools Mays attended. Their teachers, mostly white, were welcoming; the classes were fine. "I pulled mostly Bs," Jeff tells me, the mildest of boasts. Any disadvantages they felt as PWT students, oddly enough, were on the athletic fields and courts. Jeff, for example, had tried to play football, but he just couldn't handle the commute to the Valley twice a day during those "Hell Week" practices in August. The PWT buses didn't operate before fall classes started, so Jeff and his inner-city peers were forced to make their own way on the RTD (L.A.'s public transportation system). "And Johnson geared the whole offense around Sam and Gary," Jeff recalls, somewhat bitterly, turning his attention to our basketball team. The bitterness, however, almost immediately gives way to amused mockery. "Get it to Gary! Get it to Gary!" he parodies Coach Johnson's exhortations, constricting his voice to effect the tonalities of archetypal whiteness (à la Dave Chapelle), which elicits laughter from all of us, all of us except for Terence, who smiles silently, training most of his attention on the LSU-Arkansas football game.

Mays and Terence get up to leave before the game is over. They need to get going toward some unspecified destination. I wish I had some time to talk with Terence, the English teacher. There's a lot going on back there in that head of his, I can tell. I probably have a good bit more in common now with Terence than with my former teammates. But I suppose I'm not here to make any new friends. Terence takes some photographs of the three of us on the porch before they leave. "Now don't forget about your boys, dawg, if this thing hits," Mays ribs me, alluding to my project. We clasp hands to say good-bye.

Jeff and I head back inside to watch the rest of the game and talk a bit more. We share a few fond memories of our time together on the varsity. Like the time Jeff experimented with chewing tobacco on the bus taking us to the Birmingham game, then fainted as he loped down the court during the first quarter, collapsing onto the hardwood floor. And the time that Jeff's father and TMac's stepfather "went off" on the refs after a series of unfortunate calls, getting themselves tossed out of the gym. I thank Jeff for those two selfless assists during the Monroe game, which got my name in the box scores and meant a lot to me at the time, as Jeff (a starter) surely knew. We wonder, together, what happened to some of our teammates with whom we've lost touch. "Now Dennis was one humble cat," Jeff recalls. "He was as good a baller as Sam. There's no reason Johnson couldn't have run more plays around Dennis," he suggests. Not much heat here, but lingering bitterness nonetheless, which surprises me.

5. Jeff Inzar and Andrew Furman.

"Let me take you to lunch," I suggest abruptly. I'm anxious, suddenly, to leave this space, which seems somehow more bleak with just the two of us, now that Mays has departed, taking with him all his kinetic energy and humor.

"I still got all these leftovers from Thanksgiving," Jeff demurs.

I had prepared to ask Jeff a series of rather academic questions I haven't yet broached: do you think that your experiences in the PWT program equipped you to succeed in the larger society beyond the inner city? Do you feel more comfortable now as a citizen in an increasingly diverse city and world? Did your educational experiences in the Valley prepare you to succeed in a white-dominated society? Yet I can't quite bring myself to ask these questions outright, given all that is manifestly apparent before me.

I don't know what, exactly, I had expected, or hoped for, in this visit with Jeff. I knew going in, from our phone conversations, that he wasn't exactly living large; that he had only attended a semester of community college after graduating from Granada; that he had tried out for the basketball team and, when that didn't work out, pretty much lost interest; that he resided in the same inner-city duplex where he was raised (his parents still occupy the top floor); that he worked in the Sony Corporation mailroom in Culver City and deejayed gigs on the side while hoping to cut another album someday, a possibility that seems altogether remote given Jeff's apparent lack of what might best be described as zip, the general disarray of the place, and (let's face it) his advanced age. It may be that I'm projecting my own bourgeois sensibilities upon my former teammate's state of affairs, but, glancing over toward the unmade twin bed in his small bedroom, it's tough not to feel sorry for Jeff. I can't help but think that those who fought to integrate the schools in the Los Angeles Unified School District, and Jeff's parents too, had envisioned more positive outcomes for the PWT students, that Jeff himself had glimpsed more fruitful prospects waking in the frigid predawn darkness to greet the early morning bus.

The increasing afternoon chill through the steel-reinforced screen door tells me that it's time to leave. I have an appointment to keep with TMac, who lives in the Lynwood neighborhood of south L.A. Before leaving, I ask Jeff if I can use the bathroom. He accompanies me to the door, opening it for me and peeking inside, checking it for cleanliness, I presume. "It's fine," I assure him. I do my business quickly and wash up. "SPIDER MAN 2," I read the stitching on the small navy blue towel on the rack as I dry my hands, a likeness of the masked superhero embossed just beneath. Perhaps I'm only overwrought by this reunion, but there's something about this towel that I find unutterably sad.

"You sure you don't want to get out of here for a bit, grab something to eat?" I ask once again as I reenter what I suppose is the family room. "My treat."

"Nah," he repeats. "I'm good, Fur-dog."

We say our good-byes—Jeff promises to send me a copy of his CD—and I leave.

The evocative opening chapter of William Faulkner's *Intruder in the Dust* will only surface unbidden to my consciousness a few days later, once I'm on the airplane headed back home to Florida, my head dizzy with the whirlwind experiences of an emotionally charged week. What *was* all that business about treating Jeff to lunch? Why had I been so oddly insistent? Why had Jeff just as insistently declined? Early in the first chapter of Faulkner's novel, his adolescent white protagonist, Chick, falls into an icy creek while hunting with a friend for rabbit. The black landowner, Lucas Beauchamp, brings Chick back to his paintless wooden house and provides him a place beside the fire, a quilt, and a plate of "collard greens, a slice of sidemeat fried in flour, big flat pale heavy half-cooked biscuits, [and] a glass of buttermilk."[1] The chapter ends as Chick insists, vehemently, that Beauchamp accept money for his kindness, even throwing the coins to the floor and yelling "Pick it up!" after Beauchamp refuses.[2] Chick, Faulkner suggests, wishes to control the terms of this human transaction, transforming a gift by a black man into a mere service rendered for payment. For to accept the simple generosity of a black man would upset the social order to which our young protagonist (note the illustrative nickname) has already grown accustomed. In the American caste system, the subservient black citizen might accept the patronage of a white benefactor, but not the other way around.

I've taught this scene to any number of eighteen-year-old students over the years, all of whom readily enough get the point. Even Faulkner—in a book not untainted by various problematic racial assumptions of its day—limns this particular confrontation with great moral acuity. Beauchamp, importantly, refuses to pick up the money from the floor, instructs Chick's friend to place the coins back into Chick's hands, and sends our young hero off in shame to hunt his rabbits. It's a fairly easy scene to teach in the rarified, controlled setting of a college classroom. Book knowledge, however, doesn't always travel so well.

For all my right-minded predilections, visiting my old high school friend on his own turf proved more complicated than I had anticipated. Flustered by what struck me as Jeff's sad state of affairs, I had clumsily insisted upon sporting him a meal. While I would like to think that the offer was wholly innocuous, I can't help wondering whether something more insidious was afoot. Was I somehow unable, or perhaps only unwilling, to share a few hours with Jeff on equal terms? Surveying the wreckage, had I sought comfort in assuming that oh-so-magnanimous role as Jeff's white benefactor for the day? Had I thereby instinctively hoped to replicate the essential, interracial calculus that Faulkner's young protagonist wishes so desperately to affirm? Further, had Jeff just as instinctively recognized the overture for what it was and rejected it, accordingly—Thanksgiving leftovers aside? I can't quite dismiss these possibilities.

All of which probably goes some way toward explaining that vague but palpable queasiness I feel as I beat my retreat from Jeff's front porch, striding toward the rental car, tasting again certain sour phrases in my mouth.

Let me take you to lunch. . . . My treat.

"I'm just a couple freeways over from Jeff," TMac had assured me this morning, over the phone, offering me directions. It struck me as a funny way to describe his whereabouts, but it's probably the way most Angelenos offer directions to visitors. A tangled web of interstates in greater L.A. crisscross countless distinct neighborhoods (Compton, Carson, Inglewood, Pico Rivera, Monterey Park) and often demarcate their borders. From Jeff's, I hop back on the Santa Monica Freeway east for a mile or two before reaching freeways utterly foreign to me—the 110 south, which I must traverse for longer than I had anticipated, then the 105 east toward TMac's Lynwood community. My map tells me that Watts is close by, so I must have traveled here by bus with the basketball team in the summer of 1985 to play in the Watts Games, even though I can't remember anything about the commute.

Lynwood seems far livelier than Jeff's neighborhood. Bustling, multilane streets lead me gradually to smaller, quieter streets until I reach TMac's block. His neighborhood, while not quite verdant, seems almost suburban. Small, single-family stucco homes on one side of the road face a large open park space across the way. Tidy rose gardens, lawns, and trees accent the front yards of these freshly painted homes. TMac, I know, works for Verizon, installing DSL and other services into residences, and so the Verizon van in a driveway announces his home to me before I confirm the address on the doorpost. The house is painted orange, a cheery hue that effectively counters the harsher tone set by the iron bars on the windows and doors. I park my rental car and try ringing the bell, but no one answers. This doesn't surprise me. TMac warned me that he had errands to run with his boys and didn't expect to be home for another half hour or so. I'm early. I return to my car and jot down some notes in the driver's seat while I wait, feeling somewhat suspicious sitting out there. I know that I'm not casing the joint, but it somehow feels like I am.

After only a few minutes, a car pulls up just behind the Verizon van in the driveway. Yep, that's him, I think, as TMac exits the driver's seat, prompting me to exit my car and make my way over. His two slim boys, one of them nearly as tall as his father, emerge from the back seat and lope ahead toward the front door. TMac, who's spotted me, hangs back to greet his visitor. "Hey, good to see you made it, Andy," he says. His sons look back toward me, seeming only mildly interested in my presence. They're twelve and eight, TMac told me over the phone. He also raised a step-daughter, now in her twenties and living on her own.

"Glad to be here," I reciprocate. We share a handclasp and half-hug. He looks good, TMac, physically fit, with handsome metal eyeglasses, a neat goatee, and close-trimmed hair. Back in high school, he had sported a look that seemed to me an unstylish throwback to the seventies: a longish, lacquered 'fro, nearly a Jerri-curl, untamed tendrils trailing off behind, a wispy mustache. Off the court, he wore enormous clunky eyeglasses. "Thanks for making some time for me," I declare. "I know you're busy with the holidays and all." TMac shrugs off my appreciation and invites me inside the front door to the family room.

The first thing I notice isn't the Christmas tree, or the multitude of family faces beaming down toward me from the framed professional photographs on the walls, or the large-screen television, or the tall wooden end piece, featuring various crystalline collectibles across its glass-fronted shelving, or the formal wooden table in the adjacent dining room, or even the general tidiness of the place. Rather, the first thing I notice is the couch, its impossibly puffy cushions tightly wrapped in plastic. "Have a seat," TMac suggests, as if he had noticed me noticing the couch. I haven't seen a plastic-covered couch like this since I was a child visiting my elderly Jewish relatives in Scranton, Pennsylvania. I had been confused at the time—which is probably why I remember the occasion—chancing upon so many plastic-covered sofas, chairs, and love seats in so many living rooms. Was it possible that all our relatives had just returned from the furniture store at the same time? My parents would explain to me later that fancy furniture was expensive for my relatives, that it was important to them to protect it from damage, even if the plastic wasn't particularly comfortable. Respectful of their elders to a fault, my parents did their best to describe these odd proclivities vis à vis upholstery maintenance without even a whiff of condescension. Even so, such extreme prophylactic measures seemed unbelievably silly to me at the time. A plastic-covered couch? What was the point?

While I wouldn't presume to know the precise whys and wherefores of TMac's plastic-covered coach, and while I'm reluctant to draw facile parallels between my former teammate and my long-dead relatives, I can't help but think that there's something illustrative about this piece of furniture in the larger context of its environs: the abundant family photographs on display, the Christmas tree with its tantalizing ornaments, the crystalline knickknacks in their display case, the dining room table. Indeed, there's something about the whole place that bespeaks not only pride, but something greater . . . hope, it occurs to me, that vital, if somewhat intangible, substance that seemed in shorter supply at Jeff's bleak quarters, utterly bereft of scrupulously protected furniture or (come to think of it) family photos. "Look at you," I say, rising abruptly from the noisy couch, one photo having captured my eye—TMac and his bride in the back seat of a limousine. It's the old TMac, sporting an ample 'fro, enormous eyeglasses, and a frilly tuxedo. His pretty wife, her face peeking out from beneath layers and layers of bridal taffeta, beams jubilantly toward the camera. "She's pretty, your wife," I say. "She keeps me on the straight and narrow," TMac replies, sinking back into the squeaky sofa, casually adjusting the tilt of his spotless gray baseball cap from the nape. Jeff, to his credit, was right about one thing. TMac *is* doing "real good." That much is clear.

TMac started taking the buses in sixth grade, he tells me. His neighborhood wasn't "too good," he says, so his parents urged him to take advantage of the opportunity. It wasn't an easy adjustment for him. He and some of his friends from the bus got into fights from time to time with "the stoners" at Patrick Henry Junior High, a Valley school close to Granada. "The Stoners," I reflexively repeat the phrase. It's been a while since I've heard a reference to this ubiquitous social clique in the Valley, mostly white kids who skulked around wearing dirty jeans, long hair, and oversized plaid shirts. "I got into some trouble at Patrick Henry" TMac recalls, smiling mildly at his long-ago transgressions.

"So would you say you experienced a lot of racial tension with the white students in the Valley?" I inquire, dully.

TMac shrugs off the suggestion. While there was a bit in junior high, he admits, some racial scrapes with the stoners, he didn't have any trouble with his white classmates at Granada. Or with the white teachers, except for maybe one. It was on the athletic fields and courts that he felt most at a disadvantage owing to his inner-city address. "I dealt with favoritism all the time. All the coaches for football," TMac recounts, "knew all the white kids from the Pop Warner leagues in the Valley. They didn't know me." When I ask TMac about basketball, he tells me that he liked playing on our JV team with Coach Lou more than he liked playing on our senior varsity team. "I enjoyed Lou more," TMac puts it. "Johnson," he says, "wanted to run everything around Gary and Sam. You could *see* that."

Here, TMac reinforces Jeff's sense of things rather precisely, which surprises me, as I didn't quite see Johnson's favoritism, at least not in these terms. TMac would recall, somewhat bitterly, Johnson's misuse of his talents during subsequent phone conversations we'd have once I returned to Florida. ("Well, you can't go backwards," he rationalized during one such rueful moment.) Even though I didn't care much for Johnson's style, even though I felt as constricted by his offense as TMac and Jeff apparently did, it never occurred to me to question his motives, to speculate, even, that he might have favored Gary and Sam for reasons other than his perception of their talent level.

"I got tired of the busing by high school," TMac continues. "Getting home at 5:30 or 6:00 every night, sometimes as late as 7:00 after practices.

I wanted to go to Dorsey back in my neighborhood, but my parents made me go to Granada."

Given such recollections, tinged with bitterness, I'm surprised when TMac proceeds to reminisce favorably about his experiences in the PWT program. "Looking back on it, I'm glad I went to Granada, though. I didn't really appreciate it at the time, but it helped me, I think . . . it taught me things, even when I didn't realize it. I was learning all the time how to deal with different ethnicities. At Granada there were whites, Asians, Mexicans, blacks . . . that's what L.A. *is* now. I deal with all kinds of people every day on the job."

"So it was still worth it," I say, "even dealing with all the favoritism."

"Well, that taught me something, too," he says, a glint in his eye. It's a smart remark. TMac himself is awfully smart, it occurs to me (and I had always thought that Jeff was the smarter of the two), which is probably what prompts my next question:

"You never thought about going to college?" I ask. While he attended CSUN for a semester, he informs me, it failed to hold his interest. He asks me about my education, my current career, and so I tell him, sketching the broad, anyway.

"You found something you liked," he utters brightly, almost paternally pleased.

Just then his cell phone rings. It's his wife, TMac explains, apologetically, taking the call. I try not to listen as they touch base, as he explains to her that he's talking with "that old friend from high school I told you about." I rise from the couch, take in the family photographs on the wall.

"Hold on," I hear TMac utter into the phone, and then, to me at a separate pitch, "Can you take me to pick up my truck from the shop, Andy? That way we can talk for a bit longer." I tell him sure. I have nowhere else to be. He issues the favorable report to his wife, who now has some more time, TMac tells me, to do her holiday shopping. Before leaving for the shop, we visit his older son's room to tell him where we're going. TMac tells him to look after his brother. Shiny basketball trophies decorate most of the available surfaces in the bedroom. "Lots of trophies there," I utter, trying to muster up a bit of conversation with TMac's son. "You must take after your father."

"Yeah," the boy acknowledges, cracking a shy smile.

"I coach his travel team," TMac tells me. "It keeps me close to the game, anyway. We played in a tournament in Chicago a few months ago."

The drive to the shop is, indeed, a short one. After TMac settles up the bill, I follow his gleaming truck back to his house, keeping close so I don't get lost. MY SON IS STUDENT OF THE WEEK AT THE 98TH STREET SCHOOL, his bumper sticker reads. We follow a different, more circuitous, route back to his house, winding our way slowly through narrow neighborhood streets adjacent to the large park. It's the scenic route, it occurs to me. He wants to show me this park of his. And why not? It seems like a nice park, replete with playing fields, what must be a community center, a large running fountain, and a well-equipped playground, at which several parents, mostly mothers, have gathered with their wards.

"That was quite the route home," I declare, neutrally, once we finally reach his home and exit our vehicles.

"I wanted you to see the fountain," he confirms my suspicion. "It's really nice at night," he continues, unbolting the front door. "The sound. It's soothing. You can hear it from our bedroom."

I slap TMac's shoulder from behind, in partial response, as he opens the front door. "You've done all right for yourself, big man," I declare in that mock facetious tone men tend to affect when saying things they truly mean, but for whatever reason feel abashed about articulating.

We talk for a while longer in his family room, reminiscing mostly about our various teammates and their peccadillos: Dan Meyer's quirky sense of humor, Sean Brown's manner, oddly quiet for such a prodigious talent, Terrell's cockiness on the court ("he could back it up with game," TMac remarks). TMac had seen Terrell from time to time at the alumni games when they were both still playing. "But last time I made it out to the Valley," TMac recalls, smiling broadly, "the game got kind of heated. This was, like, five years ago." Apparently, Terrell almost got into a fistfight with one of the high school players, who kept hacking him. "We've sort of outgrown the alumni game, I think," TMac observes. "That was pretty much my sense the other night," I assure him, "even though it was good to see Coach Lou."

"Do you know whatever happened to the Cohens?" TMac asks, pretty much out of the blue. Amy Cohen, a junior during our senior season, was our pretty statistician. I have no idea what happened to her, or to her family. They were members of my family's synagogue, just a mile or so down Devonshire Street from the high school. Mr. Cohen, who worked in a men's formal clothing store in the mall, was a hulking, bearish figure at the temple. He volunteered at Friday night and Saturday morning services, manning the sanctuary door with implacable severity. You didn't dare stroll past him into that sanctified space without a *kippah,* or while talking with a friend, or with gum in your mouth, God forbid. His thick bejeweled fingers would fairly swallow your hand when he clasped it, growling "Good Shabbos." Mr. Cohen embodied certain physical characteristics that warm the cockles of Jew-haters' hearts. Edith Wharton or T. S. Eliot might have modeled their odious Jewish types after him. It wasn't only his girth or balding pate. His facial features were bloated and coarse, as well. There was something about his mouth, particularly. His lips and tongue seemed to protrude, fishlike, as if his oral cavity were too small to contain these fleshy organs.

"I don't know what happened to them," I admit. "He was a pretty scary guy, that Mr. Cohen." Why this bit of commentary? I'm ashamed of Mr. Cohen, it occurs to me—ashamed at what I imagine TMac might have seen when he looked at Mr. Cohen. And so I had sought, instinctively, cruelly, to distance myself from him, this coarse Jew.

"I liked the Cohens," TMac counters mildly, smiling at his memories. "They were friendly people."

His simple recollection turns my shame inward, where it properly belongs. Why shouldn't TMac have appreciated the Cohens? As he goes on to recollect (more vividly than I can remember), we had spent many a pregame afternoon at their home. Mr. and Mrs. Cohen were only too happy to host our interracial squad. Their door was always open. Mrs. Cohen would put out refreshments. While I was hung up on superficialities, TMac of Lynwood held a truer vision of the Cohens. *I liked the Cohens. They were friendly people.* I suppose that I had sold both my fellow Jews and TMac short.

"Yeah, I enjoyed the Cohens," TMac sums up his memories, as if putting them to bed. It's the second time he's uttered this curious sentiment. I had never thought about enjoying people, per se. Yet it strikes me now as an estimable skill, one that TMac seems to have cultivated at Granada, where he enjoyed a particularly diverse range of folks: his teammates, Coach Lou, the Cohens. Why else had he attended, as he goes on to inform me, our twenty-year reunion a few months ago?

All the same, there are certain realities I cannot ignore about TMac's life now, and about Jeff Inzar's and Jeff Mays's lives, and about my life—realities that only fully sink in once I'm back home in Florida. It's abundantly clear, for one thing, that since high school I've reaped a far greater share of the material rewards of our democracy than my former teammates have enjoyed. Moreover, while they all might claim that they realized concrete benefits from the PWT program (and while I believe that they mean what they say), it's impossible to ignore the largely segregated texture of their daily lives today. In the workplace, they all might visit the "White family"—as the popular African American radio host Michael Baisden refers to white America—but they all live and play in predominantly minority neighborhoods. TMac and his wife send their children to predominantly minority public schools close to their Lynwood home. "It was the most convenient option," he tells me later over the phone. All the same, they weren't particularly happy with their older son's middle school experience. "His solid grades," TMac declares, "weren't reflected in his low standardized test scores." The McBrides are currently exploring magnet middle school options for their younger son, which would likely involve a bus trip, which would surely (given the court-ordered integrationist goals of the magnet program) include a more diverse peer group.

What to make of all this? These facts on the ground send me to books for ballast once I return to Florida. Specifically, I wade through the prolific (and hardly univocal) studies of the African American experience written by a number of leading intellectuals, including Manning Marable, Steven F. Lawson, bell hooks, Cornel West, Shelby Steele, Charles Ogletree, Patricia Williams, John McWhorter, Stanley Crouch, Kate Dossett, and Randall Kennedy. It scarcely demands such reading to contemplate the significance of our disparate economic fates. Desegregated schooling may very well have benefitted my teammates, but it couldn't be expected to serve as a panacea against the entrenched structural racism that continues to plague the African American community. The vicious Jim Crow era may be behind us, but nearly fifty years after the Civil Rights Act of 1964, African Americans continue to face political disenfranchisement, mass incarceration based on antiblack criminal enforcement and sentencing guidelines, police brutality, neighborhood gentrification, unequal access to basic health care and other social services, and a brave new world of "colorblind" racism, which manifests itself most prominently in perennial assaults on affirmative action.[3] Small wonder that my teammates' brief immersion in the PWT school desegregation program hadn't catapulted them into the upper middle class.

It's partly on account of this deeply entrenched racism that African Americans have long been skeptical of integration, at least as the sole means of achieving empowerment. "Jim Crow segregation" is a phrase that continually crops up in studies on the black experience. The "Jim Crow" modifier, I eventually gleaned, distinguishes this pernicious mode of segregation from the alternative mode of voluntary self-segregation that African Americans have long pursued to combat cultural loss and promote economic independence and agency within the black community. The advocacy of *both* integrationist approaches and race-based approaches toward black empowerment have existed within the African American community at least since the emancipation from slavery. Frederick Douglass, for example, stressed the importance of the social and cultural integration of African Americans into mainstream "white" society, whereas his contemporary, Martin R. Delany, advocated race-based strategies associated with black nationalism.[4] "Integration," as Marable writes, "was never universally accepted as the best method or approach for achieving racial reform."[5] Indeed, my earlier research on the *Crawford* case in L.A. revealed that a voluble cohort of the inner-city African American community resisted forced busing and, instead, favored efforts to improve their minority-dominant neighborhood schools.

Our brains seem designed to embrace simple dichotomies, and so we have tended to view these two impulses (integrationist and separatist) as mutually exclusive. Further, we've tended to align historical figures in black history with either one or the other intellectual movement (e.g., Douglass versus Delany, W. E. B. Dubois versus Booker T. Washington, Malcolm X versus Martin Luther King, Jr.). As Marable, Lawson, Dosset, and others have recently suggested, however, our polarized understanding of these two modes has simplified and even distorted the more nuanced narrative of the Civil Rights movement and the figures involved.[6] Rather than mutually exclusive modes of thought and action, a broad swath of the African American community—and even the icons listed above—have long embraced *both* integrationist and separatist modes, depending upon specific circumstances. Put simply, these strategies have complemented each other to a much greater extent than has been acknowledged.

All of which makes me ponder the voluntary component of my teammates' segregated lives, specifically TMac and his wife's decision, thus far, to send their boys to minority-dominated public schools. I can't deny my initial visceral disappointment. But it was a disappointment grounded, I now recognize, in my reductive notions of integration and segregation. The skewed terms of our national discussion, as I've suggested, have demanded that we pick sides. Integration *or* separatism; Martin Luther King, Jr., *or* Malcolm X. While I was determined to undertake this project without preconceptions, without prejudices—without, in short, an agenda—it would be disingenuous not to acknowledge my strong integrationist impulses, the side that I had chosen. Surely part of me hoped to find reinforcement for my preconceived notions. Part of me, specifically, was disappointed that TMac and his wife hadn't pursued integrated learning environments for their children. But given the manifold variables—not least of all convenience—the neighborhood schools that TMac and his wife chose for their boys probably made perfect sense for them; and, given their disappointment with their older son's middle school experience, they may pursue the more integrated option of a magnet middle school for their younger son.[7] The long-standing African American embrace (and interrogation) of both integrationist and separatist modes of empowerment affirms this possibility. It also suggests how a historically black university, Florida A&M, continues to serve fruitfully in my state university system alongside my increasingly diverse Florida Atlantic University. The following chapter—inspired by yet additional reading—will make it clear that I continue to view integrated learning environments as a vital social good for children of all races and ethnicities. All the same, self-selected, race-based modes of education, I expect, will (and must) continue to serve various segments of the African American community.

But I'm not thinking any of these thoughts while I'm still in TMac's living room. Instead, we're thinking about our varsity season. Our memories lead us to specific games, particularly to our heartbreaking loss to Jefferson in the playoffs, which we talk about for some time, breaking down the final, frustrating minutes, play by play. The Canoga Park game was one of the least memorable games of the season. They were probably the weakest team in our league, which is why I received so much playing time. Still, I can't keep myself from rambling on about this game, reminding TMac about my performance. It sounds like special pleading even to my own ears, before TMac interjects. "I was there, Andy," he assures me. "I remember."

Soon it's time to leave. We promise to keep in touch, and I think that we actually might manage to do so. TMac calls his sons out to say good-bye and to snap a few photos of the two of us. We pose shoulder to shoulder in the family room as his older son clicks a few shots. "You grew, Andy," TMac remarks between shots. "Apparently so," I tell him. We all head outside and I take a few photos of TMac and his boys.

I was there, Andy. I remember. I contemplate TMac's words as I make my way along the increased evening congestion of the 105, 110, and 10. Could it be that TMac had unwittingly put his finger on my pulse with this remark? I had fled L.A. over twenty years ago without the slightest intention of ever returning. I was on to bigger and better things. Off the basketball court, adrift between the various cliques of our gargantuan student populace, I wasn't a particularly happy or well-adjusted high school student. Flipping through the signatures in my high school yearbook at the beginning of all this, I was struck by how many friends seemed to have sensed my malaise. "I'm very sad that your [*sic*] leaving," one sophomore girl I knew had written in purple ink, "but I know that you will be happier in Penn than here." Pretty somber stuff for a fifteen-year-old, but a prescient observation, nonetheless. I *was* happier, I *am* happier, on the

6. Thomas "TMac" McBride, at home with his two sons, Thomas, Jr., and Terrance.

East Coast than I ever was in L.A. Even so, it is just as true, I realize as I make my way back to Santa Monica, that I had never truly escaped this place. My L.A. They say you can't go home again, but the reverse is just as true, in its way. Maybe I had only undertaken this reunion of sorts having finally glimpsed this truth. Having dragged L.A. around with me these twenty years, perhaps it was time to come in for a closer look. Sure, TMac was there, as he claimed. But so was I. *I* was here, in L.A. during the turbulent 1970s and 1980s, which marked the height of the city's school desegregation efforts. *I* remember too.

My reunion with L.A.—its in-the-flesh component, anyway—is over. It's tough to say what those proponents or skeptics of school integration programs might make of all this. I imagine that readers can make of these visits what they will. For my own part, that curious line from F. Scott Fitzgerald's *Great Gatsby*, a line that has always perplexed me, springs to mind once I'm on the airplane, gazing distractedly out the window across the barren runway. "It was just personal," Gatsby utters, cryptically, after the delicate scaffolding of his whole world comes tumbling down.[8] Yes, I think. Above all else, it was personal, this reunion of mine. As fleeting as those two basketball seasons were, there was something large and human about those years, something I wanted to reclaim by glimpsing L.A. once again through these older eyes. And I do feel that my world has grown palpably larger once again, having renewed contact with my coaches, with assorted Valley friends, and with some of these inner-city teammates I knew back when, having been received in their neighborhoods and their homes, only a rumor to me as an adolescent. I couldn't find everyone. Not on this particular trip. But I found three of the four PWT teammates in my graduating class.

What's more, my own efforts from the East Coast seem to have started something on the West Coast. I finally manage to get hold of a few additional teammates from the Valley only after I return to Florida: Sam, Kevin, and Mark. They all still live in the L.A. area, scattered about the Valley and beyond. After attending Columbia University, Sam worked as a teacher for a time, then attended law school, and now works as an attorney for the Securities Exchange Commission. Kevin holds a high-powered job in the financial industry. Mark works in sales for a pharmaceutical company. They're all married and have young children. Like TMac. Like me. Sam sends me a photograph over e-mail of his newborn child sporting a robust shock of black hair. I share their contact information with TMac and with Jeff Inzar. TMac, I soon learn, has gotten in touch with Mark; Mark has gotten in touch with Kevin; Jeff has called Sam, Kevin, and Mark. Subsequent telephone conversations I share with Jeff suggest to me, thankfully, that he's doing better than I had initially thought. He's been at Sony for three years already and will soon be given a promotion. He asks me when I'm coming back to visit. "We'll *all* get together next time," he says, "for dinner." After a twenty-year hiatus, the Valley and the City are once again talking.

Return

SINCE 1986 (my high school graduating year, incidentally), we observe the Martin Luther King, Jr., National Holiday on the third Monday of every January. This year, the holiday falls on January 15, not too long after my return from L.A., and my thoughts are still whirring about my improvised high school reunion. My children greet the holiday enthusiastically. Like me, they have the day off from school, so once lunchtime rolls around I take them to Taco Bell. For Henry and Sophia, this qualifies as a special culinary treat; for me, it's simply the path of least resistance.

"So, do you know why you have the day off from school?" I ask my kids over the tabletop chaos of burritos, quesadillas, tacos, and their crinkly paper wrappings. I've found that at six and eight my children have, without warning, reached ages at which they demand thoughtful, well-reasoned conversation.

"It's Martin Luther King Day," my son replies through a full mouth. Then, anticipating my pesky line of follow-up questions, he elaborates through a single exhale: "He was a great man, who gave an important speech, 'I Have a Dream,' and then he won the Nobel Prize."

"Yeah," my daughter, seated beside me, chimes in with a bit more spirit. "He wanted both white people and black people to be treated equally. Black people couldn't use the same bathrooms as white people, they had to sit at the back of the bus, they used different drinking fountains . . ." She nearly sings this litany of racial wrongs.

"Wow," I hear myself reply. It surprises me that they've learned as much as they've learned about King and the Civil Rights movement in school, my kindergartner's font of information, especially. Sophia knows that she has impressed me.

"You're very proud of me, aren't you?" she inquires, wearing a Cheshire grin.

I *am* proud of her. I'm proud of my son too. For Black History Month—a month never celebrated during my childhood—Henry has been working feverishly on a rather detailed poster-board project on Shirley Chisholm, the first black woman elected to the U.S. Congress. It would be folly, indeed, to claim that we haven't enjoyed significant racial and interracial advances since the time I attended elementary school. But something about the scripted, rote quality of my kids' remarks unsettles me. Their public school, I've noticed, adheres to a fairly traditional pedagogy, owing in part to the unrelenting pressures of the FCAT (Florida Comprehensive Assessment Test), administered to students in grades three through eleven, the results of which carry significant consequences for schools, administrators, teachers, and students. Accountability, bordering on the draconian, is the name of the game in Florida these days. Public schools in my state—institutional funding and salary increases on the line—understandably teach to the exam, equipping their students with the "right" answers to any number of mathematical, reading, science, and writing questions. This isn't all bad. There's a place in the curriculum, I believe, for memorizing one's multiplication tables. (I've been working doggedly on the 4s with Henry for several weeks now.)

All the same, schools should teach children to utter at least as many questions as answers, and this mode of thoughtful inquiry, I've noticed (along with second-language acquisition, music, and art), is not a particularly salient feature of the public education my kids have enjoyed, perhaps because it's so difficult to assess in an exam. And so, treading warily—they're only eight and six, after all—I pursue a different tack, one that seems required given their almost too self-assured remarks on King.

"An important thing to know, kids, is that it's not like everything's all better now. Black people and other minorities, even Jews, still aren't always treated equally by everyone, everywhere, even though they should be."

"I know," my son utters, chomping down on his taco, unimpressed with my observation.

"When you look around at our own town," I continue, "at the jobs that black people and Latino people have, and the jobs that white people have, in the restaurants we go to, for example . . . at the neighborhoods where white people live, and the neighborhoods where black people and other minorities live, what does that tell you?"

My son shrugs his shoulders. My daughter silently takes a bite of a quesadilla wedge. I've gone a bit overboard, I suppose. Perhaps this is a conversation to pursue down the road some.

"Yes," I belatedly answer my daughter's earlier question. "Daddy's very proud of you, Sophia."

What I would tell my children, if they were older, is that the controversies regarding the school integration programs that defined their father's experiences in the LAUSD in the 1970s and 1980s remain a current event in L.A., South Florida, and throughout the nation. California's vertiginous relationship with school integration, since its landmark Supreme Court *Jackson* decision in 1963, fairly epitomizes our nationwide ambivalence regarding race and public education. Currently, policies promoting the integration of public schools at the primary, secondary, and collegiate levels find themselves increasingly embattled in California and beyond. First, Prop 1 in California effectively ended the most energetic desegregation programs (i.e., forced busing) in that state by 1981. Then, amid a zeitgeist increasingly hostile toward immigrants and torn between the arguably competing principles of meritocracy and affirmative action, California voters passed controversial Proposition 209 in 1996, further tightening the screws. No longer a mere proposition, the state law "[P]rohibits the state, local governments, districts, public universities, colleges, and schools, and other government instrumentalities from discriminating against or giving preferential treatment to any individual or group in public employment, public education, or public contracting on the basis of race, sex, color, ethnicity, or national origin."[1]

Interestingly, Prop 209 sharply divided the Jewish community in California in much the same way that forced busing divided Jews in L.A. some twenty years earlier. As the controversy leading up to the vote raged, synagogues and Jewish Community Centers throughout the state hosted forums and debates. Those Jews against Prop 209 viewed the anti–affirmative action measure as a step backward in the historical Jewish effort to ensure racial and ethnic equality in America. These Jews joined a progressive, multiethnic coalition of historical allies.

Jewish supporters of the measure, however (and it should be noted that the bill's co-chair, State Senator Quentin Kopp, was Jewish), argued that racial and ethnic equality could only be predicated upon a strict, "colorblind" meritocracy. The Jewish experience in higher education, proponents of Prop 209 pointed out, supported this contention. After all, it had only been the racial preference for white Anglo-Saxon Protestants that had severely restricted the numbers of Jewish Americans accepted to the nation's elite, Ivy-League schools in the first half of the twentieth century. Had institutions such as Harvard and Yale admitted students based upon merit alone, Jews would have threatened the primacy of monied white Protestants on the Ivy-League campus. Enough Jews had infiltrated Harvard by the 1920s that its president, Abbott Lawrence Lowell, set about to fix its "Jewish problem." Under his leadership, Harvard implemented a particularly insidious strategy for limiting Jewish enrollment by favoring applicants from the U.S. South and West and limiting the number of applicants they accepted from New York City and Boston. As Susanne Klingenstein notes in *Enlarging America: The Cultural Work of Jewish Literary Scholars, 1930–1990,* "[t]he informal quota limiting Jewish enrollment [at Harvard] was not given up until after World War II."[2] Once Harvard and its peer institutions eliminated their program of racial preference, Jews gained entry to these elite institutions in disproportionately high numbers.

Today, the implications of Prop 209 on the racial composition at California's flagship institutions have been no less staggering. Specifically, black and Latino enrollment has plummeted while Asian American enrollment has skyrocketed. "At Berkeley," a recent *New York Times* article notes, "the number of blacks in the freshman class plunged by half the year after the ban, and the number of Hispanics nearly as much."[3] Some ten years later, in the fall of 2006, black students represented only 2 percent of UCLA's freshman class (a thirty-three-year low) and 3.6 percent of Berkeley's freshman class.[4] Simultaneously, as Timothy Egan reports in a separate, incisive *New York Times* article, "Little Asia on the Hill," while Asian Americans represented 12 percent of California's population in 2006, Asian American students represented a whopping 46 percent of the freshman class at Berkeley.[5] The upshot: over the past half-century, Jewish and Asian Americans have been the clear beneficiaries of strict, merit-based admissions criteria at our elite institutions of higher learning. Such policies, by contrast, increasingly squeeze out African Americans and Latinos, who attend in higher (though hardly staggering) proportions when race is considered as a factor in admission decisions.

The national mood currently favors merit-based, "race-neutral" admissions criteria, while race-conscious admissions criteria draw increasing fire. In the wake of California's Prop 209, three other states—Michigan, Washington and, yes, my current home state of Florida—have enacted bans on racial preferences at their public universities. What makes Florida unique among this cohort is that it didn't take a judicial order or ballot referendum to abolish race-conscious affirmative action. Rather, Governor Jeb Bush issued an executive order in 1999, the One Florida Initiative, which compelled the overseeing Board of Regents of the ten state universities (including my own university, FAU) to "implement a policy prohibiting the use of racial or gender set-asides, preferences or quotas in admissions to all Florida institutions of Higher Education, effective immediately."[6] As part of the One Florida Initiative, Governor Bush—vowing to increase student diversity without affirmative action—instituted his Talented 20 Program. The plan guarantees admission to one of the state universities (though not necessarily to one of its two flagship institutions, UF and FSU) for all Florida high school students graduating in the top 20 percent of their class. It should also be noted that unlike California's more restrictive Prop 209, the One Florida Initiative stipulates that race and gender can still be considered in awarding scholarships, conducting outreach, or developing precollege summer programs. However, while Governor Bush was quick to proclaim the program a success in terms of increasing higher education access for underrepresented minority students—even a model for the rest of the nation—an exhaustive report released in 2003 by Professor Gary Orfield's Civil Rights Project at

Harvard, "Appearance and Reality in the Sunshine State: The Talented 20 Program in Florida," calls the governor's enthusiasm into question. After extensive interviews with staff at five universities in the state university system and a thorough review of available data, the report concludes that "the promises made about the program have proven to be largely illusory."[7] Leading scholars of African American history have been quick to cry foul, as well. Steven F. Lawson notes that the enrollment of black freshman at Florida's flagship institution of higher learning, the University of Florida, fell by 44 percent during the first year of the Talented 20 Program, while Manning Marable highlights equally disturbing statistics: "Under Florida's 20 percent admissions plan, black enrollment of first-year students in all state universities declined from 11.8 percent in 2000 to only 7.2 percent in 2001; for Latinos in the same years, the decline was 12 percent to 11.1 percent. White enrollment in the state's freshman class surged from 66.3 percent in fall 2000 up to 72.3 percent in fall 2001."[8] Still, emboldened by the anti–affirmative action developments in Florida, Michigan, and Washington, Ward Connerly, the architect of California's Prop 209, was preparing similar ballot initiatives in a host of additional states in anticipation of the 2008 elections.[9]

The consideration of race as a factor in admissions decisions in public colleges and universities having been effectively quashed in California and elsewhere, a long-awaited ruling from the U.S. Supreme Court issued on June 28, 2007, precludes any explicit consideration of race in school assignment to *secondary* schools, a factor that the public high schools involved in the litigation heretofore considered—among several other factors—to ensure a reasonably integrated student populace. The case, *Parents Involved in Community Schools, Petitioner v. Seattle School District No. 1 et al.,* was presented to the court right around the time of my visit to L.A. and involved desegregation programs at public schools in Seattle and Louisville. Although both programs had been upheld by lower federal courts, the increasingly conservative John G. Roberts, Jr., court ruled by a narrow 5–4 margin that public schools may not seek to achieve or maintain a reasonably diverse student body through programs that take an individual student's race into account. The strident language of both the majority and dissenting opinions reflect the bitter divisiveness nationwide on the issue of school integration programs. Justice Clarence Thomas, for example, writing in concurrence with the majority, remarks of Justice Stephen Breyer's dissent that his colleague's "'good intentions, which I do not doubt, have the shelf life of Justice Breyer's tenure.'"[10] Justice John Paul Stevens offers a parting shot of his own—"It is my firm conviction that no Member of the Court that I joined in 1975 would have agreed with today's decision"—to conclude his brief dissent.[11]

Interestingly (if unsurprisingly), both the majority and dissenting opinions claim the landmark *Brown* decision as a key legal touchstone. Writing the majority opinion, which will surely exacerbate the segregated character of public schools, Chief Justice Roberts declares, "Before *Brown*, schoolchildren were told where they could and could not go to school based on the color of their skin. The school districts in these cases have not carried the heavy burden of demonstrating that we should allow this once again—even for very different reasons. . . . The way to stop discrimination on the basis of race is to stop discriminating on the basis of race."[12] Justice Breyer, for his part, seeks to reclaim *Brown* toward the close of his 77-page dissent:

> Finally, what of the hope and promise of *Brown?* For much of this Nation's history, the races remained divided. It was not long ago that people of different races drank from separate fountains, rode on separate buses, and studied in separate schools. In this Court's finest hour, *Brown v. Board of Education* challenged this history and helped to change it. . . . Indeed, the very school districts that once spurned integration now strive for it. The long history of their efforts reveals the complexities and difficulties they have faced. And in light of those challenges, they have asked us not to take from their hands the instruments they have used to rid their schools of racial segregation, instruments that they believe are needed to overcome the problems of cities divided by race and poverty. The plurality would decline their modest request.[13]

Justice William Kennedy's swing-vote opinion for the majority curiously straddles the line between Breyer's integrationist fervor and Roberts's equally vehement resistance. Kennedy sides with the majority, primarily because he cannot countenance any "crude system of individual racial classifications," as he characterizes the Seattle and Louisville admissions criteria.[14] Yet, he takes Roberts to task for his cavalier dismissal of *Brown's* underlying principles:

> The plurality opinion is too dismissive of the legitimate interest government has in ensuring all people have equal opportunity regardless of their race. The plurality's postulate that 'the way to stop discriminating on the basis of race is to stop discriminating on the basis of race' . . . is not sufficient to decide these cases. Fifty years of experience since *Brown v. Board of Education* . . . should teach us that the problem before us defies so easy a solution. . . . To the extent the plurality opinion suggests the Constitution mandates that state and local authorities must accept the status quo of racial isolation in schools, it is, in my view, profoundly mistaken.[15]

Kennedy's opinion would appear to leave the door at least slightly ajar for modified school integration programs. All the same, most observers in the know speculate that the key language of his decision will hardly embolden school board proponents of such programs. Instead, school boards that wish to realize diversity on their campuses will likely resort to less effective, "race-neutral" measures to achieve racial integration, however illustratively contradictory and confused such measures sound. The *New Yorker's* Hendrik Hertzberg summed up the majority opinion— which holds sway despite Justice Kennedy's equivocation—most pithily when he remarked that the court "ruled that conscious racial integration is the moral equivalent of conscious racial segregation."[16]

Whatever one might think of the decision, it's a near 180-degree shift from the spirit of the California Supreme Court ruling in *Jackson* back in 1963, which shaped my experiences, and that of my teammates, in the public system. "Residential segregation is in itself an evil," the court argued and, later, continued, "The right to an equal opportunity for education and the harmful consequences of segregation require that school boards take steps, insofar as reasonably feasible, to alleviate racial imbalance in schools regardless of its cause."[17] From such egalitarian vim, we have arrived at Kennedy's painfully cautious proposal that school authorities "are free to devise race-conscious measures to address the problem in a general way and without treating each student in different fashion solely on the basis of a systematic, individual typing by race."[18]

Ongoing litigation in the Los Angeles Superior Court offers an indication of how *Parents v. Seattle* will resonate throughout school districts, nationwide. In the fall of 2007, The Los Angeles Superior Court heard arguments in *American Civil Rights Foundation v. LAUSD*. The terms of the suit closely resemble *Parents v. Seattle*. (The LAUSD, in fact, well aware of the import of the outcome in that case, filed an *amicus* brief to the U.S. Supreme Court in support of the Seattle and Louisville School Districts.) In *American Civil Rights Foundation v. LAUSD*, the curiously named plaintiffs, Ward Connerly's anti–affirmative action group, allege that LAUSD's magnet program and PWT program—instituted in 1977 for the express purpose of desegregation—violate the race-neutral principles of California's Prop 209.

The irony of the current situation is staggering. Little more than twenty-five years ago, the courts, via *Crawford*, compelled an intransigent LAUSD to create and implement a meaningful desegregation program. Having created the magnet and PWT programs in response to this judicial mandate, the district finds itself in court defending these very programs against charges of racial discrimination.

Back in Florida, I keep close tabs on the progress of *American Civil Rights Foundation v. LAUSD*. I call my contact at the LAUSD General Counsel office every few weeks, pestering him for updates. It's likely, he tells me, that the case will drag on for quite some time. The outcome won't affect my schoolchildren in Boca Raton. Lord knows it won't affect me. But I find myself curiously invested in the decision, as if the possible abolishment of the PWT program threatens, retroactively, to alter the composition of my high school basketball team. In my mind's eye, I see our team photo in the yearbook and imagine certain players gradually vanishing from the frame. Jeff Inzar, Sean Brown, Dennis Bishop, and TMac. This is sheer melodrama, of course. The current court decision cannot change the past, but it does threaten to exacerbate the racial isolation of minorities in L.A. just a generation younger than my African American teammates.

Superior court judge Paul Gutman issues his decision on December 10, 2007. In what seems an unlikely turn of events, given judicial trends, Judge Gutman grants the LAUSD's summary judgment. "We won!" my contact at the LAUSD General Counsel office jubilantly informs me over e-mail. It doesn't take long to read the relatively brief decision. The essential facts of the case, according to Judge Gutman, are "crystal clear."[19] "*The LAUSD*," he writes in an underscored subheading, "*Was Required By The Trial Court's Remedy Order [Crawford, 1981] To Implement The Desegregation Plan It Submitted Which Included A Race-Based Selection Process For the Magnet School and PWT Programs.*"[20] Consequently, the selection process for these programs falls under an important provision of Article I, Section 31 of the California Constitution (adopted by voters in 1996 by way of Prop 209). This provision stipulates that the race- and gender-neutral mandates of Article I, Section 31, "shall apply only to action taken after the section's effective date," and that "Nothing in this section shall be interpreted as invalidating any court order or consent decree which is in force as of the effective date of this section."[21] As "even the Plaintiff has acknowledged that the September 10, 1981 remedy order has never been reversed, overruled, vacated, revoked, modified, or withdrawn . . . that the 1981 *Crawford* remedy order has never expired," the race-based selection process for the Magnet and PWT programs, Judge Gutman argues, clearly fall under the above provision of California Constitution, Article I, Section 31.[22]

The decision—particularly Judge Gutman's strong, decisive language—offers cause for some hope that the judicial system hasn't wholly abandoned its efforts to desegregate our public schools. But we probably shouldn't forget that only a small fraction of the LAUSD's seven hundred thousand students participate in the Magnet and PWT programs, just over sixty thousand. Plus, it seems likely that Judge Gutman's decision will be taken up by the court of appeal, which has established a more conservative track record on such matters dating back to *Crawford*. Taking the broad view, Judge Gutman's ruling represents a small (and, perhaps, temporary) victory for proponents of school integration, but it seems more likely that the increasingly conservative judicial rulings at the federal and local levels will accelerate the ongoing resegregation, the increasing racial isolation, of blacks and Latinos in public school districts nationwide.

Preceding the *Parents v. Seattle* and the *American Civil Rights Foundation v. LAUSD* decisions, a 2002 report by Harvard University's Civil Rights

Project, "Race in American Public Schools: Rapidly Resegregating School Districts," examined the segregation trends in large school districts throughout the country and found that

> *virtually all* school districts analyzed are showing lower levels of inter-racial exposure since 1986, suggesting a trend toward resegregation, and in some districts, these declines are sharp. As courts across the country end long-running desegregation plans and, in some states, have forbidden the use of any racially-conscious student assignment plans, the last 10–15 years have seen a steady unraveling of almost 25 years worth of increased integration.[23]

While general school enrollment reflects our increasing diversity, the report's analysis of the racial composition within individual districts suggested a "disturbing pattern of growing isolation."[24] Perusing the data, I was unsurprised to discover that my former school district of Los Angeles ranks among the twenty districts nationwide with the lowest white exposure to blacks in 2000.[25] The demographics at my old high school, Granada Hills, bear out this finding. While Asian American and Hispanic representation at Granada Hills has skyrocketed to 22 percent and 27 percent, respectively, the percentage of African American students at the school has plummeted from the 13 percent of my graduating year to roughly 6 percent today, owing largely to the decline of the PWT program in the district. "Many Americans believe that there is nothing that can be done about these problems," the Civil Rights Project report concludes, "and that desegregation efforts have failed. This report suggests that a great deal was done, particularly in the South, and that, after a series of court decisions sharply limiting desegregation rights, it is being undone, even in large districts where the desegregation was substantial and long lasting."[26] It seems unlikely, indeed, that current and future generations of high school graduates will enjoy the opportunity to form, and then renew, cross-town friendships. Even Derrick Bell, a prominent legal scholar who worked for the NAACP Legal Defense Fund in the 1960s and supervised hundreds of school desegregation cases, sounded a defeated note in the immediate wake of the *Parents v. Seattle* decision. "It is painful for many of us," Bell wrote, taking the measure of our more conservative court and nation, "but it is time to acknowledge that racial integration as the primary vehicle for providing effective schooling for black and Latino children has run its course. Where it is working, or has a real chance to work, it should continue, but for the millions of black and Latino children living in areas that are as racially isolated in fact as they once were by law, it is time to look elsewhere."[27] By "elsewhere," Bell refers at least in part to separatist modes of school-building and education reform within racially isolated school districts. While such strategies ought to be deployed with vigor, it seems a shame that our collective failure to desegregate our schools in the wake of *Brown* has lent such urgency to the task.

What might the Honorable Paul Egly think, I wonder, about the current landscape? Egly, recall, had been appointed to *Crawford* in 1977 during its remedy stage upon Judge Alfred Gitelson's tragic death aboard a cruise ship. Egly had rejected the toothless, initial integration plans of the L.A. school board as "wholly ineffective" and impelled the board to draft that more rigorous plan, which included forced busing. He had wrangled with Bobbi Fiedler's Bustop organization and the court of appeal for the next four years, until the implementation of Prop 1—tethering California to the more conservative, federal desegregation guidelines—effectively ended forced busing. Removing himself from the case in 1981, Egly had castigated the school board for "short-changing" its minority children.[28] After leaving the bench, he returned as a professor to the La Verne School of Law just east of L.A., which he had founded years earlier. He still teaches there today, a quick Internet search reveals. And so how must Egly feel now, given the palsied breaths of school integration programs nationwide?

I send him a quick e-mail message and, within a day, his assistant replies to my query over my voicemail. Judge Egly would be happy to speak with me, she reports. She gives me his cell phone number.

"It's serendipity that you've called," the retired judge greets me over the phone. "I've been thinking about these issues quite a lot, lately. I'm about two-thirds done with a legal text I'm writing about school integration." His breath is labored, his voice broken with age. To make matters worse, our phone connection is poor. An echo repeats every word I utter back into my ear, over Judge Egly's responses. I turn the volume up on my desk phone to discern his words. "I'll help you any way I can," he continues after I tell him a bit more about my project. "Maybe you can help me, too. I'd like to hear about the PWT students you've contacted. Your former teammates. And Bobbi Fiedler. That political career didn't work out so well for her. But she's still around, eh?" No invective here. There's something wistful, even sweet, about the way he alludes to this old adversary. We decide to continue the dialogue over e-mail. He's half blind now, he tells me, so his assistant will have to read my messages to him and write his responses to me upon his dictation. It might take a few days, he warns, raspily. I assure him that this will be fine. No problem.

When Judge Egly responds to my open-ended prompts on these matters, he hardly sounds like the integrationist firebrand I had anticipated, given his former rulings from the bench and some of the quotations attributed to him following Bustop's victory in the courts. Rather, he sounds guarded, equivocal, and even weary. "As a judge," Egly writes,

> you are never sure that you are doing right. You can never remove yourself outside of the mandate of the California Supreme Court nor the directions of the US Supreme Court in 1982 respecting the constitutionality of Proposition 1. . . . I was assigned to oversee the preparation and implementation of the school district's response to the mandate found in the 1976 decision of Crawford vs. LAUSD. My job was to follow the law and not to initiate my own ideas; that is, the primary job of desegregation belonged to the district and only if they did not comply could the court step in.

Regarding the more recent judicial rulings against racial preference at the federal and state levels, Judge Egly writes, "I think our culture is rapidly changing and school assignments by race is gradually becoming irrelevant. If you need more, let me know . . . but it is complicated."

Yes, I immediately think upon reading these lines. I need more. It's tough for me to reconcile Judge Egly's dispassionate remarks about his judicial role in the 1970s, his apparent complacency regarding the current climate, with the implacable judicial stances he took against the district and Bustop in 1977 on through 1981. He hadn't coolly applied the law, as he seems to suggest. One discerns deeply felt conviction in his rulings, which he surely knew would be met with fierce resistance. Following his *Crawford* decision, Judge Gitelson, Egly's predecessor, had been derided by California's governor, Ronald Reagan; the mayor of Los Angeles, Sam Yorty; and even President Nixon; he was fairly ridden off his judicial bench on a rail by L.A. voters shortly thereafter. A more restrained, cautious judge might have simply accepted the initial plans offered up by the district in 1977 and surely might have acceded to the imperatives of Prop 1 rather than deny its applicability in L.A. (reversed by the U.S. Supreme Court, as Egly notes above, in 1982). So I press Judge Egly to elaborate. How, exactly, is our culture rapidly changing to render school assignments by race irrelevant?

"Affirmative action," Egly responds, "is no longer the darling of race relation remedies." Rather, such programs continually prove "too disruptive" for the mainstream to embrace. Popular feeling, according to Egly, holds that racial preferences are "unfair to the majority," while "to a large extent, minorities are not in love with it." While Egly still believes that "affirmative action for a short term is valuable," the courts, along with the general public, "think otherwise." This, despite the fact that studies (Egly alludes to the work of Professor Gary Orfield's Civil Rights Project at Harvard) convincingly demonstrate a "more rapid resegregation than in the desegregation of the 60's and 70's." In sum, then, when Judge Egly remarks that "our culture is rapidly changing and school assignments by race is gradually becoming irrelevant," he refers primarily to the changing, anti–affirmative action temperament of the popular, and judicial, will—*not* to our realization of a more integrated school system. "I think the issue should be alive," Egly contends, "but it isn't."

This is either a problem, or it is not a problem.

It seems to me that we face two distinct issues with regard to race and our public schools: the degree to which integrated schools ought to be pursued to ameliorate longstanding and persistent inequities at schools attended primarily by minority children, and the degree to which an integrated learning environment ought to be pursued, regardless of whether such inequities exist. This first issue cannot be so readily dismissed, even some fifty-odd years after the landmark *Brown* decision. In *The*

Shame of the Nation: The Restoration of Apartheid Schooling in America, Jonathan Kozol, citing abundant hard data to buttress countless interviews with school administrators, teachers, and students in districts across the country, makes a compelling case that the desegregation of black and Latino students, which surged from the time of the *Brown* decision up through the 1980s, has since steadily receded in our primary and secondary schools at an alarming rate; that the racial isolation of minority students in low-income school zones grows ever more entrenched; that the schools attended by predominantly minority children are the most egregiously overcrowded; that physical disrepair, and even squalor, continues to plague our most segregated, minority schools (Kozol offers particularly horrifying accounts of an elementary school and a high school in L.A.); that owing to public subsidies and local PTAs, the predominantly white students attending public schools in higher-income zones enjoy a grossly disproportionate share of school funding compared to the minority children attending schools in low-income neighborhoods; that more experienced teachers teach at schools attended by predominantly white students and less experienced teachers, however well-intentioned, teach our minority children in the inner city; that the achievement gap persists between the races, some seven years after the implementation of President Bush's No Child Left Behind Law, while the gap narrowed dramatically during the desegregation efforts of the 1970s and 1980s; and that "compensatory" educational programs geared toward minority students living in low-income areas—though all the rage these days—simply do not yield results as favorable as desegregated schooling.[29]

One doesn't necessarily need Kozol, however—or Judge Egly, or Harvard's Civil Rights Project—to glean the persistent racial inequities at our public schools. Like many parents with children enrolled in public school, I need only look about my immediate environs. There are three public elementary schools within a three-mile drive of my home: Addison Mizner Elementary (1.3 miles), J. C. Mitchell Elementary (2.44 miles), and Boca Raton Elementary (2.51 miles). My wife and I didn't give much thought to our attendance zone when we bought our house in 1996. We had just gotten married, and children seemed a prospect on the distant horizon. We bought our three-bedroom house largely because it was just across the street from the university where I would be working and because the neighborhood struck us as "normal," by which I mean that it was both un-gated and unencumbered by a homeowner's association, which police many of the more affluent, stuccoed neighborhoods in our little burg with implacable severity. Further, it didn't occur to us that we might remain in this first home by the time our prospective wards reached kindergarten. Still, on account of the financial disincentives of relocating locally and our general resistance to change, we've decided to stay put, and so our students both attend Addison Mizner.

From the first day we escorted our son to kindergarten, then reviewed the class roster, it was clear that the school was not only predominantly white, but that (uncharacteristically for Boca Raton), there wasn't even a particularly large cohort of Jewish students at the school. A quick on-line scan of Palm Beach County's Gold Report reveals that 79 percent of Addison Mizner's students are white, 9 percent are Hispanic, and only 2 percent are black. Meanwhile, 48 percent of the students at nearby J. C. Mitchell are white, 23 percent are Hispanic, and 17 percent are black, and 40 percent of Boca El's students are white, 25 percent are Hispanic, and 26 percent are black. While the students at J. C. Mitchell and Boca El enjoy a recently rebuilt campus, the monies generated by the PTAs at these respective schools bear out Kozol's assertions regarding dispropor-tionate private subsidies, based largely upon demographics. For the past three years that my children have attended Addison Mizner, its PTA has raised between $50,000 and $75,000 each year, funds principally gener-ated through its annual silent auction. These monies have been budgeted over the past several years to hire the school's few teachers' aides—an essential expenditure, most would agree—which the district has refused to fund. Meanwhile, the technology center and recreational equipment at Addison Mizner grow more and more antiquated. And we're the white-dominant, fortunately endowed school. Boca El and J. C. Mitchell, whose PTAs raise only a fraction of the amount Addison Mizner raises per year, must pursue alternative lines of funding, or must rely upon parent volun-teers, or must simply do without.

Such facts on the ground, to my mind, at the very least complicate blithe references to "colorblindness" and "meritocracy." We are a culture of charged words and phrases. Colorblind. Merit. Double standard. Reverse discrimination. Equal protection. We know how we are supposed to feel about these terms, and others, that immediately connote "rightness" or "wrongness." But rarely do we interrogate, with any intellectual rigor, the realities that might, say, cry out for the implementation of a "double standard," or complicate our understanding of how we might "protect" students across the races "equally." However we ultimately come down on issues of integration and race-based admissions policies, individually and collectively, it may be constructive simply to jettison the charged phrases from the debate, which only encourage the most facile treatment of issues that demand our more concerted attention. And so I won't speculate that the attendance zone of the public school my children attend has been "gerrymandered" to include neighborhood white students and exclude nearby minority students. I will only say that the demographics betray the entrenched dis-integration of my children's elementary school zone, like school zones throughout the nation, despite a *Brown* decision over fifty years ago that sought to address this problem.

How to explain, despite all hard evidence to the contrary, the curious view, which only seems to gain traction, that school segregation was a problem of our past, but not our present? That programs of school integration are by now a shopworn concept? It's a view shared, as Judge Egly suggests, by a broad swath of the country, and residents in L.A., specifically. The public radio station in the area, KCRW, airs a well-regarded program, *Which Way L.A.?* (which one can access on the KCRW Web site), dedicated to examining policy issues of the region. The very tag-line of the January 17, 2007, broadcast, "Have Magnet Schools Outlived Their Usefulness?"— almost a full year before Judge Gutman's ruling in *American Civil Rights Foundation v. LAUSD*—illustratively evokes the impatience of L.A. residents over the original, integrationist goals of the magnet program (the voluntary program that remained, along with the PWT program, in the wake of forced busing). "All over the district," the host, Warren Olney, introduces the show, "parents are trying to game an admissions system that's based in part on racial quotas that are thirty years out of date." The overarching theme of the broadcast, one that becomes a returning motif, is that while the magnet program remains wildly popular (approximately sixty thousand children applied for just fifteen thousand spots in 2007), the program's original mission—school integration—seems to many an increasingly obsolete, and arguably unconstitutional, goal. What attracts parents and students to the program, Olney posits throughout the broadcast, is "academic excellence" rather than "integration," per se.

Against this apparently pre-scripted thesis of the program, Sharon Curry, the assistant superintendent of student integration services at the LAUSD, affirms the enduring relevance of the magnet program's raison d'être, integration. Referring to the "harms of racial isolation" that continue to plague children living in inner-city L.A., Curry defends the program's selection mechanism, a point system that takes race into account to realize diversity at the magnet schools. "The whole objective is to maintain an integrated school," she remarks, clearly exasperated by her host's repeated implication that the quotas are obsolete. "Believe it or not," Curry insists to her skeptical host,

> there are parents, who still want their children to attend a magnet for that purpose. They have the opportunity to learn from other children who are different. They have an opportunity to participate in programs of interest with excellent teachers, high standards, rigor. So we are really providing, we believe, the jewel program in the district, because more than anything it is providing the opportunity for integration for all our children, because we all understand how important that is.

Olney, an accomplished broadcast journalist, is too gentlemanly a host to challenge Curry's assumption outright. "Sure," he responds, without conviction. Still, one gleans from the tenor of the entire broadcast, and from Curry's increasingly defensive stance, that fewer and fewer of us, in truth, understand or accept the importance of integration for all our children.

To my mind, the most provocative moment of the show emerges when Olney doggedly pursues the "academic excellence" versus "integration" chestnut with Paul McCudden, a local parent with children enrolled in both magnet and nonmagnet public schools. After McCudden speaks about the benefits of an integrated learning environment, Olney responds,

"Would it be fair to say, though, that your primary goal is to get them the best education you can?"

"Well," McCudden replies, "those two are pretty much identical." It's a bold and incisive argument from this layperson on the panel, but it's also an increasingly embattled argument, apparently. Suspecting that McCudden's views are "unusual," as he characterizes them, Olney turns to one of his panelists, the political scientist Ryane Strauss, for clarification. Strauss, who wrote her doctoral dissertation on L.A.'s magnet program, affirms Olney's suspicions. "If you look at some of the public discussions," she declares, "the way in which they are portrayed in the media . . . people rarely talk about the integration benefits." It would appear that most Angelenos, despite a lingering few McCuddens out there, view academic excellence and an integrated learning environment as discrete items and, further, value the former more than the latter. What had Bobbi Fiedler, founder of Bustop in the 1970s, told me over the phone? "I think that education should be the principal goal of education."

Closer to home, even—and despite my oh-so-progressive predilections—hadn't my wife and I accepted, more or less, Olney's reductive distinction between "academic excellence" and "integration"? Indeed, I have been less than fully honest about our complicity with the segregated character of my children's elementary school experience. I would like now to set the record straight. Like most parents of adequate means, my wife and I enrolled our children in a private pre-K program, in our case the small school at our Reform synagogue. The classes were small, our kids received sterling instruction, and both their teachers recommended that we hire a private psychologist to test them for "gifted" status. Without flinching, my wife and I paid upwards of $500 for the tests, which our children passed. And here's the rub: had we *not* tested their giftedness, our children would have attended J. C. Mitchell instead of Addison Mizner. Under normal circumstances, that is, we live in the J. C. Mitchell attendance zone. But as neither J. C. Mitchell nor Boca El boast a gifted program, students designated as gifted who reside in these zones attend Addison Mizner instead, a fact on the ground that exacerbates its segregated character. According to the most recent Gold Report from November of 2006, 309 of Addison Mizner's 868 students participate in the gifted program, 250 of whom are white. (While the district performs its own student assessments upon a teacher's recommendation, this cost-free track to the gifted program is a cumbersome process, our school's exceptional student education coordinator reveals, and one that surely overlooks several low-income students.) My wife and I, then, were presented with a clear choice. Send our children to a predominantly white public school with an educational program equipped to challenge them, or send them to an integrated public school without a gifted program. We chose the former. A desegregated school, simply put, must not have counted for as much, in our eyes, as a school with an accelerated and enriched pedagogy.

Am I simply duplicating, through my children, our nation's resurgent pattern of segregated education, to the detriment of both my white Jewish kids and their minority peers, most of whom attend J. C. Mitchell and Boca El in disproportionately high numbers? The demographics at my children's public school strike me as almost eerily similar to the segregated demographics at my own Valley elementary school, Topeka, before the vigorous integration efforts of the 1970s and 1980s. And so I find myself brooding over the not-quite-rightness of things. While I can't say that I regret our decision (which we could reverse at any moment), I don't feel particularly good about it, either, and mostly I wish it were a decision we didn't have to make in the first place, that school districts in my state were afforded the means, financial and legislative, to offer a full range of academic programs without sacrificing student diversity in the bargain.

Fortunately, the public middle and high schools within walking distance of our house, which our children will attend, boast gifted programs *and* a substantially more integrated learning environment. That I look forward to these years for my children reflects my own view that integrated classrooms and athletic fields and courts represent goods to pursue in their own right, and for all children, above and beyond those antidotal arguments on their behalf anchored in past racial wrongs. This feeling I have is mostly personal, even visceral, derived largely from my experiences on the integrated JV and varsity basketball squads at Granada, and reinforced upon my recent visit with former teammates in L.A. Forced busing probably wasn't the answer, especially given the prohibitive geographical realities of sprawling L.A. But, on the whole, the voluntary integration efforts of the 1970s and 1980s, in L.A. and beyond, didn't fail, and integrated learning environments continue to succeed in those rarified spaces where they are permitted to thrive.

Lee C. Bollinger, the former president of the University of Michigan and current president of Columbia University, has been a vocal proponent of race-conscious affirmative action policies. By a narrow margin, the U.S. Supreme Court in *Gratz v. Bollinger* and *Grutter v. Bollinger* (2003) upheld these admissions policies over which Bollinger presided at the University of Michigan. In *Parents v. Seattle,* the majority opinion defers at some length to this precedent, taking pains to distinguish between the substance of the University of Michigan's admissions program (and the distinctive compelling interests of higher education, generally) and the Seattle and Louisville desegregation programs at the secondary level. All the same, given the U.S. Supreme Court's increasingly dis-integrating temperament, it seems likely that any number of other race-conscious affirmative action programs in our public universities will soon face its scrutiny. Anticipating this siege against the landmark *Brown* decision on its fifty-third anniversary, Bollinger was compelled to defend such policies in the *Chronicle of Higher Education*. Writes Bollinger, "We know that connecting with people very—or even slightly—different from ourselves stimulates the imagination; and when we learn to see the world through a multiplicity of eyes, we only make ourselves more nimble in mastering—and integrating—the diverse fields of knowledge awaiting us."[30]

I wholeheartedly agree with Bollinger's remarks here. But as I read on, I can't help but find something depressing in what strikes me as his obligatory deference to our corporate sensibilities. Diversity matters not least of all, Bollinger implies later in his article, "because in an increasingly global world, it is impossible to compete without already knowing how to imagine, understand, and collaborate with a diverse and fluid set of colleagues, partners, customers, and government leaders." Selling diversity, Bollinger seems to recognize, means convincing a skeptical public that integrated learning environments will make our students more "competitive" in an increasingly globalized society. While true, it seems a pity that proponents of student diversity, if they hope to appeal to a broad spectrum of the public, must appeal to our most mercenary instincts.

Perhaps it's the renegade English Department chair in me—facing increasing pressure by the Florida Department of Education to defend the "learning outcomes" of our majors in these corporate terms—but I recoil against such a rhetorical tack on behalf of integration programs, or English Departments. My world, and the world of my African American teammates, had simply grown larger for the vigorous efforts in the 1970s and 1980s to integrate the public schools. I don't think I recognized it at the time, and I doubt that my teammates did either, but those integrated classrooms, ball fields, and basketball courts productively challenged our complacent assumptions about the world through introducing us to other ways of being, seeing, and knowing. Moreover, the integrated campus equipped us with the readiness to contemplate alternative frames of reference in the years that lay ahead. Like many high school students, my basketball teammates and I would fall out of touch in the years after graduation (and we may not maintain our renewed correspondence), but those early relationships across ethnic and racial lines made us more receptive, I know, to forging such friendships in the future, as adults. In short, our immersion in an integrated public high school broadened our humanity by measures of empathy. This constitutes a social good, in and of itself, which scarcely needs the ballast of an associated, remunerative payoff.

I find myself contemplating once again that team photograph in my yearbook. My teammates and I had reflexively segregated ourselves across the frame. It had taken the photographer's discomfort, and Coach Johnson's subsequent directive, to integrate our squad along the midcourt semicircle. Even our coach, not exactly a liberal firebrand, had recognized that segregation didn't look so good. Via unapologetic race-conscious manipulation, he had desegregated our ranks. A simple, uncomplicated fix—but, in spirit, not unlike the race-conscious desegregation efforts that provoked the creation of the PWT program in the first place, which brought Jeff Inzar, Jeff Mays, Thomas McBride, Dennis Bishop, and Sean Brown to Granada Hills High School. Who knows how substantially this episode before the photographer jostled us free from our narrow comfort zones and prepared us to work, collectively, toward our undefeated regular season? This story is only one of thousands, I realize. There are any number of thirty- and forty-somethings out there who attended public schools during these heady integrationist days. We may wish to speak with some more of my peers before we give up utterly on a system of education that worked.

Giving Up the Game

"YOU'RE NOT PLANNING ON PLAYING STILL, ARE YOU?" my wife inquires over dinner, an afterthought apparently, shortly after I return from L.A. It was a Friday night, the night before my regular Saturday morning game. I had only returned to the routine at the Boca High gym to prepare for the alumni game at my old high school in the Valley. Having played that game, Wendy hopes that I will once again retire, in earnest this time. She has long worried over my injuries (both actual and prospective). Plus which, she's never been crazy about being stirred from sleep at the crack of dawn on the weekend as I lumber groggily around the bedroom groping for a stray sock, or my mouth guard.

"I don't know," I answer, sheepishly. "I was thinking of just playing, like, tomorrow. See how that goes."

Wendy rolls her eyes.

I suppose that I hadn't anticipated how difficult it would be to hang up the high-tops once and for all. Instead of playing hoops this past spring, I watched my son and daughter play in a youth league at the Boca High gym, beautifully run by the school's varsity coach. This would seem a satisfying, even poetic, changing of the guard in the Furman family. Yet I can't deny the palpable, if inchoate, sense of loss I felt during those initial months.

I sought to fill the void with alternative activities. I regularly lifted weights and rode the elliptical trainer at a local fitness center. I took up saltwater fishing, pretty much out of the blue, which prompted puzzlement from my wife's quarter and even some mild concern over my mental health. These activities proved worthwhile and rewarding in their own way, but scarcely ameliorated that inchoate sense of loss. These replacement activities, I came to recognize, were solitary, on the whole, whereas basketball is principally a social activity. Only after giving up the game for six months or so, only after undertaking my makeshift reunion in L.A., did I realize how much the sport has meant to me in this regard. And more, how integrally the social quality of basketball has informed the person I take with me beyond the baselines and sidelines of the court.

For years, I suppose, I've refused to recognize the powerful and positive way in which the sport resonates throughout my life. It's always seemed tangential to my more serious scholarly and professional endeavors rather than tightly connected with these pursuits. A healthy form of exercise, yes (despite the countless ankle sprains and facial lacerations from errant elbows). A constructive diversion from the serious business of life. But nothing more.

It's poor form, I realize, to blame one's parents for one's own shortcomings, but I can't honestly deny their influence here. Like many Jewish Americans of their generation—two generations removed from immigrant status, but clinging to an immigrant ethos, nonetheless—they viewed academic prowess as a primary and principal good toward which to aspire. It wasn't that they held an exalted view of the life of the mind. Rather, they knew that the surest path to socioeconomic comfort for their three children lay in respectable university degrees and, preferably, in advanced degrees in medicine or law. They weren't opposed to athletics, outright. But they made it abundantly clear to me and to my siblings that playing organized sports was a reward for performing acceptably in the more important scholastic arena. It was a privilege that could be taken away the moment our grades slipped. Golf, the sport in which my older brother excelled, was viewed somewhat differently by our parents. On occasion, my mother exhorted me to cultivate a greater interest in the activity. Here was a sport, unlike basketball, that would likely come in handy later on in life. "With clients," she declared, presuming that I would pursue a career that included these drab-sounding entities. Clients.

As much as I may have resented my parents' rather mercenary view of matters athletic—and I do remember harboring mild feelings of resentment—I certainly internalized these values to an appreciable extent. The people I admired in high school weren't my fellow athletes, primarily, but my Chinese American and Korean American peers, and some of my fellow Jews, who weren't necessarily any smarter than I was, though many of them were, but who seemed to possess an intellectual drive and focus that eluded me at the time. They would be going on to UC Berkeley, UCLA, Stanford, and other prestigious institutions, while my SAT scores precluded such aspirations. They were the ones, it seemed to me, who had their priorities straight while I was fooling around on the basketball court. Later on, at graduate school, and now as a professor, I've continued to view the scholarly and athletic realms as well nigh mutually exclusive. I rarely broach the topic of basketball, or sports period, with my academic peers and colleagues, as if I feel that competitive basketball were some mildly shameful activity, like listening to a Britney Spears CD.

Odd as it may sound, I had never considered until giving up the game how vitally its lessons have contributed to whatever scholarly and professional success I have been fortunate enough to achieve. Many of these lessons I have unwittingly applied strike me as embarrassingly obvious now, familiar clichés bandied about in any number of NCAA television commercials. Certainly, that is, the intense focus the game demands translated productively as I buckled down to pass doctoral exams and complete my dissertation; certainly the competitive drive I cultivated on the court contributed to the fairly rapid clip with which I generated my early publications; and certainly the teamwork element central to the sport—the importance of gauging individual strengths and harnessing these strengths toward collective synergy or flow—has served me well as chair of a large academic department.

While I've coasted along, oblivious to these simple gifts of the sport, I've experienced a more conscious and complicated relationship with its racial dimension. Specifically, I've tended more deliberately over the years to dismiss its significance. Stereotypes about the African American affinity for basketball are about as prevalent as stereotypes about Jews and money. Consequently, it had long seemed something of an embarrassment that my primary point of contact with black friends was on the basketball court. Any remotely honest account of my current circumstances, the dailiness of my own life, betrays its ongoing, segregated character. I wouldn't dismiss the circumstances of my long-term employment at one of the most diverse public institutions of higher learning in the nation.[1] Nor would I diminish the significance of my own minority status as a Jew in America. But who am I fooling? The contours of my existence (my neighborhood, my town, my tax bracket) suggest that I have been fully embraced by Caucasia. Membership to this exclusive club has had its privileges, as the old advertisement used to claim. And so I've been wary of acknowledging, even to myself, the rewarding access the sport has long afforded me to individuals and to a culture that would otherwise have remained remote. But it seems disingenuous, and even silly from the current vantage, to deny the way in which the cross-cultural texture of my experiences in basketball—beginning in earnest with my integrated Granada Hills High JV and varsity teams of 1985 and 1986—has informed my sensibilities. Surely, the friendships I cultivated over the years with African Americans on the court, this simple engagement, has to some extent shaped my politics and has facilitated the fruitful relationships I've enjoyed with colleagues of color in my department and college. Surely, my interest in the multiethnic literatures of the United States (I serve on the editorial board of a leading journal in the field) was fueled early on through the crackling African American vernacular that prevailed on the hoops court, and that I sought quite consciously—even goofily—to absorb.

But here I lapse into too rosy a reflective mode, one that diminishes the racial tensions that emerge on basketball courts nationwide, in ways subtle and overt. My trip to L.A., my visits with former coaches and teammates, clarified abundantly that the basketball court at Granada Hills High had never exactly been colorblind. Further debunking any views to the contrary, a recent study conducted by a University of Pennsylvania professor and Cornell University graduate student suggests, rather convincingly, that during thirteen recent consecutive seasons, white referees called a disproportionately high number of fouls against black players, and a disproportionately low number of fouls against white players.[2] In my experience, however, accord between players on the hoops court generally prevails—divergent personalities, races, and income brackets adhering to the common denominator of the game, its rules, its etiquette, its flow. It's mostly unspoken, this amity, taken for granted, as it should be, though small, special moments can sneak up on you.

"Happy Passover," I hear over my shoulder as I stride off the court one morning, done for the day, a few months after my return from the West Coast. The voice belongs to Nervio, a skinny, twenty-something black player whom I don't know particularly well. How did he know that I was Jewish? There's a trace of amused mischievousness in Nervio's send-off, perhaps, but not ill-intent. He means what he says. *Happy Passover.*

The new game, the music of sneakered feet, has already begun. I doubt he'll hear me. But I reply, in any case, "Thanks."

The basketball court is not an uncomplicated site of interracial harmony. But in a broader culture that grows more, rather than less, segregated, it endures as a rare site of contact, anyway, between a diverse cohort. Maybe this is why I can't quite bring myself to quit. Call the hoops court a complicated refuge from our dis-integrated culture. It's a refuge, nonetheless. In terms interracial and otherwise, I sometimes feel that the canvas of the basketball court just before a game begins—not unlike an artist's fresh canvas or a writer's blank page—is a site of limitless promise.

One final memory from my varsity season . . .

Our post-practice ritual. Before heading to the mildewed locker room, my teammates and I would congregate around the top of the key, panting, our hands on our knees, recovering from Coach Johnson's closing barrage of "suicide" sprinting drills. Regaining our breath, we'd take turns rushing the rim for dunk attempts. Johnson wasn't too crazy about this routine of ours (this reckless courting of injury and rim damage) but tolerated it. Perhaps he recognized the exercise, our youthful whooping and wailing upon each attempt, for what it was, a salutary release of pressure from the valve of his disciplined practices. Gary, Sean, and Sam could throw it down easily. So could Jeff, Dennis, and Terrell, if I recall. TMac, Todd, and Mark could just about achieve the requisite lift, but not quite. Kevin, Dan, and I were hopeless. But this didn't keep us from trying, often to the amusement of our teammates. Each afternoon, we congregated around the key for a few moments before heading to the lockers, then toward our cars in the parking lot, or toward that last yellow bus out of the Valley back to the city. Some of us perfected our dunking form, some of us struggled to gain that final inch of elevation, and some of us just did the best we could, if only to vivify our slam-dunk fantasies. Day after day after day.

During those brief afternoons in the Granada Hills High gym, during those brief moments, anything seemed possible.

Epilogue

November 20, 2008

I CONDUCTED THE BULK of the research and writing of this book in advance of Barack Obama's winning campaign for the presidency of the United States. That said, writing now in the wake of Election Day, it's difficult to ignore the implications of his sweeping victory upon this work that has consumed my attention these past two years. The ascendancy of the first African American to be elected to our highest political office casts my project against a definite relief, but hardly a clear one. The meaning of his victory and presidency for the issue of race in America at the center of this book will be hotly contested in the months and years to come.

Many observers, on both the political left and right, have called Obama a "postracial" figure, one whose rise affirms the most ambitious, integrationist vision of Martin Luther King, Jr. In a very real sense, President Obama—having attended two of our country's most prestigious institutions of higher learning and winning the presidency—embodies the successful integration of an African American into the most hallowed institutions of mainstream America. To some, his story offers evidence that our painful racial legacy is behind us. If a black man can now be elected president, the logic goes, surely we can jettison vigorous school integration or affirmative action programs. Obama's success, that is, proves to a certain cohort that we have achieved our "colorblind" meritocracy.

I don't wish to underplay the enormous achievement that Obama's victory represents. Surely, we have come a long way since the landmark *Brown* school desegregation case of 1954, since the Civil Rights Act of

1964, prior to which African Americans were *legally* precluded from the full participation in and the equal protection of our nation's democracy. But before we get swept away in the egalitarian fervor of our moment, we should pause to recognize the singular intelligence and charisma of the individual we have elected president and the limitations of any post-tracial or colorblind theories his victory might impel us to accept. If the past two years of my reunion with Los Angeles (both in books and in the flesh) have taught me anything, it's taught me that race still matters in America. Make no mistake. Obama's triumph, for example, does not overnight diminish the very real problems plaguing African American schoolchildren trapped in underperforming, racially isolated schools in cities nationwide. Nor does it diminish what should be our collective urgency to attend to this crisis. My fear is that Obama's victory will lull us into believing that, despite most evidence to the contrary, we now live in an egalitarian society; my hope is that his victory will embolden us to look clear-eyed upon the racial problems that persist so that we might repair them.

For me, working toward repair on this front has been both a scholarly undertaking and a personal one. The scholarly component of my endeavor proved especially fulfilling and was never too far away from my own sense of the personal. In the months that followed my trip to L.A., I pursued additional research and tidied loose ends as new court cases emerged and were resolved. Yet a nagging sense of anxiety dogged me as my reunion with my old teammates faded into the past. Back in Florida, I tried keeping in touch with them for a time, but it seemed likely that we would disappear once again into our own busy lives on separate coasts. This, somehow, seemed a failing, or at least a disappointment. Then, out of the blue, almost two years after my trip to L.A., I received an e-mail from TMac.

He had written to let me know that his younger son, Terrance, would be playing in the Amateur Athletic Union (AAU) basketball championships in Orlando in July, a couple of hours from my home. He hoped we could all get together that week. I replied and would later travel with my

7. Terrance McBride and Henry Furman fishing near Orlando.

son, Henry, up to Orlando to see one of Terrance's playoff games. (Terrance, as it happens, is a uniquely gifted athlete.) After the game, Henry and I introduced the McBride boys to fishing in a nearby Kissimmee lake. Good times were had by all, even though we didn't get too many bites.

This photo of Henry and Terrance, who happen to be the same age, might be seen as my modest hope for our collective future—a complement, of sorts, to the team photo that initiated this project. It's not a naïve or halcyon hope. The photo of Terrance and Henry, after all, was only slightly less orchestrated than that team photo for which TMac and I stood more than twenty years ago. I don't mean to suggest through capturing and displaying this frozen moment that African and Jewish Americans now live fully integrated social lives, or even that we ought to aspire to such total immersion. Surely both blacks and Jews, and other Americans, derive sustenance (spiritual, cultural, economic) from our in-group social networks. But we stand to realize richer collective lives if we continue to extend our notion of community, if we continue to seek membership, say, in multiple communities. And, yes, it still takes some effort to carve out these interracial spaces.

Regarding blacks and Jews, specifically, the time seems especially ripe for renewed dialogue. Jews, after all, voted for Obama more dispro-portionately (at 78 percent) than any other ethnic or religious group save African Americans (at 96 percent). How's that for a conversation starter! Obama, for his part, has thus far appointed an unprecedented number of Jews (and, curiously enough, basketball players) to key positions in his administration. Efforts toward restoring the frayed social and politi-cal alliance between blacks and Jews must be reciprocal or they will fail. The same goes for restoring individual friendships across these lines. My renewed correspondence with the McBrides cheered me, most of all because it was the first contact since my trip to L.A. initiated not by me, but by one of my old teammates. I had stopped e-mailing and calling my teammates in the immediate weeks and months following my trip to L.A. If we were going to give this renewed friendship a go, I couldn't do all the heavy lifting. So it's been a happy (and, frankly, unanticipated) develop-ment that my correspondence with TMac has settled on relatively equal terms of effort. The one-sidedness of my undertaking was something that complicated my own sense of this project from the start. What did it mean that *I* was the one to pursue this reunion? That *I* was the one who would control, through this book, the terms of its telling? If we are to solve any of the racial problems that beset us, surely we must search collectively. But someone, after all, must initiate the conversation. Perhaps it's all about making that first phone call.

NOTES

SELECTED
BIBLIOGRAPHY

INDEX

Notes

1. Photograph

1. William Faulkner, *Requiem For a Nun*, act 1, scene 3 (New York: Random House, 1950), 92.

2. Valley Boy

1. Robert Scheer, "The Jews of Los Angeles: Pursuing the American Dream," *Los Angeles Times,* Jan. 29, 1978, A3, A22.

2. Raphael J. Sonenshein, "The Los Angeles Jewish Community: An Examination of Its History of Activism for Human Rights," http://www.csus.edu/calst/government_affairs/reports/ffp34.pdf, 9.

3. Deborah Dash Moore, *To the Golden Cities: Pursuing the American Jewish Dream in Miami and L.A.* (New York: Free Press, 1994), 87.

4. See Josh Getlin, "Jewish coach, black players forged lasting bond," *Los Angeles Times,* Dec. 12, 2008, A1.

5. Moore, 42.

6. Robert Scheer, "L.A. Jews: New Set of Values for the Middle Class," *Los Angeles Times,* Jan. 31, 1978, B3.

7. Moore, *To the Golden Cities,* 265.

8. Karen Brodkin, *How Jews Became White Folks and What That Says About Race in America* (New Brunswick, N.J.: Rutgers Univ. Press, 1998), 26.

9. See Eric L. Goldstein, *The Price of Whiteness: Jews, Race, and American Identity* (Princeton, N.J.: Princeton Univ. Press, 2006), 3. Goldstein examines with great rigor the "uneasy relationship to whiteness" that has characterized Jewish negotiations with their racial identity in America.

10. Joel Kotkin and Erika Ozuna, "The Changing Face of the San Fernando Valley," http://publicpolicy.pepperdine.edu/davenport-institute/reports/changing-face/, 1.

11. Kevin Roderick, *The San Fernando Valley: America's Suburb* (Los Angeles: Los Angeles Times Books, 2002), 139.

12. Ibid., 146.

13. Ibid., 148.

14. Ibid.

15. Ibid., 188.

16. Philip J. Ethington, "Segregated Diversity: Race-Ethnicity, Space, and Political Fragmentation in Los Angeles County, 1940–1994," http://www-bcf.usc.edu/~philipje/Segregation/Haynes_Reports/FINAL_REPORT_20000719g.pdf.

3. Integration Efforts and Agonies

1. See Charles Ogletree, *All Deliberate Speed* (New York: Norton, 2004). Ogletree, a professor at the Harvard Law School, offers a thorough and compelling exegesis of the *Brown v. Board of Education* decision and its complex legacy. His detailed account of the resistance to school desegregation efforts in Boston during the 1970s in chapter 4, "*Brown's* Failure: Resistance in Boston," affirms that resistance to *Brown* was not confined to the Jim Crow South but was widespread. My own detailed account of the fierce and protracted social, political, and judicial resistance to school desegregation efforts in Los Angeles might be seen, in part, as a humble complement to Ogletree's chapter.

2. Jack Birkinshaw, "Pasadena Nears Crossroads on Integration of Schools," *Los Angeles Times*, June 18, 1967, B1.

3. David S. Ettinger, "The Quest to Desegregate Los Angeles Schools," *Los Angeles Lawyer*, Mar. 2003, 55.

4. *Jackson v. Pasadena City School District*, 59 Cal.2d 876, 878 (1963).

5. Ibid., 878.

6. Ibid., 880.

7. Ibid., 881.

8. Ibid., 881–82.

9. Lee Austin, "Board of Education Faces Suit No Matter Which Way It Moves," *Los Angeles Times*, June 18, 1967, B10.

10. *Jackson*, 882. Despite the overarching integrationist fervor of the *Brown* decision, its equivocal "all deliberate speed" clause offered, perhaps, an enabling precedent for the equivocal language here in *Jackson*.

11. Ibid., 882.

12. Ibid.

13. Birkinshaw, "Pasadena," B10.

14. Ibid.

15. *Crawford v. Board of Education of the City of Los Angeles*, 17 Cal. 3d 280, 287 (1976).

16. Ibid., 288.

17. Ibid., 289.

18. Ettinger, "Quest to Desegregate," 57.

19. *Jackson*, 881–82.

20. *Crawford*, 288.

21. Ibid., 288–89.

22. Ettinger, "Quest to Desegregate," 57.

23. "Integration in Los Angeles," *Los Angeles Times*, Feb. 15, 1970, F5.

24. William Endicott, "Judge Named as Death Plot Target," *Los Angeles Times*, Apr. 30, 1970, A1.

25. William Endicott, "Gitelson Blames Racists for Defeat," *Los Angeles Times*, Nov. 5, 1970, A32.

26. Ibid., A1.

27. Gerald Faris, "'Busing Judge' Looks for Meaningful Action," *Los Angeles Times*, June 30, 1972, D12.

28. Ibid.

29. Ibid.

30. *Jackson*, 881–82.

31. *Swann v. Charlotte-Mecklenburg Board of Education*, 402 U.S. 1 (1971).

32. *Keyes v. School District No. 1, Denver, Colorado*, 413 U.S. 189 (1973).

33. *Crawford*, 285.

34. Ibid., 284.

35. Ibid., 290.

36. Ibid., 301.

37. Ibid.

38. Ibid., 310.

39. Ettinger, "Quest to Desegregate," 58.

40. *Crawford*, 286.

41. Ibid.

42. Ettinger, "Quest to Desegregate," 60.

43. Jack McCurdy, "L.A. Busing Starts Today: Leaders Urge Compliance," *Los Angeles Times*, Sept. 12, 1978, B1.

44. Ibid., B14.

45. George Ramos, "Black, Latino Group Vows Bus Boycott," *Los Angeles Times*, Sept. 10, 1978, A23.

46. *Bustop, Inc. V. Board of Education of the City of Los Angeles*, 439 U.S. 1382, 1383 (1978).

47. "A Time for Calm," *Los Angeles Times*, Sept. 12, 1978, C4.

4. The Blacks and the Jews

1. Doyle McManus, "Boycott, 'White Flight' Cut Anglo Busing Participation," *Los Angeles Times*, Sept. 18, 1978, B3.

2. Ibid., B23.

3. *Crawford*, 303.

4. Kathleen O'Leary Morgan and Scott Morgan, eds., *City Crime Rankings* (Lawrency, Kans.: Morgan Quitno Press, 2006).

5. See Goldstein, *Price of Whiteness,* 147–49, 217; Hasia Diner, *In the Almost Promised Land: American Jews and Blacks,* 2d ed. (Baltimore: Johns Hopkins Univ. Press, 1995); Cheryl Greenberg, *Troubling the Waters: Black-Jewish Relations in the American Century* (Princeton, N.J.: Princeton Univ. Press, 2006); and Maurianne Adams and John H. Bracey, eds., *Strangers and Neighbors: Relations Between Blacks & Jews in the United States* (Amherst: Univ. of Massachusetts Press, 2000).

6. Scheer, "L.A. Jews," B12.

7. Ibid., B3.

8. Ibid.

9. Jack Salzman, introduction to *Struggles in the Promised Land: Toward a History of Black-Jewish Relations in the United States,* ed. Jack Salzman and Cornel West,6 (New York: Oxford Univ. Press, 1997).

10. James Baldwin, "Negroes Are Anti-Semitic Because They're Anti-White" (1967), repr. in *Blacks and Jews: Alliances and Arguments,* ed. Paul Berman, 34 (New York: Delacorte Press, 1994).

7. The Valley Revisited, via Santa Monica

1. "Top 100 Producers of Minority Degrees, 2007," *Diverse Issues in Higher Education,* http://www.diverseeducation.com/; "America's Best Colleges 2007," *U.S. News & World Report,* http://www.usnews.com/usnews/edu/college/rankings/brief/natudoc_campdiv_brief.php.

2. Sam Dillon, "Schools Slow in Closing Gaps Between Races," *New York Times,* Nov. 20, 2006, A1.

3. Ibid., A21.

4. Ibid.

5. Paul Tough, "What It Takes to Make a Student," *New York Times Magazine,* Nov. 26, 2006, 44–51, 69–72, 77.

6. "Proposition 209: Text of Proposed Law," http://vote96.ss.ca.gov/bp/209text.htm.

7. W. E. B. DuBois, *The Souls of Black Folk* (1903; repr., New York: Modern Library, 2003), xli.

10. The 'Hood, via Sherman Oaks

1. William Faulkner, *Intruder in the Dust* (1948; repr., New York: Viking, 1972), 13.

2. Ibid., 16.

3. A vocal minority of African Americans, including a few of the scholars listed above, oppose affirmative action. Supreme Court Justice Clarence Thomas represents the most prominent (and possibly consequential) member of this cohort. For the most convincing

arguments against affirmative action from the African American perspective, see Shelby Steele, *The Content of Our Character: A New Vision of Race in America* (New York: St. Martin's Press, 1990); *A Dream Deferred: The Second Betrayal of Black Freedom in America* (New York: HarperCollins, 1998); *White Guilt: How Blacks and Whites Together Destroyed the Promise of the Civil Rights Era* (New York: HarperCollins, 2006); John McWhorter, *Authentically Black* (New York: Gotham Books, 2003); *Losing the Race: Self-Sabotage in Black America* (New York: Free Press, 2000); *Winning the Race: Beyond the Crisis in Black America* (New York: Gotham Books, 2006).

4. Manning Marable, *The Great Wells of Democracy: The Meaning of Race in American Life* (New York: Basic Civitas Books, 2002), 38.

5. Manning Marable, *Living Black History* (New York: Basic Civitas Books, 2006), 48.

6. See Steven F. Lawson, *Running For Freedom* (New York: McGraw-Hill, 1997), 142. Kate Dosset examines the roles of various black women in the Civil Rights movement, which illustrates the extent to which African Americans embraced both integrationist and separatist strategies. See Dosset, *Bridging Race Divides: Black Nationalism, Feminism, and Integration in the United States, 1896–1935* (Gainesville, Univ. Press of Florida, 2008), 6. Manning Marable calls for a "creative synthesis" between integrationist and separatist modes. See Marable, *Great Wells of Democracy*, xv.

7. The transportation burden associated with busing minority children to more integrated schools represents a major discouragement to minority parents like the McBrides and has partly accounted for the increasing dis-integration of public schools throughout the nation. As Lawson notes, "Since 1980, the percentage of black students in majority-white schools has dropped from 44 to fewer than 31. Nevertheless, because African-American children had shouldered the burden of busing, for the most part their parents were not sorry to see busing cease." *Civil Rights Crossroads: Nation, Community, and the Black Freedom Struggle* (Lexington: Univ. Press of Kentucky: 2003), 170–71.

8. F. Scott Fitzgerald, *The Great Gatsby* (1925; repr., New York: Scribner's, 1986), 152.

11. Return

1. "Proposition 209: Text of Proposed Law," http://vote96.ss.ca.gov/bp/209text.htm.

2. Susanne Klingenstein, *Enlarging America: The Cultural Work of Jewish Literary Scholars, 1930–1990* (Syracuse: Syracuse Univ. Press, 1998), 45.

3. Tamar Lewin, "Colleges Regroup After Voters Ban Race Preferences," *New York Times,* Jan. 26, 2007, A13.

4. Timothy Egan, "Little Asia On the Hill," *New York Times: Education Life*, Jan. 7, 2007, 24.

5. Ibid.

6. "Executive Order 99-281," http://dms.myflorida.com/media/general_counsel_files/one_florida_executive_order_pdf.

7. Patricia Marin and Edgar K. Lee, "Appearance and Reality in the Sunshine State: The Talented 20 Program in Florida," http://www.civilrightsproject.ucla.edu/research/affirmativeaction/florida.pdf, vi.

8. Lawson, *Civil Rights Crossroads*, 170; Marable, *Living Black History*, 202–3.

9. Lewin, "Colleges Regroup," A1.

10. *Parents Involved in Community Schools, Petitioner v. Seattle School District No. 1 et al.*, 168 L. Ed. 2d 508, 562 (2007).

11. Ibid., 575.

12. Ibid., 541.

13. Ibid., 615–16.

14. Ibid., 567.

15. Ibid., 555–56.

16. Hendrik Hertzberg, "The Darksider," *New Yorker*, July 9 and 16, 2007, 36.

17. *Jackson*, 881–82.

18. *Parents*, 566.

19. *American Civil Rights Foundation v. Los Angeles Unified School District*, Case No. BC 341363, 15 (2007).

20. Ibid., 12.

21. Ibid., 9.

22. Ibid.

23. Erica Frankenberg and Chungmei Lee, "Race in American Public Schools: Rapidly Resegregating School Districts," http://civilrightsproject.ucla.edu/research/k-12-education/integration-and-diversity/race-in-american-public-schools-rapidly-resegregating-school-districts, 4.

24. Ibid., 22.

25. Ibid., 15.

26. Ibid., 22.

27. Derrick Bell, "Desegregation's Demise," *Chronicle of Higher Education*, July 13, 2007, B11.

28. Ettinger, "Quest to Desegregate," 66.

29. Jonathan Kozol, *The Shame of the Nation: The Restoration of Apartheid Schooling in America* (New York: Crown, 2005). See also Sam Dillon, "'No Child' Law Is Not Closing A Racial Gap," *New York Times*, Apr. 29, 2009, A1, A16, for his report on the results of the most recent federal test measuring the long-term trends, through 2008, in math and reading proficiency. The data convincingly support Dillon's assertion that "[t]he achievement gap between black and white students . . . narrowed most dramatically during the desegregation efforts of the 1970s and 1980s," A16.

30. Lee C. Bollinger, "Why Diversity Matters," *Chronicle of Higher Education*, June 1, 2007, B20.

12. Giving Up the Game

1. "Top 100 Producers of Minority Degrees, 2007," *Diverse Issues in Higher Education,* http://www.diverseeducation.com/; "America's Best Colleges 2007," *U.S. News & World Report,* http://www.usnews.com/usnews/edu/college/rankings/brief/natudoc_campdiv_brief.php.

2. Alan Schwarz, "Study of N.B.A. Sees Racial Bias in Calling Fouls," *New York Times,* May 2, 2007, A1, C22.

Selected Bibliography

Adams, Maurianne, and John H. Bracey, eds. *Strangers and Neighbors: Relations Between Blacks and Jews in the United States.* Amherst: Univ. of Massachusetts Press, 2000.

American Civil Rights Foundation v. Los Angeles Unified School District. BC 341363. 2007.

Baldwin, James. "Negroes Are Anti-Semitic Because They're Anti-White." 1967. Reprinted in *Blacks and Jews: Alliances and Arguments*, ed. Paul Berman, 31–41. New York: Delacorte Press, 1994.

Bell, Derrick. "Desegregation's Demise." *Chronicle of Higher Education* July 13, 2007, B11.

Berman, Paul, ed. *Blacks and Jews: Alliances and Arguments.* New York: Delacorte Press, 1994.

Bollinger, Lee C. "Why Diversity Matters." *Chronicle of Higher Education*, June 1, 2007, B20.

Brodkin, Karen. *How the Jews Became White Folks and What That Says About Race in America.* New Brunswick, N.J.: Rutgers Univ. Press, 1998.

Brown v. Board of Education. 347 U.S. 1954.

Bustop, Inc. v. Board of Education of the City of Los Angeles. 439 U.S. 1978.

Clotfelter, Charles T. *After Brown: The Rise and Retreat of School Desegregation.* Princeton: Princeton Univ. Press, 2004.

Crawford v. Board of Education of the City of Los Angeles. 17 Cal. 3d. 1976.

Dillon, Sam. "'No Child' Law Is Not Closing A Racial Gap." *New York Times*, Apr. 29, 2009.

Diner, Hasia. *In the Almost Promised Land: American Jews and Blacks.* 2d ed. Baltimore: John Hopkins Univ. Press, 1995.

Dosset, Kate. *Bridging Race Divides: Black Nationalism, Feminism, and Integration in the United States, 1896–1935.* Gainesville: Univ. Press of Florida, 2008.

DuBois, W. E. B. *The Souls of Black Folk*. 1903. Reprint, New York: Modern Library, 2003.

Egan, Timothy. "Little Asia On the Hill." *New York Times: Education Life*, Jan. 7, 2007, 24–27, 35.

Ettinger, David S. "The Quest to Desegregate Los Angeles Schools." *Los Angeles Lawyer*, Mar. 2003, 54–66.

Faulkner, William. *Intruder in the Dust*. 1948; reprint, New York: Viking, 1972.

———. *Requiem For a Nun*. New York: Random House, 1950.

Fitzgerald, F. Scott. *The Great Gatsby*. 1925; reprint, New York: Scribner's, 1986.

Frankenberg, Erica, and Chungmei Lee. "Race in American Public Schools: Rapidly Resegregating School Districts," http://civilrightsproject.ucla.edu/research/k-12-education/integration-and-diversity/race-in-american-public-schools-rapidly-resegregating-school-districts.

Goldstein, Eric L. *The Price of Whiteness: Jews, Race, and American Identity*. Princeton: Princeton Univ. Press, 2006.

Greenberg, Cheryl. *Troubling the Waters: Black-Jewish Relations in the American Century*. Princeton: Princeton Univ. Press, 2006.

Jackson v. Pasadena City School District. 59 Cal. 2d. 1963.

Klingenstein, Susanne. *Enlarging America: The Cultural Work of Jewish Literary Scholars, 1930–1990*. Syracuse: Syracuse Univ. Press, 1998.

Kozol, Jonathan. *The Shame of the Nation: The Restoration of Apartheid Schooling in America*. New York: Crown, 2005.

Lawson, Steven F. *Civil Rights Crossroads: Nation, Community, and the Black Freedom Struggle*. Lexington: Univ. Press of Kentucky, 2003.

———. *Running for Freedom*. New York: McGraw-Hill, 1997.

Lewin, Tamar. "Colleges Regroup After Voters Ban Race Preferences." *New York Times*, Jan. 26, 2007, http://www.nytimes.com/2007/01/26/education/26affirm.html.

Marable, Manning. *The Great Wells of Democracy: The Meaning of Race in American Life*. New York: Basic Civitas Books, 2002.

———. *Living Black History*. New York: Basic Civitas Books, 2006.

———. *Speaking Truth to Power: Essays on Race, Resistance, and Radicalism*. Boulder: Westview Press, 1996.

Marin, Patricia, and Edgar K. Lee. "Appearance and Reality in the Sunshine State: The Talented 20 Program in Florida," http://www.civilrightsproject.ucla.edu/research/affirmativeaction/florida.pdf.

McWhorter, John. *Authentically Black*. New York: Gotham Books, 2003.

————. *Losing the Race: Self-Sabotage in Black America*. New York: Free Press, 2000.

————. *Winning the Race: Beyond the Crisis in Black America*. New York: Gotham Books, 2006.

Moore, Deborah Dash. *To the Golden Cities: Pursuing the American Jewish Dream in Miami and L.A.* New York: Free Press, 1994.

Morgan, Kathleen O'Leary, and Scott Morgan, eds. *City Crime Rankings*. Lawrency, Kans.: Morgan Quitno Press, 2006.

Ogletree, Charles. *All Deliberate Speed*. New York: Norton, 2004.

Parents Involved in Community Schools, Petitioner v. Seattle School District No. 1 et al., 168 L. Ed. 2d. 2007.

"Proposition 209: Text of Proposed Law," http://vote96.ss.ca.gov/bp/209text.htm.

Roderick, Kevin. *The San Fernando Valley: America's Suburb*. Los Angeles: Los Angeles Times Books, 2002.

Salzman, Jack, and Cornel West, eds. *Struggles in the Promised Land: Toward a History of Black-Jewish Relations in the United States*. New York: Oxford Univ. Press, 1997.

Scheer, Robert. "The Jews of Los Angeles: Pursuing the American Dream." *Los Angeles Times,* Jan. 29, 1978, A3, A22.

————. "L.A. Jews: New Set of Values for the Middle Class." *Los Angeles Times,* Jan. 31, 1978, B3.

Steele, Shelby. *The Content of Our Character: A New Vision of Race in America*. New York: St. Martin's Press, 1990.

————. *A Dream Deferred: The Second Betrayal of Black Freedom in America*. New York: HarperCollins, 1998

————. *White Guilt: How Blacks and Whites Together Destroyed the Promise of the Civil Rights Era*. New York: HarperCollins, 2006

Tough, Paul. "What It Takes to Make a Student." *New York Times Magazine,* Nov. 26, 2006, 44–51, 69–72, 77.

Index